CW01618853

Oxford Studies in Lexicography and Lexicology

Series editors
Richard Bailey, Noel Osselton, and Gabriele Stein

Tradition and Innovation in Modern English Dictionaries

Tradition and Innovation in Modern English Dictionaries

HENRI BÉJOINT

CLARENDON PRESS · OXFORD

Oxford University Press, Walton Street, Oxford OX2 6DP
Oxford New York
Athens Auckland Bangkok Bombay
Calcutta Cape Town Dar es Salaam Delhi
Florence Hong Kong Istanbul Karachi
Kuala Lumpur Madras Madrid Melbourne
Mexico City Nairobi Paris Singapore
Taipei Tokyo Toronto
and associated companies in
Berlin Ibadan

Oxford is a trade mark of Oxford University Press

Published in the United States by
Oxford University Press Inc., New York

© Henri Béjoint 1994

First published 1994

All rights reserved. No part of this publication may be reproduced, stored in a retrieval system, or transmitted, in any form or by any means, without the prior permission in writing of Oxford University Press. Within the UK, exceptions are allowed in respect of any fair dealing for the purpose of research or private study, or criticism or review, as permitted under the Copyright, Designs and Patents Act, 1988, or in the case of reprographic reproduction in accordance with the terms of the licences issued by the Copyright Licensing Agency. Enquiries concerning reproduction outside these terms and in other countries should be sent to the Rights Department, Oxford University Press, at the address above

British Library Cataloguing in Publication Data
Data available

Library of Congress Cataloging in Publication Data
Tradition and innovation in modern English dictionaries.
Henri Béjoint.
Includes bibliographical references and index.
1. English language—Lexicography. I. Title.
PE1611.B44 1993 423'.028—dc20 93–1936
ISBN 0–19–823919–X

3 5 7 9 10 8 6 4 2

Printed in Great Britain on acid-free paper by
The Ipswich Book Co. Ltd., Suffolk

Acknowledgements

SO many people have helped me in the preparation of this book that it would be impossible to thank them all. Particular thanks are due to Gabriele Stein, who encouraged me to prepare the manuscript for publication, to Richard Bailey, to my colleagues in Lyon, particularly in the Centre de Recherches en Terminologie et Traduction, to the University of Lyon for giving me generous leave of absence, to Brown University, and finally to my family for putting up with it all.

H.B.

Contents

Abbreviations

ACD	*The American College Dictionary*, ed. Clarence L. Barnhart (New York: Random House, 1947)
AHD	*The American Heritage Dictionary of the English Language*, ed. William Morris (Boston: Houghton Mifflin, 1969)
AHD2	*The American Heritage Dictionary*, 2nd college edn. (Boston: Houghton Mifflin, 1982)
ALD	*Oxford Advanced Learner's Dictionary*
ALD1	*Idiomatic and Syntactic English Dictionary*, ed. A. S. Hornby, E. V. Gatenby, and H. Wakefield (Tokyo: The Institute for Research in Language Teaching, 1942)
ALD2	*The Advanced Learner's Dictionary of Current English*, 2nd edn., ed. A. S. Hornby, E. V. Gatenby, and H. Wakefield (Oxford University Press, 1963)
ALD3	*Oxford Advanced Learner's Dictionary of Current English*, 3rd edn., ed. A. S. Hornby (Oxford University Press, 1974; revised and reset 1980)
ALD4	*Oxford Advanced Learner's Dictionary of Current English*, 4th edn., ed. Anthony P. Cowie (Oxford University Press, 1989)
BBI	*The BBI Combinatory Dictionary of English*, ed. Morton Benson, Evelyn Benson, and Robert Ilson (Amsterdam and Philadelphia: John Benjamins, 1986)
CED	*Collins Dictionary of the English Language*, ed. Patrick Hanks (London and Glasgow: Collins, 1979; 2nd edn. 1986). The title as given on the dust-jacket is *The Collins English Dictionary*
COB	*Collins COBUILD English Language Dictionary*, ed. John Sinclair (London and Glasgow: Collins, 1987)
COD	*The Concise Oxford Dictionary*
COD1	*The Concise Oxford Dictionary*, 1st edn., ed. H. W. Fowler and F. G. Fowler (Oxford: Clarendon Press, 1911)
COD5	*The Concise Oxford Dictionary of Current English*, 5th edn., ed. H. W. Fowler and F. G. Fowler (Oxford: Clarendon Press, 1964)
COD6	*The Concise Oxford Dictionary of Current English*, 6th edn., ed. J. B. Sykes (Oxford: Clarendon Press, 1976)
COD7	*The Concise Oxford Dictionary of Current English*, 7th edn., ed. J. B. Sykes (Oxford: Clarendon Press, 1982)

COD8 — *The Concise Oxford Dictionary of Current English*, 8th edn., ed. R. E. Allen (Oxford: Clarendon Press, 1990)

CTD — *Chambers Twentieth Century Dictionary*, ed. A. M. Macdonald (Edinburgh: W. & R. Chambers, 1972)

CULD — *Chambers Universal Learners' Dictionary*, ed. Elizabeth M. Kirkpatrick (Edinburgh: W. & R. Chambers, 1980)

DA — *A Dictionary of Americanisms on Historical Principles*, ed. Mitford M. Mathews (Chicago: University of Chicago Press, 1951)

DAE — *A Dictionary of American English on Historical Principles*, ed. William A. Craigie and James R. Hulbert (Chicago: University of Chicago Press, 1944)

DARE — *Dictionary of American Regional English*, ed. Frederic G. Cassidy, vol. 1 (A–C) 1985, vol. 2 (D–H) 1991 (The Belknap Press, Harvard University)

DEC — *Dictionnaire explicatif et combinatoire du français contemporain*, ed. Igor Mel'čuk (Montreal: Presses de l'Université de Montréal)

DFC — *Dictionnaire du français contemporain*, ed. J. Dubois *et al.* (Paris: Larousse, 1966)

DNE — *The Barnhart Dictionary of New English Since 1963*, ed. Clarence L. Barnhart, Sol Steinmetz, and Robert K. Barnhart (Bronxville, NY: Barnhart/Harper & Row, 1973). English edition: *A Dictionary of New English* (London: Longman, 1973)

DOST — *Dictionary of the Older Scottish Tongue*, ed. A. J. Aitken (University of Edinburgh, 1931–)

EWD — *Hamlyn Encyclopedic World Dictionary*, ed. Patrick Hanks (London: Hamlyn, 1971)

FWC — *Funk and Wagnalls Standard College Dictionary*, ed. Robert L. Chapman (New York: Funk & Wagnalls, 1963; 2nd edn., ed. Sidney I. Landau, 1977)

FWS — *Funk and Wagnalls New Standard Dictionary of the English Language*, ed. Isaac Funk (New York: Funk & Wagnalls, 1963)

GID — *The Reader's Digest Great Illustrated Dictionary*, ed. Robert L. Ilson (Reader's Digest, 1984)

GR — *Dictionnaire alphabétique et analogique de la langue française*, ed. P. Robert (Paris: Société du Nouveau Littré, 1953; suppl. 1970)

L3 — *Larousse trois volumes en couleurs* (Paris: Larousse, 1965)

LDEL — *Longman Dictionary of the English Language*, ed. H. Gay (Harlow and London: Longman, 1984)

LDOCE — *Longman Dictionary of Contemporary English*, ed. Paul Procter (Harlow and London: Longman, 1978)

LDOCE2 — *Longman Dictionary of Contemporary English*, new edn., ed. Della Summers (Harlow: Longman, 1987)

LLCE	*Longman Lexicon of Contemporary English*, ed. Tom McArthur (Harlow: Longman, 1981)
NCD7	*Webster's Seventh New Collegiate Dictionary*, ed. P. B. Gove (Springfield, Mass.: G. & C. Merriam, 1963)
NCD8	*Webster's New Collegiate Dictionary*, 8th edn., ed. Henry Bosley Woolf (Springfield, Mass.: G. & C. Merriam, 1973)
NCD9	*Webster's Ninth New Collegiate Dictionary*, ed. Frederic C. Mish (Springfield, Mass.: G. & C. Merriam, 1983)
ODCIE	*Oxford Dictionary of Current Idiomatic English*, vol. 1 (*ODCIE1*): *Verbs with Prepositions and Particles*, ed. Anthony P. Cowie and Ronald Mackin (1975), vol. 2 (*ODCIE2*): *Phrase, Clause and Sentence Idioms*, ed. Anthony P. Cowie, Ronald Mackin, and Isabel R. McCaig (1983) (Oxford University Press)
OED	*The Oxford English Dictionary*, ed. J. Murray *et al.* (Oxford: Clarendon Press, 1933)
OED2	*The Oxford English Dictionary*, 2nd edn., ed. John A. Simpson and Edmund S. C. Weiner (Oxford University Press, 1989)
OPD	*Oxford Paperback Dictionary*, ed. J. M. Hawkins (Oxford University Press, 1979)
PAD	*The Pan English Dictionary*, ed. Katherine Harber and Geoffrey Payton (London and Sydney: Pan Books, 1979)
PED	*The Penguin English Dictionary*, ed. G. N. Garmonsway and Jacqueline Simpson (Harmondsworth, Middlesex: Penguin Books, 1965)
PL	*Petit Larousse illustré*, ed. C. Augé (Paris: Larousse, 1906; new edn. every year)
POD	*The Pocket Oxford Dictionary of Current English*, ed. F. G. Fowler and H. W. Fowler (Oxford: Clarendon Press, 1924)
PR	*Dictionnaire alphabétique et analogique de la langue française*, ed. P. Robert (Paris: Société de Nouveau Littré, 1967)
RHC	*The Random House College Dictionary*, ed. Laurence Urdang and Stuart B. Flexner (New York: Random House, 1968)
RHD	*The Random House Dictionary of the English Language*, ed. Jess Stein (New York: Random House, 1966)
RHD2	*The Random House Dictionary of the English Language*, 2nd edn. (New York: Random House, 1987)
RM	*Le Robert méthodique*, ed. Josette Rey-Debove (Paris: Le Robert, 1982)
SOED	*The Shorter Oxford English Dictionary on Historical Principles*, ed. W. Little and C. T. Onions (Oxford: Clarendon Press, 1933)
TLF	*Trésor de la langue française*, ed. P. Imbs (Paris: Editions du CNRS, 1971–91)
W2	*Webster's New International Dictionary* (Springfield, Mass.: G. & C. Merriam, 1934)

W3	*Webster's Third New International Dictionary of the English Language*, ed. Philip Babcock Gove (Springfield, Mass.: G. & C. Merriam, 1961)
WBD	*The World Book Dictionary*, ed. Clarence L. Barnhart (Chicago: Thorndike-Barnhart, 1963)
WNW	*Webster's New World Dictionary of the American Language*, 2nd college edn., ed. David B. Guralnik (New York and Cleveland: The World Publishing Company, 1970)
WNW2	*Webster's New World Dictionary of American English* (New York and Cleveland: The World Publishing Company, 1988)

Introduction

TIME was, not so long ago, when it was usual to start a book on lexicography or on lexis by lamenting the dearth of lexical studies and the disregard of most modern linguists for semantics in general and for words in particular. The complaints were never totally justified, at least as far as lexicography is concerned: Britain, France, and the United States have always been prolific in the production of dictionaries. It is true that lexicology has been the poor relation of linguistics, in the sense that linguists who were interested in lexis were often looked down upon by their colleagues. But the interest for lexis has always been alive, even when and where structuralist linguists were of the opinion that semantics was not part of linguistics. Whatever the situation was, it is clear that things have been improving consistently everywhere, and that the improvement is accelerating. The decade between 1975 and 1985 has been called 'a decade of the lexicon' (Nowakowski 1990: 3).

The last twenty years have been particularly rich for lexicography: never before have so many dictionaries been published, and never before has so much literature about dictionaries—what has come to be called 'metalexicography'—been produced. Several specialized journals of lexicography have been launched, a large number of specialized conferences organized, and some publishers even have special series of metalexicographical books. The latest manifestation of the new enthusiasm is the publication of a three-volume, three-language (German, English, and French) and 3,300-page *Encyclopedia of Lexicography*, which contains 340 contributions from 248 specialists from all over the world (Hausmann *et al.* 1989, 1990, and 1991).

Since 1989, when the first version of this book was written, the lexicographical scene may have become slightly more gloomy. Publishers have recently complained, at least in Britain, that dictionaries no longer sell as well as they used to. But dictionaries are certainly not on their way out. Reference books in general still sell fairly well, mostly in their traditional paper versions that we are all so familiar with. The modern, computerized descendants are already operative in places, and the progress that is expected in the near future will bring more clients, though it may take more time than was once thought before the on-line dictionary becomes acclimatized in all households. Whatever the dictionaries of the future will be like, there is still ample room for improvement, and the metalexicographer is in no danger of being unemployed: there is still much that has to be done in order to adapt the dictionary to its users and different uses.

English-language dictionaries are certainly more closely scrutinized than any others, and their observers are often non-native speakers of English. The present study should be seen in this context: English-language dictionaries examined from the point of view of a French metalexicographer. French lexicography has a long and well-recognized tradition, and establishing how far the findings of French specialists can be applied to the context of English-language dictionaries is one of the objects of the following pages.

The outsider is, in a very obvious way, at a disadvantage, but he also enjoys an angle that the native speaker does not have. He may be able to see things that the insider does not—a well-known fact in sociology or anthropology. Dictionaries are so familiar to us all, and such subtle mirrors of some of the characteristics of our societies that the outsider may find it easier to describe them than the insider would. Communication across language boundaries is not as free and frequent as could be expected from a milieu of specialists of language, except in the sense mentioned above that metalexicographers of all language communities observe English-language dictionaries. Metalexicography is still very much contained within national boundaries: many specialists tend to restrict their reading to their native language, and there is a certain amount of provincialism even for metalexicographers who are native English speakers.

Lexicography has obviously entered a phase of self-examination: we have begun to wonder why the dictionaries that we have inherited from previous generations are what they are, and whether they are adapted to our times. Different societies produce different dictionaries, as we shall see in Chapter 2, because the dictionary, particularly the 'general-purpose dictionary' (as defined in Chapter 1), reflects—to a certain extent—the society in which it is produced (Chapter 4). But general-purpose dictionaries are also very similar in many European countries, because of their common origins and their similar historical evolution, from the Renaissance to the present through the turning-point of the eighteenth century (Chapter 3), because they have played the same roles in many countries, both as almost mythical emblems of learning (Chapter 4) and as tools for the improvement of linguistic communication (Chapter 5), and also because of the mutual reinforcement of the linguistic and the lexicographical traditions (Chapter 6). The time seems to have come when those traditions should be questioned.

Many metalexicographers have recently been trying to investigate the needs and the skills of the users, hoping to draw conclusions on what dictionaries of the future should be like (Chapter 5)—a clear indication that lexicography is wondering where to go. A particularly interesting area is that of research on the psycholinguistic processes of dictionary consultation, which is based on the assumption that the quality of a dictionary can be judged in terms of how closely its organization mirrors the organization of the mental lexicon. Time will tell whether such work can reasonably be expected to reach firm conclusions. If it fails, then other research, whether practical or theoretical—some of which will be reviewed and evaluated in Chapter 7—will have to pave the way for dictionaries of the future.

The field of metalexicography, though now extensively covered by numerous publications in various forms, is still evolving. Evidence for this can be found in the terminological hesitations over some of the central concepts of the discipline: how does one say *dictionnaire de langue* in English? How does one say *dictionnaire analogique*? What is it exactly? What is the English for *dictionnaire de mots*, *dictionnaire de choses*, or for *macrostructure* and *microstructure*?[1] What exactly is a thesaurus? Also—though these are relatively less important—should one say *thesauruses* or *thesauri*, *corpuses* or *corpora*, *appendices* or *appendixes*? Is it *lexicographic* or *lexicographical*, *monosemous* or *monosemic*, etc.?

It was difficult to place limits on the present study. Many dates have been important for English-language dictionaries: the publication of Johnson's *Dictionary*, of Whitney's *Century Dictionary*, the completion of the first *Oxford English Dictionary*, the publication of the *Advanced Learner's Dictionary* or of L. Zgusta's *Manual of*

[1] There are also hesitations in French: for example, there is no ready French word for *thesaurus*, or for *lexicon*.

Lexicography. The early sixties seemed to be a convenient starting-point, because they mark two important events: the first conference on lexicography for the English-speaking world, held at Bloomington, Indiana, in 1960, whose proceedings were published in 1962 under the title *Problems in Lexicography* (Householder and Saporta 1962), and the publication of *Webster's Third New International Dictionary* in 1961. The study thus focuses on three decades that have been particularly important for English-language lexicography and meta-lexicography, though the description of what happened during those thirty years cannot be clearly separated from what took place before.

The second, more difficult limit was that of the object of study. There are far too many dictionaries in English-speaking countries, of far too many different types, for any one study to embrace them all. The monolingual, general-purpose dictionary was the obvious choice, because it is the more popular type, the one that has the closer connections with the society in which it is produced, and probably the more interesting one to study, both from a sociological and from a linguistic point of view. But it is a multi-faceted object whose actual realizations defy any attempt at a precise definition (Geeraerts 1989: 288): the contents of such a study necessarily depend on what has been identified as its object, and the discussion of what is meant by 'monolingual general-purpose dictionary' naturally assumes a central position in the following pages (Chapter 1). As it is, the book is evidently broad in scope, with all the defects of all general overviews: it cannot offer an in-depth treatment of all the aspects of English-language general-purpose dictionaries for the last thirty years. It is best seen as aiming to arouse interest in some of the most interesting developments in the field since the sixties.

Charlton Laird, at the beginning of his book *Language in America*, wrote 'Presumably, no one now living knows enough to write this book. Certainly I do not.' I am not sure how far his first sentence applies to the present work, but the second certainly does. I have done my best throughout to avoid the two traps of the metalexicographer, sticking to pure and simple description—this is at best useless, except of course in a manual—and indulging in 'dictionary-bashing'. This is a fairly popular game which is played by exposing all the faults of dictionaries without proposing any practicable solutions. In its mildest form, the symptom is only a profuse eruption of *should*'s, but it may become worse than that, a superior position assumed by linguists who refuse to envisage the practical difficulties of dictionary-writing. No difficulty is insurmountable in lexicography—or no dictionary would ever have been published—but there are few easy answers. Of course, metalexicographers are not lexicographers—*à chacun son métier*—but some time, somewhere, they must come to terms with the realities of dictionary publication. The dictionary is an artefact which is written to be used every day by human beings, and it is not much use speculating on how much better the description could be if the lexicographers were better linguists, if they were less overworked, if the publishers were more generous, if the dictionary users were more competent, if the lexicographical traditions were not so powerful, if all sorts of words did not insist on requiring all sorts of different treatments, if language varieties did not exist, if acceptability were a matter of yes or no instead of being a scale, etc.

The role of the metalexicographer is neither merely to describe nor idly to criticize; it is to help the lexicographer put current practice into perspective, and eventually participate in the improvement of dictionaries. Anything can be proposed, short of 'lexicographiction' (Descamps and Vaunaize 1983: 109).

1

Dictionaries and the Dictionary

1.1 DEFINITIONS

It is traditional to start with definitions, and this is particularly appropriate in the circumstances, since the main object of lexicography is to define words and terms.

Of course, the central notion to be defined is the notion of 'dictionary'. According to the *Oxford English Dictionary* (*OED*), the word *dictionary* is derived from the Latin forms *dictionarius*, used in 1225 by the English poet and grammarian Joannes de Garlandia (John of Garland) as the 'title of a collection of Latin vocables', and *dictionarium*, used about a century later by Peter Bechorius (or Becharius). The first recorded appearance of the word *dictionary* as such is dated 1526 by the *OED*; after that the word was used by Sir Thomas Elyot in 1538. The French word *dictionnaire* seems to have been used for the first time by Robert Estienne in 1539.

The vagueness of the concept in this early period has been mentioned by many: in French by Quemada (1968: 329), Rey-Debove (1971: 23), Rey (1977: 56), etc., and in English by, amongst others, McArthur. The word *dictionary*, he writes,

> has tended to be a coverall term for all sorts of presentations of information about 'words', however conceived. In 1340, the French compiler and friend of Petrarch, Pierre Bersuire, used 'dictionarium' as more or less meaning 'phrase-book'. . . . What he compiled was in fact an alphabetical list of more than 3,000 words used in the Bible, accompanied by moral expositions . . . The Latin term may well have been popular as a convenient title for anything remotely dealing with words. (McArthur 1986*b*: 79)[1]

But this alleged imprecision of the word only reflects the vagueness of the genre. The words *dictionary* and *dictionnaire* have been used in the titles of works that would not be considered as true

[1] On the history of the word *dictionnaire* in French, see Matoré (1968: 58–60).

dictionaries now: the most famous example may be the illustrious *Dictionnaire raisonné des sciences, des arts et des métiers*, which is the second title of the great *Encyclopédie* of Diderot and D'Alembert (1751). They have also been used of books that were not thought of as dictionaries even by their authors: Voltaire's *Dictionnaire philosophique*, Flaubert's *Dictionnaire des idées reçues*, or again Ambrose Bierce's *Devil's Dictionary*. On the other hand, true dictionaries have been published under misleading titles: Quemada (1968: 329) mentions dictionaries that were called *alphabets* or *syllabaires*, and Besterman (Matoré 1968: 21) mentions an etymological dictionary of French published in 1853 by J. Azaïs under the title *Dieu, l'homme et la parole*.[2]

1.1.1 *The word* dictionary *in dictionaries*

Littré's dictionary has the following definition for *dictionnaire*:

> Recueil des mots d'une langue, des termes d'une science, d'un art, rangés par ordre alphabétique ou autre, avec leur signification.[3]

In *Webster's Third New International Dictionary* (*W3*), the definition is slightly more detailed, but very similar:

> A reference book containing words usually alphabetically arranged along with information about their forms, pronunciations, functions, etymologies, meanings, and syntactical and idiomatic uses.

Matoré (1968: 20) finds all the definitions of *dictionary* in dictionaries less than satisfactory. The only one that satisfies him is the one that is proposed by the *OED*.[4] It runs:

> A book dealing with the individual words of a language (or certain specified classes of them), so as to set forth their orthography, pronunciation, signification and use, their synonyms, derivation and history, or at least some of these facts: for convenience of reference, the words are arranged in some stated order, now, in most languages, alphabetical; and in larger dictionaries the information given is illustrated by quotations from literature.

[2] On the various titles given to dictionaries and encyclopedias throughout the world, see Rey (1982: 12–16).

[3] 'Thesaurus of the words of a language, of the terms of a science or an art, arranged in alphabetical or some other order, together with their meanings.'

[4] Matoré calls *New Oxford Dictionary* what was at the time the *New English Dictionary on Historical Principles*.

This may be considered better, if only because it is longer than the other definitions that we have seen. But Rey has argued that it is too narrow:

> les mots ne sont pas les seules unités possibles, les mots isolés éliminent indûment les syntagmes codés, la définition est restreinte aux ouvrages unilingues, la définition et l'histoire ne définissent qu'un type très particulier de dictionnaire. . . la "grandeur" du dictionnaire n'a rien à voir théoriquement avec la présence de citations littéraires. . . [5] (Rey 1977: 57)

For him, the definition of *dictionary* in the *OED* is only a definition of the *OED*: 'En fait, ce qui est décrit, plutôt que défini, c'est un modèle socio-culturel de dictionnaire, inexistant avant 1860 et périmé un siècle plus tard'[6] (Rey 1977: 57).

It is certainly unreasonable to expect a general dictionary to provide a definition of *dictionary* that can satisfy the specialist. There is a wide range of lexicographical products that can be called dictionaries: *dictionary* is a term with a wide extension and a complex intension. If the definition is too precise, it will not encompass all types of existing dictionaries; if it is too vague, it will not differentiate between dictionaries and other types of reference works. The concept is a complex one that can only be defined by specialists.

1.1.2 *The word* dictionary *in metalexicographical*[7] *literature*

When Quemada studied the origins of French lexicography, he had to allow for all the various sorts of dictionaries that his corpus contained. Not surprisingly, he used a fairly vague definition: 'Le dictionnaire est avant tout un catalogue de vocables destiné à donner accès, de manière commode, à des informations dont le nombre et

[5] 'words are not the only eligible units, single words unduly eliminate coded syntagms, the definition is restricted to monolingual dictionaries, definitions and word histories characterize only one particular type of dictionary . . . the quality of the dictionary has nothing to do, in theory, with the presence of quotations from literature . . .'

[6] 'In fact, what is described, rather than defined, is a socio-cultural dictionary type which did not exist before 1860 and is outdated a century later.'

[7] The word *metalexicography* is derived from the French 'métalexicographie', apparently coined by Rey and Delesalle (1979). It is now frequently used to refer to the activities of anyone who writes about lexicography but does not write dictionaries. It is sometimes used with a pejorative connotation by practising lexicographers. Many metalexicographers are academics, but more and more lexicographers are also metalexicographers.

la nature sont laissés à l'appréciation de l'auteur'[8] (Quemada 1968: 14). Zgusta (1971: 17) uses a slightly more precise formulation:

> A dictionary is a systematically arranged list of socialized linguistic forms compiled from the speech-habits of a given speech-community and commented on by the author in such a way that the qualified reader understands the meaning . . . of each separate form, and is informed of the relevant facts concerning the function of that form in its community.

Rey (1970*a*: 165) defines *dictionnaire* in a noticeably different metalanguage, which is typical of a certain period in the history of French linguistics: 'suite ordonnée de messages graphiques et didactiques à propos d'unités-signes fonctionnant dans le système d'une (ou plusieurs) langue(s) naturelle(s)'.[9]

The definitions of *dictionary* in metalexicographical literature vary even more than the definitions in dictionaries, because each author writes from his or her particular point of view, and for a particular category of readers. The best definition in metalexicography is actually a list of features drawn up by Rey-Debove for her study of modern French dictionaries. For her—in typical French linguistic terminology of the sixties and seventies—a dictionary can be defined by the following eight characteristics:

(1) Suite de messages graphiques isolés
(2) Ouvrage de consultation
(3) Deux structures, parfois réduites à une seule
(4) Classement par la forme ou le contenu
(5) Caractères linguistiques du sujet de l'information
(6) Caractère didactique de l'information explicite
(7) Un dictionnaire informe sur des signes
(8) La nomenclature est un ensemble déterminé, structuré s'il n'est pas exhaustif[10] (Rey-Debove 1971: 20–7)

[8] 'A dictionary is above all a catalogue of words which is designed to give easy access to items of information whose quantity and nature are left to the judgement of the author.'

[9] 'an ordered list of graphic and didactic statements about sign-units which function in the system of one natural language or several'.

[10] '(1) A list of separate graphic statements
(2) A book designed for consultation
(3) A book with two structures, sometimes only one
(4) Items are classified by form or content
(5) The information is linguistic in nature
(6) The information is explicitly didactic
(7) A dictionary gives information about signs
(8) The word-list corresponds to a predetermined set, and is structured if not exhaustive.'

1.1.2.1 *A dictionary is a series of separate paragraphs*

The text of a dictionary is a series of separate, independent paragraphs that is not designed for continuous reading. The paragraphs are the entries; the subdivisions of the entries, or sub-entries, are related within each entry and meant to be read together for comparison.

The dictionary is not the only type of book to be made up of a series of unrelated paragraphs. Rey-Debove mentions books like La Rochefoucauld's *Maximes*, but there are also phone books, mail-order catalogues, etc.

1.1.2.2 *A dictionary is meant to be consulted, not read*

The fact that the dictionary is consulted rather than read is clearly linked to the form of the text. The consultation of a dictionary is a process whereby the user acquires or verifies a particular piece of information: the dictionary is never consulted in its entirety.

D'Alembert mentioned that characteristic of the dictionary, and he did not particularly like it: for him the consultation of a dictionary is fragmentary and superficial, and the dictionary (if it is not *raisonné*) is an inferior kind of book for lazy people—as opposed to the encyclopedia, which is serious reading:

> Ces sortes de collections peuvent tout au plus servir à donner quelques lumières à ceux qui sans ce secours n'auroient pas eu le courage de s'en procurer: mais elles ne tiendront jamais lieu de Livres à ceux qui chercheront à s'instruire; les Dictionnaires par leur forme même ne sont propres qu'à être consultés, & se refusent à toute lecture suivie.[11] (D'Alembert 1763/1965: 122)

Rey-Debove draws two conclusions from the observation that the dictionary will only be consulted. The first is that the different paragraphs that constitute the text must be arranged in such a way that the users can find easily and quickly the particular bit of information that they need: the arrangement of the paragraphs must be 'coded' (Rey-Debove 1971: 20). In the prototypical dictionary, the arrangement is the alphabetical order of the words that are used

[11] 'These collections can only procure some enlightenment to those who would not be perseverant enough to secure it for themselves without such help; but they will never replace true Books for those who seek to educate themselves; dictionaries being designed as they are can only be consulted, and do not lend themselves to proper reading.'

as entry-words. This has become so habitual in our culture that we find it difficult to imagine dictionaries that would be arranged differently (see below, 1.1.2.4).

Rey-Debove's second conclusion is that the contents of each paragraph must be kept constant throughout the dictionary; there must be a 'programme' of information that is repeated at each entry, or the users will never know what to expect when they look up a word.

One might add that the word-list must correspond to some sort of pre-existing set of words, so that the users know, more or less, before consulting the dictionary, what sort of information they can expect to find in it: 'Les nomenclatures ne sont jamais arbitraires. Elles ne sont pas une liste exhaustive d'items, mais ne peuvent être une liste quelconque d'items'[12] (Rey-Debove 1969*a*: 188). The dictionary can only be consulted if the users have an idea of the existence of certain pre-existing sets, such as the lexis of the language and some subsets within that lexis. This is true of all books that are meant to be consulted rapidly about particular points of information: their contents must be predictable to a certain extent.

1.1.2.3 *Dictionaries have a double structure*

Rey-Debove distinguishes between the *macrostructure* and the *microstructure*. The macrostructure is a rough equivalent of the English *word-list*: '[c'est] l'ensemble des entrées ordonnées, toujours soumise à une lecture verticale partielle lors du repérage de l'objet du message. La macrostructure est couramment nommée nomenclature'[13] (Rey-Debove 1971: 21). The word *microstructure* refers to the contents of each entry: 'l'ensemble des informations ordonnées de chaque article, . . . qui se lisent horizontalement à la suite de l'entrée'[14] (Rey-Debove 1971: 21).

The use of the word *structure* can be justified in both cases by the existence of a pre-established programme. The macrostructure is the result of a selection of 'words' through the use of various criteria (see

[12] 'Word-lists are never arbitrary. They are not exhaustive, but they cannot be lists of items chosen at random.'

[13] '[it is] the complete set of entries arranged in some order, part of which is always used for vertical scanning when the user is looking for a particular piece of information. The macrostructure is commonly called "nomenclature".'

[14] 'the set of pieces of information as they are ordered in every article, . . . which are meant to be read horizontally after the entry-word'.

below, 6.2.1.). As we have seen, the word-list must correspond to a set of lexical units which, in a way, exists somewhere else, if only in the minds of the users. The microstructure is the result of the application of a pre-established programme of information given in each entry.

The microstructure is a rigid structure: all modern dictionaries are characterized by the uniformity of their entries, both in terms of content and in terms of layout (Zgusta 1971: 248). This has not always been the case: Samuel Johnson had some very short entries (for example *cat*) and some very long ones (for example *armadillo*, or *opium*), for no apparent reason, and even the *OED* had inexplicable variations among entries (Burnett 1989: 139). In modern dictionaries, some information may be missing in some entries, but this can always be interpreted by the users: information not explicitly given means 'normal' information in any particular field of the entry; unknown information (for example an unknown etymology) is normally indicated as such.

The structural nature of the macrostructure is less clear. As every lexicographer knows, it is always possible to add or subtract an entry-word without destroying the quality of the word-list, whose unity is not clearly definable: no lexical set is defined with enough precision to forbid this.

It is totally impossible to imagine a dictionary without a macrostructure: all dictionaries necessarily have a list of entry-words, and if the list is not structured at all the book is clearly not a dictionary. But there are dictionaries that seem to have no microstructure: they seem to give no information whatsoever about their entry-words (spelling dictionaries, crossword dictionaries, reverse dictionaries, etc.). This, however, is only an illusion. No dictionary can avoid giving, at the very least, two pieces of information:

1. The spelling of the entry-word. This information is hidden, or implicit, since it is given in the entry-word itself. But it is clear that an entry in a spelling dictionary, for example, reads 'the word X is spelt Y', in which Y is the microstructural information, in this case the spelling.
2. The fact that the entry-word belongs to the lexical set that the dictionary purports to represent.

There are other types of books that have two structures: guidebooks, for example, or mail-order catalogues. The differentiating characteristic of the dictionary lies in the fact that its two structures interact: all the entry-words that make up the macrostructure receive microstructural information, and all the words used in the microstructure must normally be included and treated in the macrostructure: the dictionary is 'closed' (see below, 6.2.10).

Macrostructure and *microstructure* are now fairly frequent words in French metalexicography. Some use *macrostructure* as a synonym of *nomenclature*, but it is certainly preferable to use the latter as an equivalent of *word-list*, while the former can be used to refer to the set of entry-words as they are arranged in a certain way in each dictionary. In spite of their usefulness, the two words have not yet been widely adopted by English-speaking metalexicographers, who prefer their traditional terms.[15]

1.1.2.4 *A dictionary is an ordered set*

The need for an easy-to-use-arrangement of the different entries of a dictionary follows naturally from the fact that the dictionary is designed for consultation rather than for reading. In most dictionaries, the arrangement is based on the graphic form of the entry-word: entries are classified by spelling, so that the dictionary can only be consulted by users who have some idea of the spelling of the word they are looking for. Classification by sound is not impossible (Lurquin 1982), but cannot be used in general-purpose dictionaries for languages where sound and spelling are related in ways that have become complex over time. In English as well as in French, the average reader would often find it difficult to locate a word if the entries were grouped by sound.

There are several ways of classifying words by form. Kristeva (1981) mentions systems used in Sumerian, in Chinese, etc. In Arabic, many dictionaries have used classifications by type of consonant group (Zgusta 1989*b*; Boisson *et al.* 1991). The first *Dictionnaire de l'Académie* (1694) classified its entry-words alphabetically, but grouped together, in the same entry, words that were related etymologically and morphologically even in the absence of any semantic connection in synchrony (*chien*, *chenêt*, *canine*, etc.). The system was the object of so much criticism, particularly by Furetière, that it was abandoned in the second (1718) edition. Classification by morphemes has been advocated by some, mostly

[15] Ilson (1990*b*) uses *macrostructure*, sometimes spelt *macro-structure*.

structuralist, linguists (Kahane and Kahane 1962: 257; Malone 1962: 113; Antal 1963). Its advantages are obvious if the dictionary is considered as a portrait of the language, but it makes the consultation process so difficult for the dictionary user that it is probably not realistic for a general-purpose dictionary (Meier 1969: 145; Zgusa 1971: 240).

When European lexicographers began using the alphabet as a key for the arrangement of words, they decided to start from the leftmost letter. This was the more logical thing to do, but they could also have decided to classify words according to their last letters. At first, lexicographers used only the first letter of every entry-word (McArthur 1986*b*: 76). Then, as dictionaries increased their word-lists, words had to be classified within each letter by means of their second letter, then of their third, etc. Minor arrangements had to be made in individual languages for the classification of letters with diacritics, as in French, German, Czech, Swedish, etc. (Zgusta 1989*b*).

Modern dictionaries still vary marginally in their use of the alphabetical arrangement, particularly in the positioning of multi-word units, both among themselves and together with simple words. Whenever a multi-word unit must be inserted in the alphabetical arrangement, the compiler first has to decide whether the unit will be listed as such, in the normal order of its elements, or whether this has to be changed: to take a simple example, should *ice cream* be listed in the letter I for *ice* or in the letter C for *cream*? The answer is not as simple as it looks: where should one place *Alzheimer's disease*, *Virginia creeper*, *artificial insemination*, and the like? The answers surely depend on the relative importance of each element, and on where the user is most likely to look first.[16]

Then, supposing the multi-word item is listed as such, at the normal position of its first element, the second problem is how to apply the alphabetical order to the space between the elements. The lexicographer has a choice of two solutions: either the multi-word units are treated like any other sequence of letters, the space between the words being disregarded; in that case, one would have, for example, *post*, *postilion*, *post office*, etc. Or the multi-word units are classified immediately after their first word, as if the space was a

[16] Some research has been carried out on where dictionary users tend to look up multi-word units (see below, 5.2.3.1).

signal for a new internal classification (thus *post*, *post office*, *postilion*, etc.).[17]

The alphabetical order has been heavily criticized, at least since Vaugelas (1647) and particularly—for obvious reasons—by structuralist linguists (Gold 1979). It is obviously not a satisfactory arrangement if the dictionary is to be used 'onomasiologically', to find 'ideas' rather than forms (as is often the case in encoding), or for anyone who thinks that the dictionary should mirror as closely as possible the organization of the mental lexicon.

The production of reference works where words are arranged differently has two origins: one is pedagogical, namely the need to provide help for those users who start from an idea and want to find the right word; and the other is ideological: in many societies, there has been a desire to encapsulate all the words of a lexis in a form that makes sense. Such reference works 'often forget their readers' needs, as if their authors were enchanted by the idea of putting world and words in order or of revealing the hidden order of nature' (Marello 1990: 1084). This need was felt at very early periods in many societies (Boisson *et al.* 1991).

A reference work where words are arranged semantically is called a *thesaurus* or *lexicon*, or again *conceptual* (or *ideological*, *notional*, *onomasiological*, *semantic*) *dictionary*. The most famous example in Western countries is probably the *Thesaurus* of Peter Mark Roget (1852), inspired by Comenius's *Janua Linguarum Reserata* (1631) and by all the encyclopedic tradition. The main advantage of a thesaurus like Roget's is that it groups together words that are semantically related, so that the location of an entry-word in the macrostructure is in itself a piece of semantic information—a clear case where macrostructure merges into microstructure (Geeraerts 1989: 289). However, the consultation of such books is not easy, since it is based on an organization of human knowledge that is bound to vary from author to author. Rey tells the following anecdote, a good illustration of the difficulties of using dictionaries with a non-alphabetical arrangement:

> Martin du Gard, ayant remarqué sur la table de Gide un exemplaire du dictionnaire analogique de Boissière, et s'étant dit: "serait-ce le secret du vocabulaire de Gide, la source de ses trouvailles?", s'appliqua à dénicher ce

[17] Roughly, the first solution is typical of American, and the second of British, dictionaries.

livre précieux. L'ayant difficilement trouvé, et payé fort cher, il reçoit la visite de Gide. "Ah", lui dit ce dernier, "vous possédez le recueil de Boissière? Que vous en semble?,"—"Incomparable!"—"Vraiment? Moi aussi, j'en acheté un, autrefois; mais je n'ai jamais su me servir de ces outils-là."[18] (Rey 1977: 16)

Most semantically arranged reference books are equipped with an alphabetical index to facilitate consultation. Many of the modern variations on the theme of *Roget's Thesaurus*, particularly in the USA, are even totally alphabetized—a complex system in which entry-words are used for paragraphs containing lists of related words and phrases.

The alphabetical arrangement is in no danger of being replaced in general-purpose dictionaries, especially at a time when the computer invalidates the main argument traditionally used against it. In most languages now, people find it difficult to imagine dictionaries in which the entries would not be arranged alphabetically. The arrangement has become part of the social image of the dictionary (Rey-Debove 1971: 21). 'The alphabetical arrangement, though strictly conventional, is so overwhelmingly dominant that the ordinary person associates with this familiar sequence the very genre of the dictionary' (Malkiel 1962: 17).

The alphabetical arrangement has several advantages. One is that splitting up the information word by word, paragraph by paragraph, condenses the subject matter of the dictionary into short texts that are easily digestible—a feature that some consider as a defect rather than a virtue. Another advantage is that the alphabetical order is by far the easiest and the fastest system for the dictionary user (Zgusta 1971: 282; Rey 1977: 20–1), an important point particularly when the dictionary is used for decoding. But the most significant advantage, the one that no doubt explains the immense popularity of alphabetical ordering of entries in so many cultures, is the fact that it gives the dictionary users the impression that they master the totality of the lexis of the language, in a form whose completeness is

[18] 'Having noticed a copy of Boissière's analogical dictionary on Gide's desk, and having wondered whether this was the explanation for Gide's vast vocabulary and lexical felicities, Martin du Gard set about unearthing the precious book. He eventually found a copy, and paid dearly for it. When he was next visited by Gide, the latter said "Ah, I see you have Boissière's dictionary. What do you think of it?" "Wonderful!" "Really? I bought a copy a long time ago myself; but I have never been able to use these dictionaries."'

immediately apparent to the senses: 'le dictionnaire représente l'illusion de la totalité, de l'ordre immobile, de l'harmonie. Il semble épuiser le monde et les mots'[19] (Rey 1970*c*: 14). The general-purpose dictionary, in that sense, is the A to Z not only of language but also of the universe: 'Le dictionnaire, c'est l'univers par ordre alphabétique'[20] (Anatole France, mentioned in Matoré 1968: 36).

The alphabetical order may also be slightly less arbitrary than it looks: when two words start with the same spelling (often the same morpheme), they are positioned next to each other in alphabetical order (Rey-Debove 1971: 21). And some improvements have been suggested to make the alphabetically arranged macrostructure more representative of semantic links. Many modern dictionaries have a system of entries and sub-entries, and words that are semantically related can be cross-referenced—a fairly recent development (Rey-Debove 1989*c*).[21] The *Grand Robert* (*GR*) justifies its label as *dictionnaire analogique* by grouping together in its entries words that are semantically related: typically, the entry for *cheval* will have *jument*, *étalon*, *poulain*, *cavalier*, *haras*, *monter*, *trot*, *galop*, etc. as well, thus facilitating encoding operations and a better understanding of the lexical system. The *Robert méthodique* (*RM*) groups words in entries according to their elements, most of them being morphemes (Béjoint 1985). Another, more revolutionary, approach is that of the *combinatory dictionaries* developed by Mel'čuk and his colleagues and followers, in which each entry-word is the centre of a complex network of syntagmatically and paradigmatically related words.

1.1.2.5 *A dictionary is a list of linguistic units*

Every single paragraph that constitutes an entry in a dictionary is headed by a short graphic sequence, the entry-form, which is generally—but not necessarily—the object of the information contained in the entry. In the prototypical dictionary, this sequence is usually a word, in the sense of 'any uninterrupted sequence of

[19] 'the dictionary represents an illusion of totality, of an immobile order of things, of harmony. It seems to exhaust the universe and the lexicon.'

[20] 'The dictionary is the universe in alphabetical order.'

[21] Cross-references were hardly ever used before the nineteenth century (Rey-Debove 1989*c*: 932).

graphemes that is commonly felt to correspond to a concept'.[22] In many modern dictionaries, some entries are also headed by morphemes, mostly prefixes and suffixes. Dictionaries of idioms may have longer strings of words, but there is one word in each string which is used as the classifying unit. The same is true of dictionaries of proverbs—but it is not clear whether or not they are real dictionaries.

All entry-forms are linguistic units: they are signs in the Saussurean sense, double-faced linguistic entities with a *significant* and a *signifié*; they have fixed forms corresponding to fixed meanings that the members of the linguistic community memorize, recognize, and use as wholes: they are coded (Béjoint 1989*a*). In that sense, rhyming dictionaries in which entry-forms are syllables are not real dictionaries.

Proper names pose a particular problem (Rey-Debove 1971: 25): they are words, they are coded, and yet it is not totally clear whether they are signs or not. The question is whether proper names have meanings or not, and it is a question that goes much beyond the scope of this book. Dictionaries of proper names can be regarded as dictionaries if their microstructure is linguistic in nature (see below, 1.1.2.7), but this is hardly ever the case.

1.1.2.6 *A dictionary is a didactic book*

A dictionary is primarily an instrument to be used when one needs a piece of information about a word in particular, about the language in general, or about the world. During the consultation process, the users learn, or verify, something that they did not know, or had momentarily forgotten. Dictionaries are instruments for self-teaching, and they have the characteristics of all didactic books: they contain definitions, they give information which is presented as the knowledge and opinions of the community in general—as opposed to the knowledge and opinions of the lexicographer (Rey-Debove 1971: 23;

[22] The notion of 'word' has been discussed extensively for some time, with less than satisfactory results. For recent research, see Greenberg (1954), Martinet (1965), Pergnier (1986), Di Sciullo and Williams (1987), Lipka (1990), etc. Every linguist has to make do with a working definition, but there are many linguistic and sociolinguistic problems. The conclusion is clear, unfortunately: *word* is not a technical term that can be defined with any precision, even if it undoubtedly corresponds to a popular notion. Words are a fuzzy set, with more or less prototypical examples. Oddly enough, the notion of 'word' is becoming more important than it was in the recent past, because it is a crucial concept for the exploitation of lexical databases by computers (Knowles 1990: 1650–1).

Dubois and Dubois 1971: 54)— and they give this information in an 'objective', undisputable way.

This has not always been the case. Furetière's and Richelet's dictionaries were rich in personal comments (Bray 1986; Corneri 1990). Some of Samuel Johnson's definitions are so well known, if only the famous 'harmless drudge' as a definition of *lexicographer*, that only a few examples will be given here:[23]

excise: A hateful tax levied upon commodities, and adjudged not by the common judges of property but wretches hired by those to whom excise is paid.
oats: A grain, which in England is generally given to horses, but in Scotland supports the people.
pension: An allowance made to anyone without an equivalent. In England it is generally understood to mean pay given to a state hireling for treason of his country.[24]

Different countries seem to have had different attitudes towards objectivity in dictionaries: British dictionaries have a long tradition of using dictionary definitions as a support for humorous, satirical, or simply idiosyncratic remarks. The first edition of the *Concise Oxford Dictionary* (*COD1*, 1911) contained whimsical definitions, comments, or examples (Allen 1986). The most recent occurrences of fanciful definitions are to be found in the 1972 edition of *Chambers Twentieth Century Dictionary* (*CTD*). Here are a few examples:[25]

civil: polite (in any degree short of discourtesy).
he-man: a man of exaggerated or extreme virility, or what some women take to be virility.
jaywalker: a careless pedestrian whom motorists are expected to avoid running down.
middle-aged: between youth and old age, variously reckoned to suit the reckoner.
noose: a snare or bond generally, esp. hanging or marriage.
Welsh rabbit: melted cheese with or without ale, etc., poured over hot toast —sometimes written 'Welsh rarebit' by wiseacres.

In France, the bias has tended to be more political. One of my dictionaries of French, published in the early twentieth century by

[23] These definitions are only extreme examples in Johnson's *Dictionary*, and should not be taken as typical of his style.

[24] See also the definitions of *cockney*, *compliment*, *Tory*, etc. (McAdam and Milne 1963).

[25] Rosamund Moon (personal communication).

a priest in Lyon, does not have an entry for *Zola*, and the early dictionaries of Pierre Larousse are famous for some of their entries, as when the entry for *Napoleon* says: 'mort le 18 Brumaire'.

Such subjectivity—the 'Johnsonian effect' (Algeo 1990*a*: 214)—is now unthinkable in commercial lexicography.[26] This is because modern dictionaries are compiled by teams of lexicographers rather than by just one person—Johnson already had a few people working for him, but they were just copyists—and mostly because the public now expects the dictionary to be as 'objective' as possible. Modern dictionaries use all sorts of devices, scientific or Latin words, impersonal forms, the passive voice, etc. to make sure that the text has all the appearance of objectivity.

Modern dictionaries are certainly not free from ideological biases, but those are now social rather than individual. The general-purpose dictionary is a text in which a certain social group (or social class) describes the world and the language, but the users see it as a book in which society, that abstract but impressive entity, speaks to its members, with the lexicographer as a 'go-between' (Dubois and Dubois 1971: 49). Rey-Debove writes, with uncharacteristic understatement: 'Il arrive que les dictionnaires soient polémiques et que l'information apportée reflète la pensée d'une classe sociale, d'une génération, d'une intelligentzia qui veut faire triompher une idéologie'[27] (Rey-Debove 1971: 23). This is probably true of many —if not all—dictionaries, even though we find it difficult to discern the biases of a dictionary when they are those that prevail in our society. Consider the following definitions of *canoe*, compiled only a few decades ago for the *OED*:[28]

1. A kind of boat in use among uncivilized nations: a. Originally applied to those of the West Indian aborigines, which were hollowed out of a single tree-trunk, and thence to those of other savages, or of prehistoric men, of and used generally for any rude craft in which uncivilized people go upon the water; most savages use paddles instead of oars, whence 'canoe' is

[26] Though Geeraerts (1989: 290) gives the following example, translated from the Van Dale 1976 Dutch dictionary: '*kosmonaut*: a somewhat hyperbolic designation for persons who make a tiny jump in cosmic space, e.g. by having themselves shot to the moon or a planet of our solar system'.

[27] 'Dictionaries are sometimes polemic, sometimes they contain information that reflects the thinking of a particular social class, of a generation, of an intelligentsia which is out to vindicate a particular ideology.'

[28] Mentioned by Moon (1989: 74).

sometimes this construction. b. Extended to those of other races and other construction, understood to be any vessel propelled by paddles.
2. In civilized use: A small light sort of boat or skiff propelled by paddling.

Lexicographers are always, however hard they try, the mouthpieces of a particular social group in the society to which they belong: 'Chaque lexicographe, porte-parole d'une classe, truchement d'une idéologie, croit sans doute re-présenter fidèlement un ensemble de formes. Mais il n'y a pas de fidélité possible, de dessin si léché qu'il n'abolisse le modèle'[29] (Rey 1977: 88). Meschonnic, having observed Bayle's and Larousse's dictionaries in particular, argues that most dictionaries are not didactic but polemic. He writes:

> Voir du didactisme dans le dictionnaire suppose une conception de son rôle comme d'un modèle, ce qui généralise abusivement à la fois une notion particulière et une époque du dictionnaire. . . Et le retard des dictionnaires sur leur époque achève de leur retirer ce rôle d'enseigneurs, sinon qu'il en laisse à certains le fantasme.[30] (Meschonnic 1991: 59–64)

But the frontier between the two attitudes is hard to place: for Pierre Larousse, for example, didacticism was necessarily polemic, since his aim as a lexicographer was to liberate the masses by educating them (see below, 3.2.3.1). It is impossible to define the general-purpose dictionary without mentioning its role as an instrument for self-education and for social integration, even though the contents are not as 'objective' as they are made to appear.

1.1.2.7 *A dictionary gives information about linguistic signs*

A reference work can be considered as a dictionary only if the microstructural information is about signs, not about the referents corresponding to those signs. This is a very tricky distinction, which has been discussed for centuries. In France, the notions of *définition de mot* and *définition de chose* date back at least to Pascal's *Opuscules*, and they were extensively commented upon by the Port-Royal

[29] 'All lexicographers, who are the mouthpieces of a social class, the instruments of an ideology, no doubt believe that they objectively represent a set of forms. But there is no objectivity, no picture so accurate as to eliminate the model.'

[30] 'One can only see didacticism in the dictionary if one sees it as a model, thus unduly extending a particular conception of the dictionary and a stage in its historical development . . . And the delay with which dictionaries reflect their times removes any pretensions they might have of being educators, though such a role remains as a fantasy in the minds of some.'

grammarians, as well as by every linguist or philosopher of the time (Rey 1990: 14). Many metalexicographers insist that the dictionary should only contain definitions of words, not definitions of things, those being typical of the encyclopedia (Rey 1968: 70; Rey-Debove 1969*b*: 125, 1971: 180). Some, particularly in Germany and in France, distinguish between *dictionnaire de mots* and *dictionnaire de choses* (Wagner 1967: 127; Quemada 1968: 77; Rey-Debove 1971: 188).

The opposition between the sign and the thing is clear enough in some cases, particularly when a word in discourse refers to itself rather than to an extralinguistic concept. A statement like 'I don't like your Sir!' can have two interpretations; the predication '*cat* ends with a "t"' clearly applies to the sign *cat*, not to the thing, whereas 'the cat catches the mice' applies to the thing, not the word.

The underlying verb of the definition may help to distinguish the two types of definitions: the verb *be* introduces a definition which applies to the referent ('X *is* a Y that . . .') whereas *refer to* introduces a definition that applies to the sign ('the word X refers to a Y that . . .') (Rey-Debove 1970*a*: 10). Some definitions are clearly *définition de mot*, as when *poor* is defined by 'contrary of rich'. There are tendencies for nouns, particularly concrete nouns, to have 'be'-definitions, and for other words to have 'refer to'-definitions. But many can be construed with either verb.

The question is whether it is possible, and indeed advisable, to stick to *définition de mot* in a dictionary. Some linguists have argued that the two types of knowledge, linguistic and encyclopedic, can and should be distinguished. Rey-Debove (1989*a*: 308–9) says that the distinction is 'very easy' in theory, though the two often coincide in practice. For Wierzbicka (1985: 40–1), the 'dividing line is clear, at least in principle: no specialized knowledge can be regarded as part of the meaning'. For her, the linguistic concept includes only 'shared knowledge', which can be attained by introspection. If the result is not always as clear-cut as theory would have it, she says, this should not call into question the necessity of drawing a line.[31]

But most lexicographers admit that the dividing line is indeed a fine one: 'Contrairement à ce qu'un modèle sémiotique réducteur donne à penser, cette frontière est extraordinairement floue'[32] (Rey

[31] See also Mackenzie and Mel'čuk (1988: 79).

[32] 'Contrary to what an excessively simplifying semiotic model has implied, the frontier is extraordinarily fuzzy.'

1977: 181). And this is confirmed by recent research in psycholinguistics, which indicates that linguistic knowledge and encyclopedic knowledge are inextricably mixed (Kremin and Koskas 1984: 49; McNamara and Miller 1989). Much of what a dictionary definition says, particularly about concrete nouns, actually applies to the referent (Wiegand 1984; Kleiber 1988: 3–4; Fillmore 1989: 74).[33] It is impossible to define the *signifié* of a word without mentioning and to a certain extent describing the referent. Without that, the definition is reduced to virtually nothing, as Haiman has shown in his famous and highly controversial paper: a lexicographer wanting to define *elephant* without running the risk of falling into a *définition de chose* would end up with something like 'that animal which is named elephant' (Haiman 1980: 330).

The entry-forms of a dictionary are names, in the sense of linguistic labels for categories—if they were not, it would be possible to translate the dictionary. It is those names that are defined, not the referents, and the fact that dictionary definitions contain information that seems to apply to the referent simply proves that one cannot define a name without referring to the category that it applies to.

The debate is important for lexicographical practice. Some dictionaries tend to go for the minimal definition, the statement that is necessary and sufficient to isolate the word—or concept—from all the others, like Aristotle's famous example of the definition of *man* as 'featherless biped'; others prefer a more encyclopedic description that gives details much beyond what the language users should know of the concept in order to be able to use it in linguistic communication. Most dictionaries lie somewhere between these two extremes, and the dictionaries with the longer definitions—which tend to be the larger dictionaries—naturally tend towards more encyclopedicity: beyond the basic, admittedly ill-defined, evocation of the concept, any additional information is bound to be encyclopedic.

33 Maybe some of the confusion is created—or at least compounded—by the fact that all semanticians and metalexicographers tackling this question have used concrete nouns as examples: *chat* (Rey 1977), *libraire* (Rey-Debove 1970*a*, 1971: 187), *pomme de terre* (Rey-Debove 1971: 228), *carrot* (Weinreich 1962: 33), *cup* (Labov 1973), *wolf* (Leech 1974), etc. Oddly enough, they never use verbs or adjectives, no doubt under the influence of philosophers, who deal with the question from a different point of view.

1.1.2.8 *A dictionary is a structured representation of a predetermined lexical set*

As we have seen, the dictionary represents the lexis of a language, or a determined portion of that lexis. This must correspond to an entity that is perceived as such by the average language user.

Despite the claims of publishers on the dust-jackets of dictionaries, it is impossible for a dictionary to list *all* the words of a language, as every metalexicographer knows (Zgusta 1971: 246, etc.; see below, 6.2.1): 'L'exhaustivité n'est qu'un projet, jamais réalisé puisque l'ensemble n'est pas défini en extension, et c'est généralement un projet assez éloigné de sa réalisation'[34] (Rey-Debove 1971: 30).

There are several reasons why exhaustiveness is impossible. One is that the lexis of any language keeps changing and expanding, and that the dictionary—unless it describes a very precisely defined set of words—cannot avoid being partly obsolete at the time of publication.

> The half-million entries in a so-called 'unabridged' dictionary are but the tip of the lexicographical iceberg, for it is estimated that fifty thousand chemical compounds are discovered and named every year. There is no—and may never be—a complete inventory of all the slang words that have been used in English since printing was developed. (McDavid 1973*b*: 259)

But the main reason is the fact that the limits of the lexis to be described are far from clear. What exactly counts as an element of the lexis? When can one consider that a word has become part of it? Is one occurrence enough? If not, how many occurrences should one count? And how should they be counted? Or is it the case that some occurrences are better than others? What people can be considered as members of the linguistic community? Does one count regional words, children's words, words used by some native but debilitated speakers? How far should the dictionary account for 'potential vocabulary' (Tournier 1985: 33)? The number of possible words may be mathematically finite if it is accepted that there is only a finite number of morphemes and a finite number of possible combinations of morphemes (Rey-Debove 1971: 64), but it is a huge number, which no real dictionary ever approaches.

[34] 'Exhaustiveness is only an ideal; it is never realized since the set of words is never defined in extension, and the final realization is usually quite far removed from the ideal.'

Since lexicographers cannot ever hope to capture all the words of a lexis, the best they can do is to represent a reduction of the whole that must be as 'faithful' to the original as possible: 'Il ne s'agit évidemment pas de présenter un "morceau" quelconque de l'ensemble, mais d'en élaborer une réduction en y faisant figurer les éléments les plus représentatifs'[35] (Rey-Debove 1971: 30). This 'representativity' is also difficult to achieve (see below, 6.2.1), particularly for specialized dictionaries such as slang dictionaries, where the set to be represented is particularly elusive (Spears 1989: 99). Generally speaking, it is impossible to determine the quality of the word-list of a dictionary—apart from the grossest mistakes—because the model is not known. The lexis of a language has no concrete existence apart from the dictionary, thus creating a vicious circle from which it is difficult to escape.

1.1.3 *Definitions*

In addition to the list of eight points that we have just discussed, Rey-Debove proposes the following definition of *dictionnaire*:

> Un dictionnaire est un ouvrage didactique qui décrit un ensemble (généralement structuré) d'éléments linguistiques, présentés en messages séparés et ordonnés, permettant la consultation. Les éléments, qui se situent entre la lettre et l'unité supérieure à la phrase, sont suivis ou non d'un énoncé (deux structures ou une seule structure). L'information implicite (une structure) ou explicite (deux structures) réalise un programme, et concerne toujours, au moins partiellement, le signe; dans l'information explicite qui semble ne concerner que la chose, la présence de la définition vaut comme information sur le signe.[36] (Rey-Debove 1971: 27).

Not surprisingly, this definition is longer than all the definitions we have seen so far. It does not totally do justice to the accompanying discussion: for example, it does not say that the entry-forms are necessarily linguistic signs, that the whole must be representative of

[35] 'The aim is obviously not to propose a randomly chosen section of the whole set, but to prepare a reduction that will contain the most representative elements.'

[36] 'A dictionary is a didactic book which describes a (generally structured) set of linguistic elements and presents them in separate and ordered units, thus allowing for consultation. The elements, which range from the letter to elements that are above sentence-length, are usually followed by paragraphs (two structures, or only one). The information, whether implicit (one structure) or explicit (two structures), follows a predetermined programme and is always, at least in part, about the sign; in the explicit information which seems to be only about the referent, the presence of a definition is taken as information about the sign.'

a predetermined lexical set, etc., but it is the best definition available.

The word *dictionary* thus defined is inevitably polysemous: it can be applied either to the book as a whole (the thing or the contents) or to the alphabetical list inside the book, exclusive of all other components, like the front matter, the appendices, etc., or to the alphabetical list of the words, exclusive of the encyclopedic matter, etc. The 'polysemy' of *dictionary* is contextually bound (see below, 7.2).

1.1.4 *The dictionary and other types of word-lists*

1.1.4.1 *Other types of dictionaries*

Bookshops are full of 'dictionaries' that have few of our defining features: the most common type is that of the book that provides information on a given subject in separate paragraphs, anywhere between a few lines and a few pages in length, with alphabetic arrangement of those paragraphs according to a chosen entry-word. Those are not real dictionaries, since they are clearly about things, not about words: a 'dictionary of economics', for example, is only an alphabetical encyclopedia (see below, 1.1.4.4.). 'Dictionaries' of quotations are only dictionaries in the sense that their contents are arranged in some sort of alphabetical way for consultation, but they are not about coded linguistic units.

Transformational and generative grammarians make use of a list of words that has to be attached to the set of rules used to generate sentences in any given language. This is called the *lexicon*, or sometimes the *dictionary*. It is not usually a material object, because the information that is necessary for each word to fit into the empty slots of the generated sentences is not totally known. 'No one actually *uses* the lexicon, or any sub-section of it that happens to be published. Books which contain specimens of the lexicon are not actual dictionaries themselves' (Mallinson 1979: 10).

Also, the specialists of databanks use dictionaries, sometimes also called *thesauri*, which are lists of the keywords used as pointers to the location of information inside the bank (Aitchison and Gilchrist 1972). The lists of words that are *not* used in such a way are called *anti-dictionaries*.

1.1.4.2 *The dictionary and other lists of words*

An *index* is a list of words used in one book or series of books, by one or several authors (Sappler 1990). The only microstructural information it contains is the number of the page where the word can be found in the book, a cross-reference to the information contained in the book itself. The word-list of an index is only part of the total number of words used in the source work, typically chosen on account of the importance of the notion that they refer to in the subject treated. An index does not represent a set of words outside the source text to which it is attached. Most of the words in indexes are nouns, for obvious terminological reasons. Function words can only be found in the indexes of metalinguistic books.

A *concordance* is also a list of words, but it aims at drawing together the various passages of a book where a particular word is used. The first concordances were compiled on the text of the Bible, to give access to it through particular words, as early as the seventh century (Hanon 1990: 1563). Many others have been compiled in many languages since then, mostly for literary works. The concordance is usually exhaustive, containing every single word used in the work that is being studied. Concordances are now used in dictionary-making because the grouping of all the contexts of one word is of great help in compiling entries.

Glossaries, *vocabularies*, etc. are lists of specialized terms used in a particular field, with or without definitions. Like the index, they give only the terms that are considered important; unlike it, they are not limited to a particular work, but aim to represent the field in general. The word *glossary* is also sometimes used to refer to lists of regionalisms, dialect or patois words.

1.1.4.3 *The dictionary and the grammar*

Dictionaries and grammars have often been opposed (Kruisinga 1931: 7–14; Gleason 1962: 92; Mathiot 1973, etc.). Not that there can be the slightest ambiguity for the users, who know at once whether they are looking at a dictionary or at a grammar. Some of the differences between a grammar-book and a dictionary are obvious enough: a grammar has a running text that is not divided into unconnected paragraphs, and thus it can be read, not only consulted; it does not have a coded arrangement of entry-heads; its text is unambiguously about the language, not about the world; also, and probably as a consequence, it is meant for a narrower public than the dictionary.

On the other hand, the two types do have certain things in common. They are both metalinguistic descriptions with a didactic purpose, designed to facilitate linguistic communication, and they contain the general knowledge of the society. Both are necessary for the acquisition of a language.

Linguists are interested in the distinction between the grammar and the lexis of a language, and lexicographers are interested in the definition of what goes into the dictionary as opposed to what goes into the grammar. Some have claimed that the dividing line is clear: 'The grammatical statement deals with form, the dictionary with meaning' (Gleason 1962: 90). This is of course untenable: the dictionary contains many statements that are about form, and the grammar—despite the efforts of some structuralist grammarians—cannot totally escape considerations of meaning. Another solution lies in the opposition between quantity and quality: 'All matters that apply to a considerable number of items would belong to the grammatical statement; those which apply to a single item to the dictionary' (Gleason 1962: 92). This is typical of a period when grammar was thought to be totally regular and lexis totally irregular. It allowed linguists to devote all their efforts to what they thought was at the same time the most important thing, and the most amenable to study. But it leaves open the question of the frontier: how does one count the number of items to which a statement applies, and where is the limit to be placed?

In fact, recent research indicates that the dividing line between the lexicon and the grammar is not that clear. In all languages and in English in particular, there are facts that one would hesitate to attribute to grammar or to lexis: where does one classify the *-er* endings in agent nouns, for example? 'Is this a lexical rule, because it relates words of different major classes, or is it a transformation —or more generally a non-lexical rule—on the grounds that it is relatively productive and regular?' (Hudson 1988: 292). The same can be said of the *un-* prefix used before adjectives; of word order when using the adverb *enough*, or words like *someone* (one says 'someone nice', but not 'nice someone') (Hudson 1988: 292–5); of the use of specific prepositions after certain nouns or adjectives; of the rules of nominal composition (Levi 1983: 194); of the two types of adjectives in English (a red book is a book that is red, but a legal expert is not an expert who is legal) (Connor Ferris 1990); and generally of all kinds of lexical semantic regularities (see below, 7.2).

Since the end of the seventies, generative grammarians have re-evaluated the place of lexis in language. Some have been working on the 'syntactic' aspects of lexis, producing books whose titles are symptomatic of the fuzziness of the border: *Lexical Grammar* (Hoekstra *et al.* 1980), *The Semantics of Grammar* (Wierzbicka 1988*b*), etc. It is probably reasonable to think of lexis and syntax as two domains separated by a fuzzy border (Lemmens and Wekker 1991: 2). 'Grammarians and lexicographers['] respective patches turn out to be like the north end and the south end of the same field, rather than like different fields separated by a hedge' (Hudson 1988: 295).

Lexicographers cannot ignore the discussion about the distinction between grammar and lexis, but their problem is above all a practical one: What sort of information should be included in the dictionary? What is potentially useful? The answer will depend on what sort of user the dictionary is aimed at, and for what sort of linguistic operation. Dictionaries have always carried some information that was clearly grammatical. This is particularly true of the entries for function words, but there is also syntactic information in the examples, in the indications about part of speech, etc. The amount of grammar in dictionaries has recently increased noticeably, at least in France and in Great Britain, particularly in the dictionaries specially designed for foreign students (see below, 2.3.2.1). The shift towards more grammar in dictionaries may not be finished yet if we are moving towards a 'lexicography for encoding' (see below, 2.5.1.1):

> My own point of view is that the so-called grammatical information in most GPD's[37] is much too limited, and that as a result much linguistically important data finds it way neither into grammars nor into dictionaries, particularly information about the syntagmatic or collocational behavior of language. Of the two efforts to describe a language, grammar and dictionary, I feel that dictionaries have the greater capacity to absorb and organize this syntagmatic and collocational material and that they are therefore the proper archive for such information. (Sherman 1978: 100)

[37] GPD = general-purpose dictionary.

The presence of clearly grammatical information in a dictionary is now used as a sales argument by some publishers: the *Longman Dictionary of Contemporary English* (*LDOCE*), for example, has been described as 'a dictionary-cum-grammar'.

There is now mutual reinforcement between theoretical linguistics, where the frontier between lexis and grammar is becoming more and more blurred as lexis is seen as more and more regular, and lexicography, which tends to produce dictionaries that are more and more guides for encoding—an operation for which information about the syntagmatic, regular behaviour of words in discourse is indispensable.

1.1.4.4 *The dictionary and the encyclopedia*

The dictionary and the encyclopedia may have evolved historically, at least in some cultures, from a common origin (Boisson *et al.* 1991). They now differ in the nature of their entries, their arrangement, and the nature of the information given in each entry.

The entry-words of an encyclopedia are always nouns, both common nouns and proper nouns. But those nouns are not the subjects of the microstructural information contained in the entries; they are only the signs—in the sense of road signs—indicating the contents of the entries. They are labels attached to the entries for convenience of reference: typically, for example, an entry headed by the word *garden* will contain not an exploration of the concept, an explanation of the etymology of the word, etc., but a history and geography of gardening, an explanation of its techniques, etc. For many entries, a different entry-word might have been chosen, and this would not have modified noticeably the contents of the entry. That is why an encyclopedia can be translated, but a dictionary cannot.

> L'article d'encyclopédie, qui a pour objet la description du monde, utilise l'entrée comme un accès au domaine à décrire. Cette entrée n'est pas imposée comme signe, mais seulement comme contenu: tout mot voisin du même champ sémantique pourrait convenir. Au contraire, le dictionnaire, qui se propose la description des mots, présente des entrées qui sont l'objet même dont on parle en tant que signe. . . et chaque entrée, qui est envisagée dans sa forme, est déterminée: on ne peut lui substituer aucun synonyme ni aucune traduction.[38] (Rey 1982: 19)

[38] 'The encyclopedia article, which aims at describing the world, uses the entry-word as a means of access to the domain of description. The entry-word is not used as a sign, but only for its contents: any neighbouring word in the same semantic field could be used in its place. By contrast, the dictionary, which aims at describing words,

In an encyclopedia, the arrangement of the entries is usually not alphabetical but according to domain, and there is an alphabetical index of all the important words for ease of access (Rey 1982: 17–34).

The microstructural information of an encyclopedia is explicitly about the world, rather than about words. The two types, as we have seen, are not easily differentiated; encyclopedias contain information that is also to be found in dictionaries, and vice versa. Consider the following definition of *wolf* from *COD5* (the definition in *COD6* was slightly modified), as discussed by Leech (1974: 204):

> Erect-eared, straight-tailed, harsh-furred, tawny-grey, wild, gregarious, carnivorous quadruped allied to dog preying on sheep, etc. or combining in packs to hunt larger animals.

Such a definition goes much beyond the simple evocation that would be sufficient to isolate the concept. It could be found in an encyclopedia, the only difference being that the encyclopedia entry (if there was one) would contain much more. And there are thousands of similar examples. In practice, the presence or absence of linguistic information—information that is explicitly about the signs— is usually enough to differentiate the dictionary from the encyclopedia.

Dictionaries lean more or less towards encyclopedicity. An *encyclopedic dictionary* is a dictionary that has the macrostructure of a dictionary plus encyclopedic features—including entries for proper names and generally providing encyclopedic information whenever necessary. Most American dictionaries are encyclopedic at least in the macrostructural sense, as are some French ones, for example, the *Petit Larousse* (*PL*), and a few British ones, like the *Collins English Dictionary* (*CED*).

Encyclopedic dictionaries come in all sorts of designs: some have two sections, encyclopedic and linguistic, like *PL*—in which case one may wonder whether the word *dictionary* should be applied to the whole book or only to the alphabetical list of 'linguistic' entries. Some have only one macrostructure (like *CED*), and among those some have 'double entries' that separate the encyclopedic information from the rest of the entry: for example, the *Larousse trois volumes en couleurs* (*L3*) has, at the end of some entries, a paragraph or a

has entry-words which are, as signs, the objects of description . . . and every entry-word, which is taken as a form, is unique: it cannot be replaced by a synonym or an equivalent in another language.'

small essay headed ENCYCL. In the entry for *chat*, for example, this runs:

> Le chat jouit d'une excellente vision nocturne, d'une bonne ouïe, d'une grande sensibilité tactile au niveau des vibrisses. . .[39]

1.2 TYPES OF DICTIONARIES

1.2.1 *Dictionary typologies*

Many researchers, mostly over the last thirty years, have attempted to classify dictionaries in a clear typology, and this may seem surprising in view of the results obtained. The conclusion is virtually always the same: the task is impossible because the concept is too imprecise. The main interest of a typology—like sport for Pierre de Coubertin, *mutatis mutandis*—is to give occasion to explore the outer limits of a concept: a typology is a 'de-finition' in the etymological sense.

The basic question for anyone who attempts a typology is whether to derive categories from the observation of existing dictionaries or to create categories in theory and then see how existing dictionaries fit into them. Strictly speaking, the former would be a classification and the latter a typology. The two types are illustrated in the following review.

1.2.1.1 *Morphological typologies*

The simplest way to categorize dictionaries is to organize a taxonomy according to their most obvious formal characteristics. This is what librarians do, for obvious reasons (see Besterman 1943; Whittaker 1966; Kister 1977). Mitterand (1963: 104–5) distinguishes nine broad categories, each being referred to by a name that is very often, at the same time, the title of a dictionary, or part of it: dictionary of synonyms, dictionary of slang, dialect dictionary, etymological dictionary, etc.

Kister (1977: 4) distinguishes between unabridged (more than

[39] 'The cat has excellent nocturnal vision, good hearing, fine tactile sensitivity in its vibrissae . . .'

250,000 words),[40] semi-unabridged (between 130,000 and 250,000 words), and abridged dictionaries (less than 130,000 words). This poses a terminological problem: a dictionary can be technically abridged—that is, derived from a larger, more expensive version—and not fall into Kister's 'abridged' category because of its word-count. This is indeed the case of some of the American dictionaries that will be examined below (see 2.2.1.1). Also, the 'abridgement technique' seems to be practised in the USA and in Britain, but not in France, where no dictionary can be considered as the abridged version of a larger one—apart from perhaps the *Petit Robert* (*PR*).

Wagner (1967: 94, 123–6) also distinguishes between 'extensive' and 'selective' dictionaries according to the length of the word-list, while Dubois and Dubois (1971: 13) use almost the same labels, *extensive* and *intensive*, in a more subtle way that goes beyond the crude distinctions of basic morphological typologies, showing that size is not enough to classify dictionaries:

> Un dictionnaire est dit *extensif* quand sa nomenclature coïncide plus ou moins avec la totalité des items lexicaux que comportent idéalement la langue, le dialecte, le lexique fonctionnel d'une activité technique déterminée, etc. Un dictionnaire est dit *intensif* quand, procédant à un choix défini parmi ces items, il donne sur eux un plus grand nombre d'informations.[41] (Dubois and Dubois 1971: 13)[42]

Most authors until the eighties have proposed improved versions of the simple typologies outlined above. Malkiel (1962), for example,

[40] On the counting of words in dictionaries, see below, 2.2. Kister's figures must be interpreted in the context of the methods used in American lexicography. Also, because of the increase in word-count for all types in dictionaries generated by the intense competition of the American market-place, the figures used by Kister in 1977 would have to be changed for 1992.

[41] 'Dictionaries are said to be *extensive* when their word-list coincides more or less with the set of all the lexical items that ideally exist in the language, the dialect, the functional lexicon of a particular technique, etc. Dictionaries are said to be *intensive* when, having chosen some of those items with the help of clearly defined criteria, they then provide more information on each.'

[42] Read (1973*a*) uses the labels *extensive* and *intensive* in yet another way. For him, an extensive dictionary is one that tends to distinguish as many senses as possible in the entries for polysemous words, whereas an intensive dictionary is one that tends to extract a general meaning for as many as possible of the different uses of a polysemous word. Thus, an extensive dictionary will have many polysemous entries and many different senses in each, whereas an intensive dictionary will have few polysemous entries and few senses in each entry (see below, 7.2).

proposes a typology based on three main features, 'range', 'perspective', and 'presentation'. Range distinguishes between dictionaries according to the number of entries, the number of languages used, and the percentage of exclusively linguistic information. Perspective differentiates between historical dictionaries and synchronic dictionaries. Historical dictionaries describe the evolution of the language over a certain period of time: they contain obsolete words and archaic words, as well as information on the history of every entry-word, while synchronic dictionaries only describe the language as it is used at a given period, which is usually the present, and goes back a certain number of years, for example a generation (Rey-Debove 1971: 98). However, few dictionaries can afford to be really synchronic in this sense, if they are to be used in reading the literature of a society: most dictionaries of English contain words that are used in Shakespeare's plays, even if those words have rarely been used since the seventeenth century.

Presentation, in Malkiel's typology, is a measure of the precision of the definitions, the nature of the examples, the presence of pictures and certain pieces of information such as phonetic transcription and usage labels. Malkiel also distinguishes between prescriptive and descriptive dictionaries (see below, 3.2.2.4). For him, a dictionary can be either detached, preceptive, or facetious, though, as we have seen, facetiousness is hardly compatible with modern lexicography: 'Un "dictionnaire" entièrement facétieux (ou polémique) n'est simplement plus un dictionnaire: aucun utilisateur de la partie du *Jacassin* de P. Daninos qui affecte l'apparence du dictionnaire ne s'y trompe: il lit ce livre, ne le consulte pas'[43] (Rey 1977: 58). Malkiel also mentions the type of arrangement of the entries: this can be alphabetic, semantic or . . . casual (Malkiel 1962: 17).

Another distinction is used by Sebeok (1962) between dictionaries that are produced by their compilers and dictionaries that are abstracted from a corpus. This might be interesting in theory, but no real dictionary has ever been produced entirely by its author: 'le type. . . du dictionnaire généré n'existe guère à l'état pur'[44] (Rey 1977: 77).

[43] 'An entirely facetious (or polemical) "dictionary" is simply not a dictionary any more: none of the readers of the part of Pierre Daninos's book *Le Jacassin* which is presented in the form of a dictionary really believes it is a dictionary: the book is read, not consulted.'

[44] 'the purely generated dictionary scarcely exists'.

There have also been attempts at basing a dictionary typology on the type of linguistic approach used by the lexicographer.

La conformité avec la tradition ou la soumission à l'analyse linguistique scientifique sont les deux pôles entre lesquels se distribuent les conceptions des lexicographes modernes. Une typologie des dictionnaires français contemporains consistera donc à définir chacun des dictionnaires par rapport aux analyses de la linguistique et à les situer dans une gamme allant du non-linguistique au linguistique.[45] (Guilbert 1969: 28–9)

Guilbert then proceeds to distinguish five types of dictionary: the encyclopedia (*sic*), the scientific and technical dictionary, the 'linguistic' and encyclopedic dictionary, the *dictionnaire de langue* (this, interestingly enough, has no obvious equivalent in English),[46] and the 'linguistic-type' dictionary. The classification is difficult to apply to English-language dictionaries.

Behind Guilbert's analysis, there is a distinction that was popular for a while in the sixties and seventies, between commercial dictionaries and academic dictionaries (Guilbert 1969: 28–9). Commercial dictionaries have a wider public, they are smaller and cheaper, and above all they are compiled, Guilbert says, by non-linguists. The distinction has become blurred—if it was ever clear—with the increasing sophistication of lexicographers: 'il est vain d'opposer les dictionnaires "commerciaux" et les dictionnaires "scientifiques". . . Les grands dictionnaires de langue ont la réputation d'être les plus "scientifiques", sans doute parce qu'ils sont les plus développés et souvent les plus austères'[47] (Quemada 1987: 237). Some dictionaries may be good because they are big and contain a lot of information, but smaller dictionaries published by people who are trying to make a profit are not necessarily bad: 'toute opposition entre dictionnaires "commerciaux" (c'est-à-dire publiés par des firmes qui recherchent ouvertement un profit) et descriptions "désintéressées", qui seraient

[45] 'Submitting to tradition or following scientific linguistic analysis: those are the two extremities of the scale on which the ideas of modern lexicographers can be positioned. A typology of modern French dictionaries must therefore be an analysis of each dictionary in the light of the achievements of linguistics, allowing each to be placed on the scale that goes from the non-linguistic to the linguistic.'

[46] The concept exists, of course, but is has not been lexicalized. Is this because it was never an important issue in English-speaking countries? Ilson (1990*b*: 1970) uses the French term *dictionnaire de langue* in his English text.

[47] 'it is useless to oppose "commercial" dictionaries and "scientific" dictionaries . . . The larger "dictionnaires de langue" are thought to be more "scientific", probably because they are more extensive and more austere.'

plus "scientifiques", est simplement dérisoire'[48] (Rey and Delesalle 1979: 9).

1.2.1.2 *Functional typologies*

Some linguists have argued that all existing typologies miss the point, and that a typology of dictionaries should be based not on the characteristics of dictionaries but on the linguistic operations that the dictionaries are designed for. Matoré (1968: 190) distinguishes between 'quantitative' dictionaries, which are designed for a vast public which needs quick and superficial information about many different sorts of things, and 'qualitative' dictionaries, which are for people who want precise information about the language. Hartmann (1987*a*) independently reached similar conclusions: 'the fundamental yardstick for classifying dictionaries is no longer (only) the absolute knowledge of the lexicographer, but rather the relatively varying purposes achieved by the dictionary for the benefit of different groups of users' (Hartmann 1987*a*: 16). Thus, there are dictionaries for comprehension, dictionaries for production, dictionaries for translation, etc. But this eventually brings us back to the usual categories, since there is a close enough correlation between the characteristics of dictionaries and what they are used for, or what they are meant to be used for (the way they are actually used, though interesting for research, is surely irrelevant for a typology).

1.2.1.3 *A 'genetic' typology*

Rey (1977: 54–80) proposes another type of typology, based on the more or less chronologically ordered choices that lexicographers have to make when designing and compiling a dictionary: it is, in that sense, a 'genetic' typology. Dubois and Dubois (1971: 14), reacting to an earlier version (Rey 1970*b*), have called it 'la plus approfondie qu'on ait faite jusqu'à maintenant'.[49]

Rey's genetic typology uses some of the traditional classifying features, but it also introduces new distinctions and clarifications: it opposes 'observed dictionaries', that is to say dictionaries that are based on the observation of discourse, and 'observed and generated dictionaries', which use language produced by the lexicographer and

[48] 'any opposition between "commercial" dictionaries (i.e. those that are produced by publishers who are openly trying to make a profit) and "disinterested" descriptions, which are allegedly more "scientific", is simply untenable'.

[49] 'the most detailed that has ever been produced'.

informants ('generated' is Sebok's term); 'functional' and non-functional information, the former being that information which is meant to facilitate communication, as opposed to the information which is there just to educate the user on some linguistic or non-linguistic point—like, for example, etymology. Rey also applies the notion of functionality to the macrostructure: if all the entry-words belong to the same code, if they can all function together, then the macrostructure is called *functional*.

Rey himself, evaluating his own typology, finds it both too narrow to make room for all the types of dictionaries that have been published, and too loose to maintain the coherence of the concept. It is, he says, 'trop restrictive, empiriquement, alors qu'elle peut paraître trop large aux linguistes'[50] (Rey 1977: 80). At least, it shows that the making of a dictionary is the result of a series of choices, and that many of those choices are linked: many of the decisions that lexicographers make restrict their freedom for the following stages.

1.2.1.4 *The basic types of dictionaries*

The conclusion to be drawn from all the typologies proposed by various authors over the years is that it is impossible to classify dictionaries in a way that would be both orderly and applicable to all societies. Dictionaries come in more varieties than can ever be classified in a simple taxonomy. As Rey puts it with his usual elegance: 'Dans nos sociétés où l'acculturation est intense, très structurée et exigeante, les modèles concrets de dictionnaires tendent toujours à l'hétérogénéité'[51] (Rey 1970*b*: 64). Lexicographers keep finding new solutions, creating new categories and subcategories of dictionaries that will not fit into any prior classification. However, the following broad distinctions will be found useful.

General and specialized dictionaries. A dictionary can be specialized or general either in its macrostructure or in its microstructure, or in both.

The macrostructure of a dictionary can be called *general* if it includes all, or a representative section, of the elements of a lexicon, even the obsolete and archaic, and also all of its varieties in

[50] 'too narrow in practice, though it may seem too loose to linguists'.

[51] 'In our societies, where acculturation is intense, highly structured, and exacting, the concrete models of dictionaries always tend to be heterogeneous.'

synchrony, and if it has all parts of speech as entry-words. The macrostructure of the new *OED*, for example, is general. However, the label *general* is usually applied even if the macrostructure contains a much smaller section of the lexis, with particular emphasis on the words used at the period of publication: this would be the case of the *Pocket Oxford Dictionary* (*POD*), for example.

A specialized macrostructure, on the other hand, is one that is restricted to one variety, a dialect, technical jargon, slang, etc., or to one type of entry-word: verbs, adjectives, idioms, or proper names—if there are indeed true dictionaries of proper names.

A general microstructure is one that gives a 'complete' programme of information in each entry, including at least an explanation of the meaning, generally by means of a definition. Apart from the definition, general microstructures traditionally include, in varying order and with varying emphases: part of speech, examples, collocations, etymology, pronunciation, idioms, synonyms, pictorial illustrations, etc. If the dictionary gives only one of those other types of information, the microstructure is specialized: for example, a dictionary of etymology or a dictionary of synonyms.

A dictionary like *COD* has a general macrostructure and a general microstructure; a dictionary of etymology, or a dictionary of pronunciation, has a general macrostructure and a specialized microstructure; most dictionaries of slang, or dialect, have a specialized macrostructure and a general microstructure; finally, a dictionary giving the etymology of dialect words, for example, would have a specialized macrostructure and a specialized microstructure; this is clearly an infrequent type.

Monolingual and bilingual dictionaries. The distinction between the bilingual or multilingual (or plurilingual) dictionary and the monolingual (or unilingual)[52] dictionary is usually clear enough. Monolingual dictionaries are those in which the language of description is the same as the language being described: the microstructural information is given in the language from which the entry-words are drawn. A bilingual dictionary uses two different languages: one as the object of description and one as the instrument of description.

[52] French speakers hesitate beween *monolingue* and *unilingue*. The dictionaries of French are of no help since they ignore this meaning (*sic*). In English, *monolingual* seems to be the preferred form, but some use *unilingual* (see e.g. Weinreich 1962: 26–7). *OED2* has neither in the sense that can be applied to a dictionary.

'La macrostructure et la microstructure des dictionnaires bilingues . . . appartiennent chacune à un système linguistique différent'[53] (Rey-Debove 1971: 21).[54] Typically, bilingual dictionaries provide equivalents, but some bilingual dictionaries are not 'translation dictionaries': for example, the best etymological dictionary of French is written in German.

There are also many intermediate subtypes. Many Renaissance dictionaries had Latin definitions for English words. Some modern dictionaries are basically monolingual but also have translations of their entry-words into another language. Some are two monolingual dictionaries of two languages juxtaposed, like the *Diccionario Inglès, for Spanish Speakers* (Skokie, Ill.: Voluntad Publishers, Inc., 1982), which gives for each English word in the word-list an English definition (for the more advanced speakers) and a definition in Spanish (for the less advanced), with examples of usage and equivalents in Spanish.[55]

The dialect dictionary and, to a lesser extent, the slang dictionary pose a particular typological problem: are they monolingual because the explanations are given in the language of the entry-words (if one accepts a broad definition of *language*), or bilingual because the entry-words do not belong to the same functional code as the language of explanation? The answer is obviously in the evaluation of the distance between the dialect—or the slang—and the language proper. A dictionary defining Americanisms in British English might, given a certain definition of *language*, be considered bilingual (Geeraerts 1989: 294–5). The notions of 'bi-dialectalism' or 'bi-varietalism' should be taken seriously in lexicography, because they cannot be avoided in the tracing of the historical development of the genre: many of the earliest dictionaries produced in all the societies of the world were bi-dialectal or bi-varietal, and the truly monolingual dictionary as we know it is only a recent development (Boisson *et al.* 1991).

Encyclopedic and 'language' dictionaries. As we have seen, encyclopedic dictionaries have proper names among their entry-words:

[53] 'The macrostructure and the microstructure of bilingual dictionaries . . . belong to two different linguistic systems.'

[54] Oddly enough, with such a definition, a picture dictionary would qualify as a bilingual dictionary (Geeraerts 1989: 294).

[55] See also the *Robert-Signorelli*, a special kind of bilingual (French–Italian) dictionary.

geographical names (names of countries, regions, rivers, towns, mountains, etc.), the names of famous people, plus a few categories like places of famous battles, characters in fiction, etc. Typically, their microstructure deals more or less explicitly with the encyclopedic aspects of the entry-words.

Foreign learners' and native speakers' dictionaries. The distinction between dictionaries for foreign learners of a language and dictionaries for native speakers of that language has become important only recently. It will be examined in the following chapter (2.3.2.1).

Dictionaries for adults and dictionaries for children. Dictionaries that are designed explicitly for children have a shorter word-list consisting of the most 'important'[56] words of the language, excluding regionalisms, archaisms, slang words, etc. They also use different techniques for the explanation of meaning, including, for instance, the use of illustrative examples without definitions. They are often interesting for the metalexicographer, but oddly enough they have never been the object of serious research.

Some countries, such as the USA, also have dictionaries for adolescents, but those are not really different from dictionaries for adults (see below, 2.2).

1.2.2 *The monolingual general-purpose dictionary*

Among all the types of dictionaries, one occupies a particular position in all societies: the monolingual general-purpose dictionary. It is the one that every household has, that everyone thinks of first when the word *dictionary* is mentioned, it is the type that is most often bought, most often consulted, the one that plays the most important role in the society that produces it. It sells in huge numbers everywhere,[57] and it is also the one that metalexicographers describe most, sometimes even exclusively. In fact, some of the definitions of *dictionary* that we have seen are only definitions of that particular type: the general-purpose dictionary is the prototypical dictionary.

[56] On the 'importance' of words, see below, 6.2.2.

[57] There are probably as many general-purpose dictionaries in Britain as there are television sets, and more than there are cookbooks (see Stein 1984*c*: 3).

The monolingual general-purpose dictionary is characterized by:

1. Its use of only one language as the object of description and as a tool for that description;

2. A general word-list, which can be either exclusively linguistic or mixed. Practically, the presence of function words in the word-list is enough to identify the dictionary as a general one. However, the word-list must also be reasonably extensive for the dictionary to qualify as general: it must be useful to the average adult. Children's dictionaries are not general-purpose dictionaries;

3. A general microstructural programme, giving at least the meaning of each entry-word, by means of a definition.

> The prototypical dictionary . . . is monolingual rather than multilingual, provides linguistic rather than encyclopedic information, contains primarily semasiological rather than onomasiological or non-semantic data, gives a description of a standard language rather than restricted or marked language varieties, and serves a pedagogical purpose rather than a critical or scholarly one. (Geeraerts 1989: 293–4)

The general-purpose dictionary, in its turn, has many subtypes that vary according to time, space, and other factors. The examination of those subtypes will be one of the objects of this book.

2

The Lexicographical Scene of English-Speaking Countries

2.1 INTRODUCTION

The lexicographical scene[1] of a society is a complex thing to describe. A true portrait implies the study of the sociological conditions in which dictionaries are called for, then designed, produced, and finally used. The following questions should be answered: What sort of dictionaries are the most common in that particular society? What sort are rare, or do not exist at all? What dictionaries are remarkable, for their originality, or for their quality?

The lexicographical scene of the English-speaking countries, for very obvious reasons, is characterized by the quantity and the variety of the dictionaries that are produced. Probably no other language in the world has produced so many dictionaries of so many different types, and none produces as many at present. In 1969, according to Barnhart (1969: 176), there were more than 60 general dictionaries available on the market. In 1977, Kister described 343 monolingual dictionaries of English available on the American market: this included dictionaries for children, for adolescents, or for foreign students, but excluded not only bilingual or multilingual dictionaries but also terminological, highly specialized dictionaries (Kister 1977). No doubt the figures would be even higher fifteen years later.

It would probably be impossible to draw a complete list of all the dictionaries of the English language, even within a well-defined period like the last thirty years. It would even be impossible to list all the general-purpose dictionaries of English. This is because some dictionaries are produced by fairly obscure publishers, some have a lifespan which is extremely short—as well as, sometimes, unduly extended—with few copies being produced and sold; some are

[1] Hausmann (1984) uses the French phrase *paysage dictionnairique*, which is virtually impossible to translate into English.

marketed only in places like bookshops specializing in books at reduced prices, railway-station bookstalls, or supermarkets. Also, it is sometimes difficult to be sure that a dictionary is really new, or how new it is. The dictionary market is a strange market, where the same book can be given different titles according to criteria that totally escape the customer; where, on the other hand, different books can be given the same title, no matter how different they are; where every 'new' dictionary is more or less unashamedly copied from one or several others—and where this is never properly acknowledged; where publishers re-produce old dictionaries, put new covers on them or add a few extra plates and tout them as entirely new; where many titles are published under different guises, even by perfectly serious publishers (Hausmann 1989*a*: 98 calls this 'dictionary criminality'): from one dictionary, it has become customary to 'extract' a special edition for adolescents, one for schoolchildren, one bound in plastic, one in leather, one paperbound for the less wealthy, one for some particular countries in the world, one with and one without pictures, one in colour and one in black and white, one with and one without a thumb-index, one in bigger print, one for the blind, etc. Some American dictionaries even have special editions for some states, when the local legislation requires changes for the dictionary to be officially adopted on the book-list of schools and colleges (see below, 4.2.5.1).

Many English-speaking countries now have their own lexicography. Up until the early years of the nineteenth century, Britain was the only source of dictionaries for all the countries in the world where English was used, including the USA. Then the USA began producing their own dictionaries, on American soil and from American sources. Finally, since the latter part of the nineteenth century, and especially since the mid-twentieth, many other English-speaking countries of the world have followed suit. The countries that actually produce dictionaries, as opposed to just buying them from abroad, now include Australia, Canada, South Africa, New Zealand, and a few others. Their production is less and less directly inspired by American or British dictionaries.

Finally, English may be the only language in the world for which monolingual dictionaries are published in countries where it is only a foreign language, like France, Poland, and no doubt many others.

2.2 THE LEXICOGRAPHICAL SCENE OF THE USA

The lexicographical history of the USA begins with the publication of Noah Webster's *American Dictionary of the English Language* in 1828: before that, as well as some time after, the dictionaries used by the American population were produced in Britain. The American scene is characterized by two types of dictionaries: general-purpose dictionaries that are typically encyclopedic, and dictionaries that are designed to be usage guides, like dictionaries of synonyms.

2.2.1 *The general-purpose dictionaries of the USA*

General-purpose dictionaries in the USA range from 'unabridged' dictionaries like *Webster's Third New International Dictionary* (*W3*) to 'pocket' dictionaries. There is, however, an intermediate category which is particularly popular: the 'college' or 'collegiate' dictionary, with anywhere between 125,000 and 200,000 'words' (according to the American way of counting words[2]), and to a lesser extent the slightly bigger 'desk' dictionary. All the major publishers have their own 'collegiate' but, oddly enough, the type was virtually unknown in Great Britain until very recently. As the name suggests, the college dictionary is designed for college and university students, though it is used by the population at large. All college dictionaries are very similar, in their macrostructure as well as in their microstructure: 'Most authorities agree that 90 per cent or so of the lexical content of the leading college dictionaries is rougly the same' (Kister 1977: 92). That is why the comparative studies that are published now and then in more or less specialized periodicals, journals, magazines, or even newspapers, always end with very cautious conclusions as to 'which is best?' (Yorkey 1969).

2.2.1.1 *The main general-purpose dictionaries*[3]

The monument of American lexicography is undoubtedly *Webster's Third New International Dictionary* (*W3*), published in 1961. It has

[2] American dictionary publishers do not count 'words' the same way as the British. American figures tend to be 'inflated', because not only the entry-words are counted, but also undefined derivatives, and sometimes even the different senses of words within a single entry (see below, 2.2.4). The figures given in this chapter should be interpreted in that general context. Collegiate dictionaries would be classified as 'semi-unabridged' in Kister's classification (see above, 1.2.1.1).

[3] Dictionaries will be classified according to the number of 'words' as advertised

460,000 'words' and about 6 million quotations by about 14,000 different authors. The history of *W3* goes back at least to Merriam-Webster's *A Dictionary of the English Language* of 1864, through *Webster's International Dictionary*, published in 1890, *Webster's New International Dictionary*, published in 1909, and *Webster's New International Dictionary (Second Edition)* (*W2*), published in 1934. The latter was much bigger than *W3* (it had 600,000 'words'), and it was regretted by many when *W3* was published.

W3 departs from its predecessor not only in word-count. Among its innovations:

1. It has no proper names, except in their attributive uses—a policy that can readily be understood for a dictionary that wanted to be more 'linguistic' than 'encyclopedic', but that was virtually impossible to put into practice. The only word to be capitalized in *W3*, apart from abbreviations, is *God* (in one of its entries; there is another one for *god*), for obvious reasons.
2. It omits archaisms not used since 1755, apart from those that are used in well-known literature.
3. It has few pictorial illustrations. The first printings had colour plates scattered through the text like many other American dictionaries, but all except the one illustrating the word *color* were withdrawn in 1975 because of the cost (Algeo 1990*b*: 1995)—a good illustration of how the same dictionary can be different.
4. It draws for its quotations on contemporary authors.
5. It uses an entirely new set of—more 'objective'—usage labels: the label *colloquial*, for example, was discarded and replaced by labels like *substandard* or *nonstandard*.
6. It does not have any encyclopedic supplement, etc. (see below, 2.2.1.2).

Some of these changes enraged those of the users who like their dictionaries to remain true to the tradition, so that *W3* came very near to being a commercial disaster (see below, 4.2.1.1).

A new edition—it will probably be called *W4*—is now in preparation. Pending this, Merriam-Webster has published three supplements to *W3*: *6,000 Words* (1976), *9,000 Words* (1983), and

by the publishers. The list is not meant to be exhaustive, either in the number of dictionaries mentioned or in the characteristics of each. It is only meant to give an idea of what sort of dictionaries American society has tended to produce over the last thirty years.

12,000 Words (1987). They contain all the important words that have appeared since 1961, plus a few (rare!) omissions that had been detected in *W3*, like *frog*: 'a spiked or perforated holder used to keep flowers in position in a vase' (*6,000 Words*: 17a).

The *Funk and Wagnalls New Standard Dictionary of the English Language* (*FWS*): the parent edition appeared in 1913, and the latest version in 1963. But the dictionary 'has never been entirely reset, and in spite of numerous slight emendations [it] reflects the language as it was used in 1913' (Landau 1984: 341). *FWS* had 458,000 words. Once a very successful line of dictionaries, Funk and Wagnalls has apparently disappeared from the market (Algeo 1990*b*: 1993–4).

Webster's New Twentieth Century Dictionary: the second edition, published in 1975, had 320,000 words, but is no longer available.[4]

The *Random House Dictionary of the English Language* (*RHD*) was first published in 1966. The 1987 edition (*RHD2*) has 2,500 pages and 315,000 words, 50,000 of which are new compared with the 1975 impression of the first edition, plus almost 300 pages of encyclopedic appendices. *RHD2* has dates for the first occurrences of words.

The *World Book Dictionary* (*WBD*): this was compiled by Clarence Barnhart and first published in 1963 as a supplement to the *World Book Encyclopedia*. The 1981 edition has 264,000 words. *WBD* has no proper names, since it is a supplement to an encyclopedia, and is updated every year. It is particularly useful for its extensive quotations—not a frequent feature in American dictionaries of that size.

The *American Heritage Dictionary of the English Language* (*AHD*) was published in 1969. A second edition, called 'College Edition', was published in 1982 (*AHD2*). It has 200,000 words, and comes in various formats, with or without illustrations, thumb-index, etc. *AHD* broke new ground by using a panel of about 100 experts who were consulted on about 600 disputed usages; the results are given in the entries themselves, in the form of percentages. For example, the entry for *flammable* has:

> *Flammable* is as acceptable as *inflammable* in all areas of speech and writing, according to 61 per cent of the Usage Panel, though *inflammable* is more common outside technical contexts.

[4] The dictionary, though called *Webster's*, is not published by Merriam-Webster; the name Webster can be used by anybody who wants it. In 1972 there were at least 28 different dictionaries with that name, from ten different publishers, and in 1977 Kister listed 69!

The usage panel has been heavily criticized as a commercial gimmick. *AHD* was touted as an extremely conservative dictionary, but in fact was the first American general-purpose dictionary to introduce some taboo words (see below, 4.2.5). It is now available on-line. A new edition was published in 1992.

Webster's Ninth New Collegiate Dictionary (*NCD9*), published in 1983, with 160,000 entries and 200,000 definitions. This, like *W3*, is published by Merriam-Webster. The first in the series was published in 1898, the seventh in 1963, the eighth in 1973. *NCD9* has usage notes and dates of first occurrences. Merriam's Collegiate series has been available on magnetic tape since the sixties.

The *Random House College Dictionary* (*RHC*), based on *RHD*, was first published in 1968. The latest edition, dated 1984, is notable for its extensive use of the computer in the preparation stages. It has 'more than 170,000 words'. A *Random House Webster's Dictionary* was published in 1991.

The history of the *Webster's New World Dictionary of American English* (*WNW2*) dates back to 1951. The latest edition (1988) has 170,000 words. The preceding edition was called *Webster's New World Dictionary of the American Language*—an interesting change of title. *WNW* and *WNW2* are the only general-purpose dictionaries to indicate (by means of a little star) words and usages that originated in the USA. *WNW* has been noted for its squeamishness in the treatment—or rather non-treatment—of taboo words (see below, 4.2.5.1), but *WNW2* is much more liberal.

The *Funk and Wagnalls Standard College Dictionary* (*FWC*), first published in 1963, with a new edition in 1977. It has 150,000 words. It no longer seems to be produced (Algeo 1990*b*).

The *American College Dictionary* (*ACD*), first published in 1947, with an edition in 1970, was compiled under the direction of Clarence Barnhart, who used some of the ideas put forward some time before by the psychologist Edward Thorndike: use of frequency lists to draw up the word-list, fabrication of 'artificial' examples designed to reinforce the definitions, evaluation of the competence of the potential user in order to compile understandable definitions, emphasis on the quality of the treatment of each entry-word rather than on the number of words in the word-list, etc. (Barnhart 1949).[5]

[5] Thorndike's ideas are very similar to those put forward by Sweet (1899: 139–49), which were later used by the compilers of dictionaries for foreign students (see below, 2.3.2.1).

Barnhart was helped in the design of *ACD* by well-known linguists like C. Fries and A. Marckwardt.

ACD was innovative in many ways, particularly in its definitions (see below, 6.2.9). It was also the first American dictionary to use the 'schwa' symbol of the International Phonetic Alphabet (IPA), represented by a letter 'e' upside down. *ACD* was influential in the lexicography of the USA, and even in other countries; it was used as a basis for the compilation of many other dictionaries, including *RHD*. Unfortunately, it has never been updated since 1970.

2.2.1.2 *The main characteristics of American general-purpose dictionaries*

In the fifties, according to Whitehall (quoted by McArthur 1986*b*: 137), American general-purpose dictionaries were characterized by:

American spelling and pronunciation;
strictly limited etymologies;
numbered senses;
pictorial or diagrammatic illustration wherever needed;
selective treatment of synonyms and antonyms;
scientific, technical, geographical, and biographical information, both scattered through the main list and added in special appendices.

The description is still valid some thirty-five years later.

Most American general-purpose dictionaries have a more or less encyclopedic macrostructure. The earliest dictionaries in America were 'linguistic', but encyclopedic features were soon added because they were needed by a public who did not have many other sources of knowledge to turn to (Algeo 1990*b*: 2004). The encyclopedicity of American dictionaries ranges from the inclusion of proper names (*W3* being one of the exceptions) to encyclopedic-type definitions, through encyclopedic sections in some entries or special appendices. *W3* was heavily criticized for departing from this tradition, though the policy of its editors was perfectly logical and had been duly explained: 'Think, if you can, of an unabridged dictionary from which you cannot learn who Mark Twain was, or what were the names of the apostles, or that the Virgin was Mary, the mother of Jesus of Nazareth, or what and where the District of Columbia is' (Follett 1962, in Laird 1970: 503). One can think of the *OED* as a good example of an 'unabridged' dictionary that has none of these, but the expectations of the reading public are obviously different on the two sides of the Atlantic.

American dictionaries also have entries for all sorts of compounds and phrases that would probably not be considered as entry-forms in other lexicographical traditions: for example, one page of *NCD8* chosen at random has entries for *ground ball*, *ground bass*, *ground cloth*, *ground cover*, *ground-effect machine*, *ground floor*, *ground glass*, etc. In Britain, most of these would be included in the entry for their main component, *ground* (for example *ground bass*), and others would simply be omitted (for example *ground glass*) because they would be considered semantically 'regular'.

W2 even had the names of associations, of colleges, of books, foreign quotations, etc., none of which would be treated in the macrostructures of general-purpose dictionaries in other countries.

> le Webster de 1934 annonce 400.000 mots (*words*). On s'avise alors que sont comptées comme mots des entrées telles que *Home Owner's Loan Corporation*, *Angle of incidence* (et 49 entrées du type *Angle of —*), *Blenheim Spaniel*, *Book of Common Prayer*, *Characteristic of a surface*, *Engagement ring*, *Ils ne passeront pas*, *Lex Talionis*, *Tobacco brown*, *Poor in spirit* etc.[6] (Rey-Debove 1971: 63)

There is a clear desire in such dictionaries to record not only the language but also the names of things in the culture. The American general-purpose dictionary is an all-purpose reference book.

American dictionaries also tend to be synchronic: they tend to ignore obsolete or archaic words, and to give less space to words that are only used in some great literary works of the past. This is a tradition that may go back to the early nineteenth century, when American lexicographers wanted to produce specifically American dictionaries but had little native literature to draw from (Simpson 1990: 1958).

American dictionaries are not particularly generous in their representation of other varieties of English. The number of Briticisms is typically limited (Read 1962: 221), British spellings are usually not indicated, and even Canadianisms were often omitted up until the very recent past (Read 1962: 222). This is slowly changing, and the inclusion of Canadianisms, for example, is now facilitated by the publication of specifically Canadian dictionaries.

[6] 'the 1934 Webster announces 400,000 words. But then one realizes that the count includes such entries as *Home Owner's Loan Corporation*, *Angle of incidence* (as well as 49 entries of the type *Angle of —*), *Blenheim Spaniel*, *Book of Common Prayer*, *Characteristic of a surface*, *Engagement ring*, *Ils ne passeront pas*, *Lex Talionis*, *Tobacco brown*, *Poor in spirit* etc.'

Finally, the inclusion in American general-purpose dictionaries of 'difficult' words, such as taboo words or ethnonyms, has been sketchy, and the situation only began to change in the late sixties (see below, 4.2.5).

American dictionaries usually have only one word-list, with proper names mixed with other types of lexical units, but the two- (or even three-)list type is not unknown: for example, *NCD8* has a special section for geographical names and another one for the names of famous people.

American dictionaries tend to have separate articles for complex lexical units that would be treated as sub-entries in other lexicographical traditions. Such macrostructures can be called *analytic*, as opposed to those in which the entries tend to group several sub-entries, which are *synthetic*. *W3*, the *NCD*s, *WNW*, *AHD*, etc. all have analytic macrostructures.

In polysemous entries, the ordering of the different meanings tends to be 'logical' rather than chronological: the most 'important' meaning, which is not necessarily the most frequent one, but that meaning from which most of the others can be derived with the greatest appearance of logic, is given first, and then the others by decreasing order of importance. *AHD* and *RHD* both use that system. There are, however, exceptions, like *W3*, which does have chronological ordering of meanings.

Many American general-purpose dictionaries have usage notes on the finer points of usage or of synonymy, something totally unknown in British lexicography up to the eighties. For example, the entry for *importance* in *AHD* is completed by a usage note explaining the difference between *importance*, *consequence*, *moment*, *significance*, *import*, and *weight*. Most dictionaries, even the smaller ones, have etymologies (Zgusta 1971: 251–2). They always indicate where words can be broken at the end of a line (Ilson 1986*b*: 57).

American general-purpose dictionaries exhibit a remarkable lack of 'dictionarese', that special jargon which, in extreme cases, can make the consultation process a very puzzling operation indeed: the traditional abbreviations are used relatively little. The label *fig*, for example, is never used to indicate shifts of meaning from a concrete to an abstract (figurative) meaning (Ayto 1988: 50). The label *formal* is not used either (Ilson 1986*b*: 60).

The definitions are often more clearly encyclopedic than those of British dictionaries, and are often completed by pictorial illustrations

—a tradition going back to *The Century Dictionary* in 1891. The definitions for *cat* and for *dog* in *NCD8* and in *COD7* read as follows:

Small furry domesticated carnivorous quadruped, *Felis catus*. (*COD7*)
A carnivorous mammal (*Felis catus*) long domesticated and kept by man as a pet or for catching rats and mice. (*NCD8*)

Carnivorous quadruped of genus *Canis*, of many breeds wild and domesticated. (*COD7*)
A highly variable carnivorous domesticated mammal (*Canis familiaris*) prob. descended from the common wolf. (*NCD8*)[7]

W3, though basically a 'language' dictionary, sometimes inclines towards encyclopedicity as well: it has five pages for the word *dye*, for example (as against two columns only in the *OED*), and a colour plate for *color*, the only one in the whole dictionary. The definitions of *W3* are easily recognizable: the compilers had deliberately adopted a new style of 'completely analytical one-phrase definitions' (Preface: 6a). As a result, the definitions are often long paragraphs that seem to aim at giving a 'complete' description of the referents rather than extracting what is essential for the comprehension of the concept. This is particularly noticeable in the definitions for artefacts. The following passage, which is part of the entry for *door*, has often been quoted by metalexicographers (see Algeo 1990*b*: 1995 for other examples):

a movable piece of firm material or a structure supported usu. along one side and swinging on pivots or hinges, sliding along a groove, rolling up and down, revolving as one of four leaves, or folding like an accordion by means of which an opening may be closed or kept open for passage in or out of a building, room or other covered enclosure or a car, airplane, elevator or other vehicle . . .

Clearly, what the compiler is after is an exploration of all the possible applications of the word rather than an extraction of the essence of the concept. This, in a way, is a constant trait of the larger dictionaries, in which the extended treatment of words is equated with a multiplication of the number of their 'applications'. But different dictionaries have different practices: the definition of *door* in the *OED*, for example, is shorter and expressed in vaguer terms.

[7] Interestingly, the definitions of *cat* and *dog* in each dictionary also differ in other ways. Why the definition for *dog* should mention the origin of the species while the definition for *cat* mentions the behaviour of the animal is a mystery.

Hanks (1979) convincingly argued that definitions that try to be exhaustive in this 'referential' way are self-defeating, because they can never hope to explore all the limits of the concept.

The encyclopedicity of American general-purpose dictionaries is also expressed by the presence, either before or after the dictionary proper, of several pages of information on various subjects that are not strictly linguistic. There is a long tradition of adding such information to dictionaries in Britain as well as in the USA. R. Bailey mentions an abridged edition of Johnson's *Dictionary* 'published not long after his death that includes weights and measures, a table of heathen deities, Archbishop Ussher's history of the world with principal dates from the creation in 4004 B.C., and the market days in the principal towns of England and Wales' (personal communication).

In America, the tradition goes back at least as far as Webster's *A Compendious Dictionary of the English Language* (1806), which had, among other things, tables of currencies used in different countries, weights and measures ancient and modern, a history of the world, the Jewish, Greek, and Roman calendars, and a complete list of all the post-offices in the United States (Marckwardt 1963/1967: 34). *WNW* (1969 edition) has a complete list of all the colleges and universities in Canada and the USA, a guide to punctuation, a list of the signs used in typesetting, plus a vinyl record (*sic*) of the different regional accents of the USA; *WBD* (1973 edition) has 124 pages of vocabulary tests, a guide to forms of address, the currencies of all the countries of the world, etc.; *RHD2* has nearly 300 pages including a quadrilingual dictionary (French–German–Spanish–Italian), etc. Such practices are not unknown in other societies, but they are particularly marked in the USA. The reasons may be trivial, for example the need to avoid blank pages at the end of a signature, but there is also a demand for dictionaries that are compendiums of human knowledge (see below, 4.2.3).

Among unabridged dictionaries we see no end yet to the 'encyclopedic', whether it be practical information or a miscellany of appended facts and addenda, e.g. the 29 'specialist' dictionaries of the *Reader's Digest Great Encyclopedic Dictionary* (1966) or the non-lexical supplements such as 'Wines of the Presidents' and 'How to start a club and run its meetings' in Funk and Wagnall's *Standard International*, bicentennial edition (1973). Non-lexical and encyclopedic supplements swell *The Random House Dictionary of the English Language* (1966) by nearly one-fourth its total volume. (Roe 1982: 20)

The fact that *W3* broke with tradition, Roe says, may be 'a signal that non-lexical elements may gradually disappear from large dictionaries' (Roe 1982: 20), particularly because of the competition with encyclopedias that are becoming more and more easily accessible. Time will tell.

2.2.2 *Dictionaries of usage*

The term *dictionary of usage* is used here as an encompassing term for all the dictionaries that are specifically designed to facilitate or improve the use of the language. They include thesauri, dictionaries of synonyms, dictionaries of spelling, etc. American lexicography is particularly rich in such dictionaries: it 'has always been intimately associated with questions of usage and the standard' (Algeo 1990*b*: 2005).

The American market offers many variations on the theme of *Roget's Thesaurus*. Since the original work is now public property, all major publishers have their own edition. Many are alphabetically arranged, for ease of consultation—a solution totally ignored on the British market. The commercial success of such books is clear: my own copy of the *New American Roget's College Thesaurus in Dictionary Form* (1962) says that the book has gone through 66 new editions! Other thesauri keep being published: the *New World Thesaurus* (1971), taken over by Collins, the *Webster's Collegiate Thesaurus* (1976), etc.

All the major dictionary publishers also have their dictionary of synonyms. To mention only a few: the *Webster's New Dictionary of Synonyms* (1942 through 1973), the *Modern Guide to Synonyms* (1968), etc. An interesting publication in this field is the *Word Finder* (1947), by Rodale. It is not often mentioned by metalexicographers, and yet it is an innovative work that provides the user with thousands of collocations that are classified by part of speech. It is huge, dense, and somewhat chaotic, but it had the merit of anticipating modern reference works on collocations (see below, 2.5.1.1). It has proved useful over the decades.

There are a few dictionaries of idioms in the USA, like the *Dictionary of American Idioms* of Maxine Boatner, Edward Gates, and Adam Makkai (1966 and 1975), etc.

None of the American pronouncing dictionaries, like the *Pronouncing Dictionary of American English* of John Kenyon and Thomas

Knott (1953 for the fourth edition), S. Noory's *Dictionary of Pronunciation* (1965), and the *NBC Handbook of Pronunciation* (1984), has the prestige and the influence of Daniel Jones's *English Pronouncing Dictionary* in Britain, because American English does not have the equivalent of RP (Received Pronunciation), a generally accepted pronunciation that is taught nationwide as well as abroad, and was even up to the recent past a prerequisite for anyone who hoped to climb the social ladder. America is more tolerant of regional accents, and has therefore less need for a guide to the 'right' pronunciation.

2.2.3 *Other dictionaries*

2.2.3.1 *Dictionaries of new words*

The supplements to *W3* (*6,000 Words*, *9,000 Words*, and *12,000 Words*) published by Merriam-Webster have already been mentioned. They represent a genre that has appeared recently on the market in many countries, the *dictionary of new words*,[8] which is justified by the acceleration of lexical changes, and rendered possible by the computer management of lexical databases.

American lexicography has produced another noteworthy example of the genre: the three volumes of Clarence Barnhart's *Dictionary of New English* (1973, 1980, and 1990; *DNE*). Those are designed to update all existing dictionaries of English, including the *OED*. Naturally, almost all the entries are nouns, and most of them are scientific and technical words (see Algeo 1990*a*).

2.2.3.2 *Dictionaries of slang*

The American market is richer in dictionaries of slang than the British: the *American Thesaurus of Slang*, by Lester Berrey and Melvin van den Bark (1964 for the second edition), the *Dictionary of American Slang*, by Harold Wentworth and Stuart Flexner (1975 for the second edition), and recently the *Thesaurus of Slang* by E. Lewin and A. E. Lewin (1988), etc. are only a few examples. There is a marked interest in America for the language of the underworld, and some of the lexicographers have been direct observers.

2.2.3.3 *Dictionaries of regionalisms*

American lexicographers have produced a number of dictionaries of regionalisms, particularly in the fifties, sixties, and seventies. The

[8] The French equivalent would be a Latin form: *dictionnaire de néologismes*.

main early productions are well known: the *Dictionary of Americanisms* of Mitford M. Mathews (1951; *DA*) and the *Dictionary of American English* of William Craigie (1938–44; *DAE*). The *Dictionary of American Regional English* (1985– ; *DARE*), published under the direction of Frederic Cassidy, is the result of a long and painstaking series of dialectological field studies (Cassidy 1987*a*, 1987*b*). It brings together words and phrases that refer to all the elements of daily life in rural America, even the humblest, those that belong to regional dialects and run the risk of being wiped out from the surface of the earth in the near future. The dictionary is a remarkable book, both very scholarly—it breaks new lexicographical ground by providing maps ('Spot Maps') showing the areas where words are used—and highly entertaining.

Oddly enough no comprehensive dictionary of Black English has ever been produced or even envisaged (Görlach 1990: 1479).[9]

2.2.4 *The popularity of dictionaries in the USA*

The American dictionary, on the whole, is not a remote object to be handled only by an élite; it is designed for use by the general public in all sorts of everyday situations: the absence of 'dictionarese', the easy-to-use phonetic notation, the encyclopedic flavour all contribute to a certain 'user-friendliness'. It is reasonable to think that this was inherited from the colonial period, when American settlers needed a handy reference work to help combat their 'linguistic insecurity' and to try and improve their social status. In the early days of the colony, the dictionary was, together with the Bible, one of the two books that any American household had to possess: 'most rural estates, be they ever so humble, boasted a dictionary' (McDavid 1979: 17). No doubt the arrival of millions of immigrants from other linguistic communities only reinforced the tendency.

American society apparently still has a profound respect for the general-purpose dictionary (Algeo 1990*b*: 1987), and the genre is as prosperous in the 1990s as it was before: 'Clearly, dictionaries are in demand, and play an important role in American society—a society that is not notorious for the purchasing of books' (McDavid 1979: 17). According to Algeo (1989*b*: 37), 87 per cent of American homes have a dictionary.

[9] There are some interesting attempts, like Clarence Major's *Dictionary of Afro-American Slang* (New York: International Publishers, 1970).

This prosperity is not linked to any frenzy of innovation. American dictionaries have not changed very much over the last thirty years, and the few changes proposed by lexicographers have not been particularly well accepted. Even in the last few years, when dictionaries have been evolving so rapidly all over the world, the evolution has tended to be more timid in the USA, so that *W3*'s attempt at representing contemporary usage may be considered as the most important development in the American lexicographical world since 1960. Yet American dictionaries are prosperous in a quiet way, as their influence over British lexicographers in the last few decades amply testifies (see below, 2.3.2.2).

The American dictionary is an object that is advertised and sold, and that has a place in the competitiveness of American society. Publishers naturally want to make money, and they advertise aggressively, particularly by flaunting the number of words that their dictionaries contain—one of the surest ways to sell a dictionary, in all countries. The competition between the publishers explains why the figures that are bandied about are the result of rather mysterious computations, and are consistently overinflated (Landau 1984: 84). For example, the dust-jacket of the 1973 edition of *WNW* announced 157,000 entries, but a rapid calculation based on the number of entries on some ten or twenty pages chosen at random indicates that there cannot be more than 80,000. The same calculation for *AHD* (1969 edition) reveals 75,000 instead of 155,000. Where are all those entries? Of course, the publishers never say how they arrive at such results, but it is clear that undefined derivatives listed at the end of many entries, and possibly even the sub-entries are sometimes—though perhaps not always—counted. Has any research been carried out on the efficacy of such commercial methods? They probably pay, or if they did not the publishers would just stop trying.[10]

2.2.5 *The future of American dictionaries*

Where does American lexicography go now? The question is difficult because there are few tell-tale signs of any impending changes. Some

[10] The least unreliable way of evaluating the richness of a dictionary is by counting all the words that it contains. Thus, *CED* has 3 million, the *Great Illustrated Dictionary* (*GID*) 4 million, etc. (Ilson 1986*b*: 54). Needless to say, this is virtually impossible for a metalexicographer working with the paper version of a dictionary. And after all, some dictionaries may be wordier than others without being markedly 'richer'.

British dictionaries are imported on to the American market, particularly dictionaries for foreign students—a field where American lexicography is conspicuously absent—but this has not prompted American publishers to claim their share of this highly profitable market. Ilson notes that American children's dictionaries are probably more innovative than any others, particularly in the domain of the explanation of meaning:

> The American children's dictionary as a genre is a remarkable achievement. There is a marvellously creative use of illustrations in such books. They have experimented with unorthodox defining techniques and sometimes with the replacement of definitions by examples only, as C. K. Ogden did in *Basic by Examples* (1933). Even more interesting, some have done in practice what many semanticists have advocated in theory: grouped senses by semantic categories across part-of-speech boundaries, as when the military senses of *charge* are explained next to each other even though some are nominal and some are verbal. (Ilson 1986*b*: 70)[11]

Time will tell whether these changes will affect the general-purpose dictionary in America.

2.3 THE LEXICOGRAPHICAL SCENE OF GREAT BRITAIN

The lexicographical scene in Great Britain is more difficult to describe than in the USA. It is characterized by the presence of a long and solid line of traditional dictionaries—mostly those produced by publishers like Chambers and, above all, Oxford University Press—and by a large number of other dictionaries, some of which are very innovative. The situation of Britain is unique: the boom in the industry of the teaching of English as a foreign language throughout the world since the Second World War has been much more profitable, so far, to British than to American publishers, because of the prestige of RP and the British colonial empire. The

[11] The idea of grouping senses semantically rather than grammatically, Ilson says, goes back to Thorndike in the thirties. As for replacing definitions by examples, it is an idea that crops up periodically in metalexicographical literature. It was used in Richardson's *New English Dictionary* (1835–7) (Simpson 1990: 1957), and to some extent in the *New York Times Everyday Dictionary*, 1982 (Ilson 1990*b*). Marcel Cohen's attempt in France was a failure (Rey-Debove 1971: 31). Some psycholinguistic research indeed indicates that examples are not necessarily very good conveyors of meaning, but this is not totally conclusive (see below, 5.2.3.3).

money earned has been partly reinvested in an effort to improve dictionaries, particularly through the hiring of competent lexicographers. This, in turn, has inspired metalexicographical activity.

2.3.1 *The traditional dictionaries*[12]

The *Oxford English Dictionary* was first published in 1928 in 12 volumes under the title *A New English Dictionary on Historical Principles*, then in 1933 in 13 volumes under the title of the *Oxford English Dictionary on Historical Principles*, the thirteenth volume being a supplement. The *OED* had 16,500 pages, 252,259 entries, 414,825 defined words (headwords and subentries), and 42,514,696 words of text.[13] It was revolutionary in many respects at the time of publication. Its methodology was characterized by:

1. A focus on the historical development of words. For that reason, the *OED* is classified as a *historical dictionary*. It has all 'words now in use, or known to have been in use since the middle of the twelfth century' (*OED*: xxviii), chronological ordering of the senses in polysemous entries, and the most careful and precise delineation of etymological evolution ever published for English. In the *OED*, this means the 'etymology or derivation of each word, that is, taking back the current shape or spelling of each word to its earliest form in English, and the establishment of its cognates in other Germanic languages, or, if it is a loan word, of its form in the borrowed-from language' (Burchfield 1986: 19).

2. A literary orientation of the language of reference. The sources used by *OED*—the 'corpus', of a kind (see below, 3.2.2.2)—were mostly literary (though they occasionally included cheap novels and even newspapers): figures published recently after the computerization of the *OED*[14] indicate that the most often quoted writer is Shakespeare (32,886 times); then come Walter Scott (15,499), Milton (11,967), and Chaucer (11,000). The bias towards literature is so strong that *OED* has literary *hapax legomena*—words that seem to have been used only once—if they are used in great literary works

[12] The use of the word *traditional* is naturally relative—and devoid of any pejoration. The *OED* can be considered as traditional now, but it was revolutionary a few decades ago.

[13] The figures are provided by *OED* staff. They are the result of the recent computerization of the text.

[14] Source: the *DSNA Newsletter* 12/2, Summer 1988, p. 14.

(Schäfer 1980: 13). 'Words of marginal importance used by these preferred authors are rarely omitted, and their vocabulary is usually assigned main lemma status. The *OED* was clearly conceived as an aid in reading great literature' (Schäfer 1980: 13).

3. Numerous citations (as opposed to examples), illustrating every sense of every word. The compilers had 5 million citations drawn from more than 5,000 works, covering a period of more than 700 years. The citations were selected by about 1,300 readers between 1884 and 1898. Out of those, 1,861,212 were finally selected for publication, or 1,827,306 for the first twelve volumes, that is an average of more than seven citations per entry.

4. No pictorial illustrations, so that even the word *colour* is defined only by linguistic means.

5. No proper names, no highly specialized scientific and technical words, and as little encyclopedic information as possible. Of course, such a large dictionary is bound to include encyclopedic information in many of its entries (see above, 1.1.2.7), so that the *OED* is indeed a rich source of information about the world, though it purports to be a purely linguistic dictionary.

6. A highly synthetic macrostructure: compound words, idioms, etc. are normally treated within the entry for the most 'important' of their component words. This is in sharp contrast with the American tradition.

A four-volume *Supplement* to the original edition was published in the seventies and eighties: A–G in 1972, H–N in 1976, O–Scz in 1982, and Se–Z in 1986. Each volume has between 15,000 and 20,000 new words or senses not included in the original edition. The third, for example, advertises 18,750 words and 28,000 senses.

Up until the mid-eighties, everything in the dictionary division of Oxford University Press was done 'by hand', with millions of slips provided by readers, and lexicographers working at their desks, in the traditional way described by Hulbert (1955) and Murray himself (see Murray 1977). The first indication that the methodology of the *OED* was being modernized was the transfer of all the data contained in the first thirteen volumes plus the four supplements on to a CD-ROM (actually available as one or two CDs). A worldwide survey of users and potential users of the system was carried out to determine user preferences (Benbow *et al.* 1990), and the results were used to organize a complex consultation system which considerably enhances the value of the data for research purposes. The user can now access the thousands of pages through any word contained in the definitions or in the examples, through the languages mentioned in the etymologies, through the dates of first occurrence, through the names of the authors of citations, through the labels of domain, or again through any combination of all these. Some reviewers have expressed dissatisfaction with certain aspects of the system: for example, the data can only be accessed through a proper word, not through an idiom or a series of words. Also the program does not differentiate between lower-case and capital letters, so that if for example you type in ON (for Old Norse), the system will also give you all the occurrences of the preposition *on* (Kaye 1989: 85). But these are only teething troubles for an entirely new dictionary type.

The second, more important, step in the modernization of the *OED* was the publication, in paper form, of the second edition in 1989. This has twenty volumes, 21,728 pages, about 500,000 definitions, and about 2.4 million citations.[15] Much of the original text of the *OED* and its supplements has been kept, but some 5,000 new words and senses were added. It is, the publicity says, 'more than five times the size of any other dictionary of English'. Some other improvements were made: for example, the entry words are now in lower case, not in capital letters, and the pronunciation is now indicated in IPA (Weiner 1987), etc.

The *OED* has been, and will no doubt continue to be, extremely influential, not only in Britain or even the English-speaking countries, but also in the whole world. It has been the object of innumerable articles, reviews, and books. It has inspired numerous historical dictionaries, compiled with the same, or similar, methodological principles, so that the category of historical dictionaries is considered by many English-speaking metalexicographers to be a major category of dictionaries (see Read 1986: 28).

Examples of dictionaries compiled with an *OED*-influenced methodology are: the *Dictionary of Old English*, published at the University of Toronto (D was published in 1986, and C in 1988; the work goes on); the *Dictionary of the Older Scottish Tongue* (*DOST*) begun in 1931 (PO–QUH was published in 1988); the *Middle English Dictionary*, begun in 1954 by Hans Kurath at the University of Michigan, which does not seem to be finished yet (Aitken 1987); the *Dictionary of*

[15] The figures are rough approximations because they are drawn from publicity material rather than from scholarly reviews.

Canadianisms on Historical Principles begun in the forties, then continued by Walter S. Avis, and finally published in 1967 (there is an abridged edition, *A Concise Dictionary of Canadianisms);* the *Dictionary of South African English on Historical Principles*, published for the first time in 1978; the *Australian National Dictionary*; the *Dictionary of Americanisms* of Mitford M. Mathews and the *Dictionary of American English* of William Craigie, already mentioned, etc. Typically, these projects are ambitious ones, which cost a lot of money—so much so that some were at a standstill for long periods for lack of funding, and one at least is not yet finished.

The *OED* methodology has also been influential abroad: some would say that the *Trésor de la langue française* (*TLF*; 1990 for the last volume but one) is a French version of the same school (Rey and Delesalle 1979: 10), with its literary bias, its use of a corpus, the absence of illustrations and encyclopedicity, etc.

Shortly after it had been published, the *OED* was reduced to a more practical and affordable size. This was the *Shorter Oxford English Dictionary on Historical Principles* (*SOED*), which came out in 1933. It was based on exactly the same principles as its parent dictionary. The 1944 edition was supplemented by 5,000 new words in 1973, so that it now has 2,500 pages, 80,000 entries, and 163,000 words (Burnett 1988: 229). The new edition in preparation (compilation was at the letter P in late 1989) will be based on a careful re-evaluation of the text of the *OED*. So far, this has brought to light some hitherto unnoticed inconsistencies: for example, the 'shoe-size sense' of some figures is only mentioned for *nine*, *six*, *twelve*, and perhaps *thirteen*.

> Temperatures cannot be up in the eighties—only, on OED evidence, in the nineties, and implicitly, through a quotation, in the twenties. One can be aged eighty, but not eight, eighteen, or eleven—nor explicitly, later in the alphabet, two, four, five, nine, thirteen, fourteen, fifteen, nineteen or ninety. (Burnett 1989: 140)

Other strange omissions had been turned up by earlier researchers. Thus, Schäfer (1980: 29) notes that the *OED* has '*East Indies, England, Holland, Iceland, Lapland, Poland, Portugal,* etc.', but not '*France, Germany, Ireland, Scotland, Wales,* etc.': 'it has been suggested that some of them were included in the *OED* for the simple reason that readers had registered these names on their slips' (Schäfer 1980: 29).

The first edition of the *Concise Oxford English Dictionary* (*COD*) is dated 1911. It thus antedates the *OED* by seventeen years: when it was published, the compilation of the *OED* was reaching the letter R, so that the compilers could use the data accumulated for the *OED* from A to R, and were then rather embarrassed to finish the dictionary (Allen 1986).

The methodological principles underlying the *COD* were not quite the same as those of the *OED*, for obvious reasons. McArthur describes them as follows:

— not to be encyclopedic
— to give adequate space to common words and their idioms
— to supplement the definitions with illustrative phrases only when really necessary to clarify the meaning
— to order the senses of words according to casual logic and present-day appropriateness . . .
— to have a layout involving 'the severest economy of expression—amounting to telegraphese—that readers can be expected to put up with' (McArthur 1986*b*: 136)

Some of those principles were dictated by the design of *COD* as a guide to everyday language—the non-historical ordering of the senses, for example; others were imposed by the need to save space: for example, the telegraphic metalanguage (Allen 1986: 1). *COD* goes to extreme lengths in this economy of style, to the point where it is sometimes difficult to use because its abbreviations are puzzling. Not surprisingly, this was remarked on by an American lexicographer and metalexicographer, accustomed to other practices.

> Definitions are written in a compressed but flowing style that is very different from American styles of defining. COD covers many more senses than one would expect in a dictionary of this size, but its definitions are therefore often very brief amounting sometimes to a kind of shorthand reminder rather than a definition. When it works, it works very well indeed; one feels in private converse with a friend. When it fails, one is utterly lost and feels by turns stupid and abandoned. (Landau 1984: 338)[16]

COD has been through several editions since 1911. It is probably one of the best sellers on the British market—though it is of course impossible to obtain figures from the publishers. *COD7*, published in 1982, had 40,000 entries and 76,000 definitions. The latest

[16] For a French point of view on *COD7*, see Tournier (1985: 373–80).

edition, regrettably presented as the *New Edition*,[17] is dated 1990. It announces 120,000 entries (20,000 new ones) and 190,000 definitions!

Finally, there is an apparently inexhaustible series of smaller dictionaries more or less clearly derived from the *OED*, like the *Pocket Oxford Dictionary of Current English* (*POD*), published for the first time in 1924, with an edition in 1984 (it is an abridged version of the *COD*), the *Little Oxford Dictionary*, the *Oxford Minidictionary*, etc.

Though it does not belong to the *OED* line strictly speaking, and though the Chambers lexicographers are justly proud of their ancestors, the *Chambers Twentieth Century Dictionary* (*CTD*) can be considered as one of the 'traditional' dictionaries on the British lexicographical market. *CTD* was first published in 1901. The 1983 edition has 138,000 entries and 198,000 definitions in only 1649 pages. It is extremely useful because it contains more Scotticisms than any other readily available general-purpose dictionary of English, and also because it is particularly rich in 'Milton words' or 'Shakespeare words'. It is also remarkable for the humorous tone of many of its definitions (see above, 1.1.2.6). Lastly, *CTD* has appendices with Latin, Greek, and foreign quotations, the Greek and Russian alphabets, Roman figures, mathematical symbols, etc.

CTD is, even more than *COD*, the archetype of what Landau called the 'friendly' dictionary (Landau 1984: 338), in the sense that it 'talks to you' as a friend would, but you have to belong to the inner circle to understand: the print is very small, the different senses in a polysemous entry are—strangely—separated by a colon; the definitions are so compact that some of them are virtually useless; and there is not a single example or quotation. Yet it is an endearing dictionary, because of its compactness and its many redeeming features. A new edition has recently been published.

Chambers has recently published several other dictionaries: the *Chambers Everyday Paperback Dictionary* (1980), the illustrated *Chambers Family Dictionary* (1981), the *Chambers Concise Twentieth Century Dictionary* (1985), etc.

Oxford University Press produces a few dictionaries that do not belong to the *OED* range, but that remain very traditional in every

[17] A way, for the publishers, to avoid displaying the date of publication, which would only be attractive for a brief period. The word *New*, in contrast, keeps its (superficial) appeal for ever.

aspect: the *Oxford Illustrated Dictionary*, first published 1962, then 1975; the *Oxford Senior Dictionary*, published 1982, for secondary schools, etc. The *Oxford Paperback Dictionary* (*OPD*), published in 1979, was used as a basis for the *Senior Dictionary* and adapted for the American market under the title of *Oxford American Dictionary*, published in 1980—not a great success in the USA, perhaps because 'in the modern British tradition, it is unyieldingly lexical, with none of the encyclopedic content Americans have come to expect' (Ilson 1990*b*: 1969).

Two other dictionaries are worth mentioning here, though they are still further away from the *OED* tradition. The *Penguin English Dictionary* (*PED*) was first published in 1965, with a new edition in 1979. It has 45,000 entries, and is useful because it is especially rich in colloquial words and phrases. Unfortunately, it does not have any examples. A new edition has just been published.

The same publishers published the *Penguin Wordmaster Dictionary* in 1987. Despite a preface by David Crystal and a publicity that emphasized the book's originality ('a pioneering concept in word books'), it is not particularly interesting from a methodological point of view, though it is good browsing: its most innovative feature is that it has a large number of 'boxes' in the text that concentrate on more or less trivial or anecdotal aspects of usage or etymology.

The *Pan English Dictionary* (*PAD*), published in 1979 (apparently the same text exactly had already been published under the title *Heinemann English Dictionary*), has 30,000 entries. It is a very simple dictionary aimed at the less educated user. Its layout is easy to read, the definitions are simple, and there is absolutely no 'dictionarese'.

The dictionaries that we have called traditional are typically characterized by

1. an exclusive focus on words, as opposed to things, with very little 'encyclopedicity';
2. the fact that they are basically tools for decoding—mostly for reading literature;
3. a relative 'élitism'. British lexicographers make no particular efforts to ease the consultation process for the less educated user. The metalanguage is often enigmatic—even in the *OED*—the page cluttered, and the citations (if any) from 'good' authors.

Finally, traditional British dictionaries are also characterized by a relatively poor representation of regionalisms, either from Britain or from other English-speaking countries. According to Read (1962: 222), there were only about a dozen Australianisms in the 1964 edition of *COD* (*COD5*). The policy of the *OED* 'with regard to all kinds of regional lexis was ill-defined from the beginning' (Görlach 1990: 1478). The first edition had virtually no Americanisms, no doubt a comment on how the British intelligentsia regarded American culture at the time. The first supplement (1933) admitted that this was a mistake, and many Americanisms were added. After that, the tendency to include more regional words increased.[18] The fact that one recent editor-in-chief of the *OED* was a New Zealander (Robert Burchfield) probably helped the inclusion of New Zealandisms in the latest edition. *COD* started indicating American spellings in its 1976 edition. The contrast between *OED* and *OED2* in that respect is striking. The computerization of the *OED* was carried out at a Canadian university (Waterloo, Ontario), and the compilers now use American databases (Simpson 1988: 440).

The differences between dictionaries like the *COD* and American dictionaries are clear enough. The best explanation is that the two types of dictionary are designed for different users. British dictionaries aim at giving the educated user an *aide-mémoire* or a source of philological information, while American dictionaries provide the less educated person with a guide to linguistic usage and a handy source of reference for all sorts of extralinguistic facts.

2.3.2 *The 'new' dictionaries*

The main innovations in the lexicographical world of Great Britain came from two directions: the first is the dictionary specially designed to cater for the needs of students learning English as a foreign language, which appeared during the forties; the second is a dictionary based on the American college dictionary, which arrived in Britain during the seventies.

2.3.2.1 *The dictionaries for foreign students*

The first dictionaries specially designed for foreign students appeared in the thirties. Their arrival was unnoticed outside the circles of teachers of English as a foreign language, in a lexicographical world

18 With, inevitably, some errors. Forgue (1981: 91) notes that *chicano* is not in the 1972 supplement (A–G).

that was exclusively dominated by the prestige of the *OED* and its family of dictionaries. Yet those dictionaries would eventually turn out to be important in the evolution of lexicography.

The dictionary that we now know as the *Advanced Learner's Dictionary of Current English* (*ALD*) was published first in Japan in 1942 under the title *An Idiomatic and Syntactic English Dictionary*. The authors were A. S. Hornby, E. V. Gatenby, and H. Wakefield, who were teachers of English as a foreign language. The dictionary was then brought back to Britain, for obvious reasons, and taken over by a new department of Oxford University Press, the dictionary department having refused to touch what was not, in their eyes, really a dictionary (Strevens 1978: ix). It was published as the *Advanced Learner's Dictionary* in 1963, then in 1974, 1980, and 1989 (*ALD4*), the last two being under the direction of A. P. Cowie. *ALD4* has 57,100 words and phrases, and 81,500 examples.[19]

ALD had been preceded by Michael West and James Endicott's *New Method English Dictionary* in 1935, which worked on the same principles. Both implemented some of the ideas expressed by Sweet as far back as 1899, such as the need to limit the word-list to only the most 'important' words, but to treat them more fully, with pronunciation indicated through phonetic transcription, with grammatical information, explanation of idioms and use of examples, and meaning conveyed in simple terms (Sweet 1899: 139–49). The main features of *ALD* were:

1. The indication of the syntactic patterns of verbal constructions by means of a code using letters and figures, which had been designed by A. S. Hornby and based on the work of Harold Palmer (*A Grammar of English Words*, 1938). This was certainly the most innovative feature in the dictionary.
2. The systematic indication of other information necessary for encoding: whether nouns are *countable* or *uncountable*, what are the plurals of nouns, the comparatives of adjectives, irregular verbal forms, etc.
3. A large number of examples. *ALD* had more examples than any other dictionary of comparable size had ever had before. They

[19] *ALD3* had announced 50,000 entries and 100,000 words, but the mode of calculation must have been changed, no doubt under the pressure of the competition (see below the figures announced for the *Longman Dictionary of Contemporary English* in 1978).

were all fabricated—as opposed to citations culled from a text—and all representative of current usage—as opposed to literary styles. The space occupied by all those examples had been saved by a severe reduction of the word-list, based on the reasonable idea that foreign students would only need a limited proportion of the English lexis.

4. The indication of pronunciation by means of the IPA, which had been used before only by Wyld for his *Universal Dictionary* in 1932 (Ilson 1986*b*: 55).[20]

5. Pictorial illustrations. This had been common practice in the USA for decades, but was infrequent in Britain since the *OED*.

6. The presence of a certain number of appendices (8 pages in the 1942 edition, 30 in *ALD2*, 33 then 35 in *ALD3*, and finally 49 in *ALD4*): illustrations (trees, flowers, animals, birds, musical instruments, furniture, maps, etc.), irregular verbs, punctuation, numerical expressions, weights and measures, geographical names, common forenames, family relationships, military ranks, chemical elements, and the International System of Units. Clearly, *ALD* is a book to be used for the teaching of English as a foreign language, and it must transmit British culture as well as the English language.

ALD4's real originalities when compared with its predecessors are the drastic simplification of the coding system for the syntactic patterns and the particular care taken in the indication of collocations. This was done by A. P. Cowie, the compiler of the two volumes of the *Oxford Dictionary of Current Idiomatic English* (*ODCIE*; see below, 2.5.1.1).

The second dictionary for foreign students to appear, in terms of pure chronology, was the *Collins English Learner's Dictionary* (1974). It was much smaller than *ALD*, but based on very similar principles.

The *Longman Dictionary of Contemporary English* (*LDOCE*) was launched in 1978 deliberately to compete with *ALD* for the vast market of students of English as a foreign language throughout the world. It soon became, like its predecessor and competitor, a huge commercial success. The 1978 edition had 55,000 entries and

[20] The use of IPA was limited to the learners' dictionary for several decades. General-purpose dictionaries for native speakers, both in the USA and in Great Britain, used all sorts of codes for the indication of pronunciation that were supposed to be easier to use for the average reader. The trend is now back to IPA in Great Britain—not in the USA—with even the new *OED* using it. Oddly enough, French lexicographers used the A(lphabet) P(honétique) I(nternational) much before the English did.

100,000 words. The second edition (*LDOCE2*), published in 1987, was drastically revised; it has 56,000 entries. *LDOCE* was made available on magnetic tape, which allowed some metalexicographers (particularly at Liège and Amsterdam) to carry out research that had hitherto been impossible (Boguraev and Briscoe 1989).

LDOCE had a few original points compared with *ALD*. It used a coding system not only for verbal constructions but also for nouns and adjectives. This led to an even larger quantity of codes that the users had to memorize, or at least understand. *LDOCE* also indicated the changes of stress on compounds in discourse.

Contrary to the British lexicographical tradition, and contrary to *ALD*, *LDOCE* has a very analytic macrostructure, separating as much as possible the different senses of a form in different entries instead of organizing complex entries with all the senses under one heading. For example, the adjectival uses of *good* are scattered over a large number of entries, including *good book, good-humoured, good looker, good-looking, good looks, good-natured, good offices, good sense*, etc., whereas *COD* or *ALD*, for example, have them all in a single entry.

LDOCE had a strict alphabetical ordering of all the entry-words. This sometimes makes it difficult to locate an entry. For example, the following entry-words were all treated in separate entries in the following order: *put over, put over on, putrefaction, putrefactive, putrefy, putrescent, putrid, putsch, putt 1, putt 2, puttee, putter 1, putter 2, putter about, putter away, put through*, etc. With this sort of ordering, there is very little grouping of words and phrases that are semantically related. This might be justified to a certain extent in a dictionary that would be used exclusively for decoding activities, but looks strange in a dictionary like *LDOCE*. *LDOCE2* has come back to a more traditional ordering, with, for example, all the phrasal verbs with *put* in the entry for *put*.

LDOCE tended to distinguish as many senses as possible in polysemous entries, sometimes to absurd lengths. The most often quoted example is the verb *walk*: *LDOCE* distinguished seven different meanings, the first two definitions being introduced by, respectively: '1 (of people and creatures with 2 legs)' and '2 (of creatures with 4 legs)'. This distinction can hardly be justified (Stein 1979: 8). Why not, some smart reviewers remarked, a special definition for creatures with six legs? And one for spiders as well? *LDOCE2* wisely reverted to a more traditional definition.

LDOCE and *LDOCE2* have only 'real' examples, drawn from the corpus constituted at the University of London for the Survey of English Usage by Randolph Quirk—the same corpus that had already been used for the compilation of the huge *Grammar of Contemporary English* (1972) by Quirk *et al.*, and that was to be used again for Quirk *et al.* (1985).

Above all, *LDOCE* and *LDOCE2* use a defining vocabulary of 2,000 words, given in a list in one of the Appendices. All the definitions in the dictionary were written with those 2,000 words only (2,166 actually). The idea had been first used in the *New Method Dictionary* in 1935, where the 24,000 entry-words had been defined with 1,490 words only.

The use of a restricted defining vocabulary is based on the idea that a monolingual dictionary can only work if the vocabulary is organized in 'strata', so that each stratum can be used to define the words belonging to the next one, and so on (see below, 6.2.11). This makes it possible for the lexicographer to define words by means of words that are 'easier'[21] than the word being defined.

Yet the technique also raises all sorts of practical and theoretical questions. A general problem is that the use of a restricted vocabulary blocks the chains of definition. If *cat* is defined as 'mammal that . . .', then the users can take the word *mammal*, look it up, etc., thus enlarging their vocabulary and their knowledge of the world; but if *cat* is defined as 'animal that . . .', the chain is, so to speak, 'short-circuited' (see below, 6.2.11). This is clearly a case of conflict between the dictionary as a quick reference tool and as an instrument for self-teaching.

Another difficulty in the use of a controlled defining vocabulary is the precise identification of the words that are used. In the case of *LDOCE*, many—not all—words on the list of 2,000 are polysemous and frequent: 'Although there are only about 2166 words [*sic*] in the "controlled" vocabulary, over 24 000 of the 74 000 senses defined in LDOCE are senses of these words.' Each, says Wilks, 'has about twelve senses' (Wilks *et al.* 1989: 201). Of course, the dictionary does not say which of the senses are used, or whether they are all used, or how many. The notion of 'word', in that particular case, is misleading.

[21] The difficulty of a word may be roughly equated with its relative position in the linguistic development of the native speaker, the easier words being acquired first.

The final, and most serious drawback of the defining vocabulary is that it sometimes forces the definers towards formulations that sound stilted, unnatural, or—worse—simply wrong. The definition for *volcano*, for example, reads:

a mountain with a large opening (CRATER) at the top

This sounds like child-language. Interestingly, *NCD8* defines the same word as 'a vent in the planetary crust from which molten or hot rock and steam issue', which for the user is certainly a case of jumping from the frying-pan into the fire. But there is worse. Stein (1979: 6) takes the example of *bemoan*, which is defined by *LDOCE* as 'to be very sorry because of'. The definition, she argues, misses the point, which is that *bemoan* is a way of *expressing* sorrow; the word cannot be used of someone who is silently sorry. For the same word, *ALD* has 'moan for, show great sorrow for', which is definitely better. But that sort of wording was impossible in *LDOCE*, given the limitations of the defining vocabulary: neither *moan* nor *sorrow* are part of the 2,000 defining words.

LDOCE's defining vocabulary has been extensively discussed. Some conclude that on the whole it works quite well (Herbst 1990: 1381); others—probably more numerous—think that, though the idea is interesting, it is much less useful than it appears at first (Michiels and Noël 1984; Jansen *et al.* 1987).

LDOCE has been extensively discussed in many journals, not only for its defining vocabulary (see Carter 1989; Fillmore 1989; Hausmann and Gorbahn 1989, among others). Like all innovative dictionaries, it has been the subject of heavy criticism. The features that were the most criticized were the ordering of the entries, the quality of the definitions, and the excesive analyticity of the treatment of polysemous words. As a result of this criticism, *LDOCE2* has simplified its coding system, adopted a less mechanical use of the alphabet, and modified slightly its definitions: now *bemoan* is defined as 'to express sorrow or disappointment because of', and *volcano* as 'a mountain with a CRATER (= large opening) at the top'.[22]

[22] The change from the first version is not impressive, but it means that the word *crater* is now accepted in the definition. Also, an interesting feature—actually a compromise with the techniques used in *LDOCE*—is the explanation of the difficult word (*crater*) within the definition itself. A small but significant improvement that no one else had implemented before, paving the way for a 'two-speed dictionary' (see below, 6.2.11).

The *Chambers Universal Learners' Dictionary* (*CULD*) was published in 1980. It is slightly smaller than either *ALD* or *LDOCE*: 54,000 examples, as against 69,000 for *LDOCE* and 81,000 for *ALD4*. It does not have any pictures, and makes great efforts to avoid all dictionarese: it does not even use a coding system for the indication of syntactic patterns.

The *Collins COBUILD English Language Dictionary* (*COB*) was published in 1987 by a team of lexicographers working in Birmingham under the direction of John Sinclair. Though not presented as a dictionary exclusively for foreign learners, it is mostly used as such.

COB does not have any pictures or any cultural addenda—not even linguistic ones, not even a list of irregular verbs, which all other dictionaries for foreign learners have. Yet it is innovative in many respects:

1. It is based on an entirely new, 7.3-million-word corpus, the COBUILD corpus, which is the property of Collins and of the University of Birmingham.[23] All the examples provided by *COB* were extracted from that corpus, with only minor adaptations. This ensures a total authenticity of the language, but it also has unfortunate consequences. The examples, when taken out of their original contexts, sometimes make no sense at all. For example, one meaning of *every* is illustrated by: 'One woman out of **every** two hundred is a sufferer . . .' (noted by Hausmann and Gorbahn 1989: 46).

2. The syntactic patterns of verbs, nouns, and adjectives are indicated in coded form in a special column to the right of the main text, so that the two types of information, semantic and syntactic, are clearly separated. The coding system has been criticized for being as complex as the one used in the early editions of *ALD* and *LDOCE* (Carter 1989: 36), but at least it does not clutter the text.

3. The words are defined in an entirely new way. Each word is inserted in a complete, grammatical sentence instead of the traditional, formulaic definition. The word is used in a typical syntactic pattern and accompanied by its typical *collocates* (see below, 7.1.2.2).

[23] The COBUILD corpus is composed of the following parts: non-fiction 3.1 million words, fiction 2 million, written press 1 million, and oral documents 1.2 million; 5 million words are British English, 2 million are American English, and the rest come from other English-speaking communities. All those figures are tokens, not types. The COBUILD corpus is part of the Birmingham Collection of English Text (BCET), which contains 17.78 million tokens and 246,000 types (Renouf 1987; Hanks 1989).

Bemoan, for example, is defined as 'If you bemoan something, you express sorrow or dissatisfaction about it'; the definition for *careworn* is 'A person who looks careworn looks worried, tired and unhappy', etc. The new style is very often convincing, but fails in places. Some definitions are long, inelegant, and sometimes even ambiguous. Hausmann and Gorbahn (1989: 47–8) mention several examples, among which some of the verbal meanings of *throw*:

If something **throws** a person or a thing into a particular situation or state, especially an unpleasant one, it suddenly causes them to be in that situation or state. [24]

4. The macrostructure is extremely synthetic, as if the dictionary were meant to be used only for the decoding of isolated, context-free forms. This is taken to extreme lengths, unknown in English-language lexicography. For example, there is only one entry for the form *wind*. This is how the entry begins:

wind, winds, winding, winded, wound. The word **wind** is pronounced /wɪnd/ for paragraphs 1–10 and /waɪnd/ for paragraphs 11–13 and the phrasal verbs. **Winded** is the past tense and past participle of the verbs in paragraphs 4 and 6, and **wound** is the past tense and past participle of the verbs in paragraphs 11–13 and the phrasal verbs. 1. A **wind** is a current of air . . .

Such solutions may have been dictated by a desire to facilitate consultation, but they rest on mistaken assumptions about the skills of the dictionary user.

COB has been very successful; many learners of English find that, after all, its defining technique works quite well. A simplified version, aimed at British schoolchildren, the *Essential English Dictionary* (with a few pictures), was published in 1988, and another in 1990, the *Collins COBUILD Students' Dictionary* (40,000 entries).

Other dictionaries for foreign students have been published in the seventies and eighties. Most of them were adaptations of *ALD* or of *LDOCE* for less advanced students, and none was as innovative: the *Oxford Intermediate Learner's Dictionary* (1978), the *Oxford Elementary Learner's Dictionary* (1981), the *Oxford Student's Dictionary of Current English* (1978 for the first edition, then 1981; an American edition was published under the title *Oxford Student's Dictionary of*

[24] For other examples of dubious definitions in *COB*, see Fillmore (1989: 62–4).

American English in 1983), the *Longman Active Study Dictionary of English* (1983, with an American edition published in 1983 under the title *Longman Dictionary of American English*), etc. Other publishers, such as Heinemann, Macmillan (*Macmillan's Learner's Dictionary*, 1983), or Nelson, have also published their own learner's dictionaries. The *International Reader's Dictionary*, actually a revised edition of the *New Method Dictionary*, was published in 1977.

A recent development in the field of dictionaries designed for foreign students is the monolingual dictionary with translations into the native language of the students. For example, a special edition of the *Oxford Student's Dictionary of Current English* has been published in Israel: it is an exact reproduction of the original English edition, with Hebrew equivalents added on to each entry and sub-entry (Reif 1987: 146). There are similar dictionaries for Japanese, Greek, Brazilian Portuguese, Arabic, Polish, Italian, Norwegian, Chinese, etc. (see below, 2.5.1.3).

Dictionaries for foreign students are usually called *learners' dictionaries*, or *MLDs* (for *monolingual learners' dictionaries*).[25] Their most interesting features are their efforts to develop new ways of defining words and to provide information necessary for encoding. It is the latter feature that explains most of their characteristics:

1. the language described is the usual, everyday variety, not the formal or literary;
2. preference is given to the quality of the treatment of words rather than to the quantity of words;
3. particular care is taken in the treatment of the more frequent words;
4. the obligatory or preferred syntactic patterns of verbs (at least) and sometimes nouns and adjectives, the countability or uncountability of nouns, the irregular forms of plurals, comparatives, conjugations, etc. are all indicated;
5. pronunciation is indicated by means of the IPA;
6. many examples, sometimes authentic but always representative of normal, everyday usage, are given.

[25] This is, in itself, a misleading label, since all dictionaries are designed for people who have something to learn—but this is 'l'arbitraire du signe'. French does not even have a generally accepted equivalent: French metalexicographers say *dictionnaire pédagogique*, *dictionnaire pour apprenants*, *dictionnaire d'apprentissage*, *dictionnaire pour étrangers*, etc.

Finally, learners' dictionaries are also innovative in the sense that they have extensive introductions on 'How to use the dictionary'.

Learners' dictionaries differ more or less from the dictionary for native speakers. The traditional British dictionaries for native speakers are meant to be used mostly for the reading of literature, and American dictionaries are compendiums of the culture as a whole: both are 'cultural dictionaries' (Rey and Delesalle 1979; Dubois 1981). Learners' dictionaries, on the other hand, are instruments for the acquisition of foreign words, and of the foreign language in general. They are 'functional dictionaries': 'La description de ces dictionnaires doit éliminer ce qui n'est pas pertinent dans l'apprentissage du système et de l'usage considéré comme le meilleur. Ce sont des dictionnaires synchroniques à dominante fonctionnelle'[26] (Rey 1977: 133).

Until very recently, learners' dictionaries were not even recognized as a category worthy of study,[27] and most dictionary typologies simply ignored them. Yet they obviously display many innovative features that could usefully be adopted in dictionaries for native speakers (Quirk 1986: 3–4). Ilson believes that their influence has already been felt in the lexicographical world at large: 'Certainly the learner's dictionary, with its emphasis on the encoding aspect of language and in some cases its use of a controlled defining vocabulary, is an important centre of innovation which may already have begun to affect native-speaker dictionaries' (Ilson 1986*b*: 69). At least one native-speaker dictionary, the *Longman New Generation Dictionary* (1981), meant for teenagers, was based on a learners' dictionary, *LDOCE* (Ilson 1990*b*: 1972).

2.3.2.2 *The American model*

The emergence of the learners' dictionary can be explained by the extraordinary development of the industry of teaching English as a foreign language since the Second World War. The importation of an American model of dictionary into Britain has more complex causes. Why did the British public, which is certainly no less traditional than in other countries, suddenly discover a taste for a new type of dictionary? Does the change mean that dictionary

[26] 'In those dictionaries, the description must omit anything that is not instrumental in learning both the system and what is considered as the best usage. They are synchronic dictionaries which are predominantly functional.'

[27] This has changed recently: see e.g. Battenburg (1991) and Diab (1990).

publishers are trying to reach new categories of users, hitherto untouched by the traditional dictionaries? Is it only a passing fashion, or will it last? Has the dictionary become, in Britain as well, just an item in the consumer's society that must be changed periodically, like washing powder, cars, or ties, to keep the consumers interested?

The lexicographical relations between Britain and the USA are older and more complex than one might think. During the colonial period, and until the beginning of the nineteenth century, the only dictionaries in America were British. But the exchanges did not remain unilateral for very long after that: Webster's dictionaries were used and even copied by the British (Sledd 1972: 122). This was also true of Worcester's dictionaries, published during the same period.[28] Then the relations were reduced during the first half of the twentieth century, with only a few exchanges: for example, 'an American edition of the POD was published in 1927 but soon went out of print and was not revived' (Allen 1986: 7). After the Second World War, the relations became more intense again. A few commercial agreements have been signed between British and American publishers: Longman and Merriam, for example, and Collins and World—though this was short-lived (Ilson 1990*b*: 1968). The British sell a few dictionaries in the USA, and the USA sells some—probably more—in Britain. Some dictionaries produced in Britain have been adapted, or redone, for the American market, and the reverse started taking place a few years ago (Ilson 1986*b*: 51–2). But the clearest sign that the relations between the two countries have changed is that American dictionaries are now providing models and ideas for the British.[29]

The dictionary type that the British have imported from the USA lately is the college dictionary: an encyclopedic dictionary in one volume, slightly bigger than the *COD* in size, with particular

[28] The first dictionary published by Joseph Emerson Worcester appeared in 1830. It was a small dictionary for schoolchildren, which was not very successful. The last he published (1860) was a big dictionary of 1,786 pages that was launched to be a competitor for Webster's *Dictionary*, and the competition was fierce indeed (Laird 1970: 286).

[29] An interesting aspect of the relations between Britain and the USA is the 'dictionary' of lexical peculiarities of each country. Many 'dictionaries' of Americanisms have been published since the end of the eighteenth century, and very few dictionaries of Briticisms (see, however, Schur 1980). The word *Briticism* itself is rare. Allen Walker Read has been preparing a dictionary of Briticisms for a long time (Read 1987). See also Algeo 1987.

emphasis on the present language and on non-classical culture—particularly scientific and technological. The first notable example of such dictionaries to be published in Britain was the *Collins Dictionary of the English Language*, often called *Collins English Dictionary* (*CED*). When this was published in 1979, it was said to have 162,000 'words'—a figure similar to all American college dictionaries, and obtained through the same sort of calculation. It was not based on any particular dictionary, but on the general type.

Actually, *CED* had been preceded by the *Hamlyn Encyclopedic World Dictionary* (*EWD*), published in 1971 and based on *ACD*. *EWD* has long been out of print. Even before that, the true ancestor was the *Longman's English Larousse* (1968, 60,000 words), an adaptation for the British market of the French tradition of Larousse general encyclopedic dictionaries like *PL*, with proper names, illustrations, and the use of IPA—a first in dictionaries for native speakers (Ilson 1990*b*: 1968). This was later re-released under the title *Longman Modern English Dictionary* (1976). But those dictionaries had not been commercially successful, perhaps because they came too early, at a time when the public was not ready for them.

CED, true to its models, has an encyclopedic and analytic macrostructure, but it has neither pictorial illustrations nor cultural addenda. It uses IPA, indicates the century when a word appeared in print, and gives some semantically related words, like *aqueous* in the entry for *water*.

CED has been very successful commercially, and deservedly so, since it is a good dictionary. Other dictionaries have followed suit. The *Reader's Digest Great Illustrated Dictionary* (*GID*), published in 1984, with its 1,917 pages and 180,000 entries, was based on *AHD*. There is also an American edition (1987) of this British American-inspired dictionary. OUP have published the *Oxford Encyclopedic English Dictionary* (200,000 definitions, and 100 pages of cultural addenda on countries of the world, music, money, and—someone had to start—ecology!). The *Longman New Universal Dictionary* (1982) was based on *NCD8*—the first product of the agreement signed by Longman and Merriam (see Ilson 1990*b*: 1970)— and was designed to compete with *COD*, though it was very different. The *Longman Dictionary of the English Language* (*LDEL*) was published in 1984, and was based on the *New Universal*, and consequently on *NCD8*. It has 90,000 entries and 225,000 definitions. The *Longman Webster English College Dictionary* was also published in 1984. Collins published a simplified version of *CED*, the *New Collins Concise Dictionary of the English Language*, in 1982; it was also a direct competitor for *COD*.

All those dictionaries share some features with the American college dictionary: an encyclopedic word-list with a rather analytic macrostructure; only one macrostructure for all types of entries, etc. Even the bad habit of overestimating the contents of the dictionary has been imported by the British publishers: 'It [i.e. the *CED*] has also caught the American disease of entryitis, boasting of 162,000 entries' (Landau 1984: 338).

Ilson notes that none of the existing British dictionaries modelled on the American tradition has all the features of the average American college dictionary:

> There isn't a single dictionary in the British list that has all the major design features of the American dictionaries. For example, CED hasn't got pictures or synonym essays. LDEL hasn't got pictures or orthographic syllabification. GID *has* got pictures, and lots of them, but for reasons of space omits the full-fledged synonym essay, contenting itself with lists of near-synonyms. So there is as yet no British dictionary with all the features one associates with the American college dictionary. The British lexicographic scene is still fluid. (Ilson 1986*b*: 58)

2.3.3 *The dictionary war*

The new dictionaries that have appeared in Britain since the Second World War have not brought about the extinction of the older traditional types. On the contrary, they seem to have spurred the more traditional publishers on to a frenzy of activity. The lexicographical scene of Britain, particularly since 1980, has been described—with some exaggeration—as the 'dictionary war',[30] a phrase already used for the Webster–Worcester competition in the nineteenth century and for the furore that followed the publication of *W3* in the early sixties in the USA.

The British situation since the late seventies is characterized by the publication of many aggressively advertised dictionaries (some of which, but not all, are lexicographically innovative), with the arrival in the field of publishers that had not published dictionaries before,

[30] Hausmann, in an article written in French, calls it 'la guerre dictionnairique' (Hausmann 1984: 25).

by a noticeable acceleration of the production in the more traditional publishing houses, and by an appeal to dictionary types that are imported from abroad—particularly the USA. The dictionary war seems to be fought through quantity as much as, if not more than, through quality.

The competition is fierce in the field of dictionaries for native speakers, where dictionary after dictionary is published, sometimes with very few noticeable original features. But it is probably even fiercer on the front of the learners' dictionaries. Each publisher has a 'major' dictionary, like *ALD*, *LDOCE*, or *COB*, and each tries to inundate the market with as many variations as possible on that dictionary. Some editions are specifically designed for the American market (the *Oxford Student's Dictionary of American English*, 1983, the *Longman Dictionary of American English*, 1983), some for the less advanced student, some—and they are by far the most interesting—concentrate on some particular aspect of the difficulties of English as a foreign language.[31] There are many dictionaries of idioms, like the *Oxford Dictionary of Current Idiomatic English* (*ODCIE*), or the *Longman Dictionary of English Idioms* (1979); of phrasal verbs, like the *Longman Dictionary of Phrasal Verbs* (1983), or the *Collins Dictionary of English Phrasal Verbs and their Idioms* (1974 and 1980); of prepositions, and, recently, of new words, like the *Longman Register of New Words* (1989), or the *Oxford Dictionary of New Words* (1991). The major publishers have not yet fully turned to specialized dictionaries (dictionaries of commerce, of the law, of science, etc.), but they still might when they run out of ideas.

Hausmann (1984: 37) sees in that frenzy of creation 'une vaste prise de conscience générale face au phénomène dictionnairique',[32] but this may be excessively optimistic. What proportion of the British population is really aware that anything like a dictionary war is going on, and really understands what the stakes are? Has the dictionary war improved the awareness of the public at large about things lexicographical? Or isn't all this basically a commercial affair? The amounts of money invested in dictionaries are colossal, Hausmann says, and the publishers naturally try to recoup their

[31] Oxford University Press has just published an 'encyclopedic edition' of the *ALD*—an interesting combination of the learners' dictionary and the encyclopedic dictionary modelled on the American college dictionary: *Oxford Advanced Learner's Dictionary*, encyclopedic edition, ed. Jonathan Crowther (Oxford, 1992).

[32] 'a general awakening to the phenomenon of the dictionary'.

investments. They do succeed in selling more dictionaries than ever, but this may be due more to the commercial handling of the product than to its intrinsic qualities.

Ilson notes that, in spite of all this activity, there are many types of dictionaries that the British have *not* produced.

> There is now no British *dictionnaire analogique* like the French *Petit Robert*, with its panoply of cross-references from a given lexeme to other lexemes in its semantic field; but analogical information was given sporadically by the *Pocket Oxford Dictionary* (POD) until its Sixth Edition. . . . Neither is there a British dictionary with a morpheme-based macro-structure like that of *Le Robert Méthodique*. Nor is there a family of dictionaries from Britain that includes (as does the Van Dale series) a monolingual dictionary and bilingual dictionaries with the same basic format, allowing users to investigate their own language or learn others with minimal change in the dictionary skills required. (Ilson 1990*b*: 1972)

One might add that there are few dictionaries of usage in Britain, as if the mastery of good English were acquired by means other than the dictionary, or not acquired at all, despite the Pygmalion myth.

On the whole, the dictionary war is probably a good thing for British lexicography, even if it produces some unwanted effects. The publishers are more prosperous than ever, and they have been hiring better lexicographers and pushing for innovations, some of which are genuinely important for lexicography.

2.4 OTHER ENGLISH-SPEAKING COUNTRIES

2.4.1 *Canada*

Canada did not start producing dictionaries until the 1960s. Before that, there had only been a few isolated attempts (Drysdale 1979: 37), and most of the dictionaries available in Canada were imported from Britain or from the USA.

Like most regions of the English-speaking world, Canada has produced dictionaries of regionalisms. The most remarkable achievement is undoubtedly the *Dictionary of Canadianisms on Historical Principles* (1967), which was later abridged to *A Concise Dictionary of Canadianisms* (1973). It is a historical dictionary like the *OED*, but with an emphasis on the cultural particularities of Canada and the words that go with them. 'One intention of the book was to show

how the distinctiveness of Canada's culture is reflected in its English vocabulary' (Drysdale 1979: 39). Some regions of Canada also have their own dictionaries: the *Dictionary of Newfoundland English* (1982) and the *Dictionary of Prince Edward Island* (1988) (see Görlach 1990).

Canada now has its own general-purpose dictionaries as well. Most Canadian general-purpose dictionaries are very similar to American dictionaries, and are sometimes even derived from them. The *Canadian Senior Dictionary* (1979), for example, published later under the title of *Gage Canadian Dictionary* (1983), uses material from the Thorndike–Barnhart line of dictionaries, to which it adds elements culled from the *Dictionary of Canadianisms on Historical Principles*. The *Penguin Canadian Dictionary on Collocational Principles* is advertised as 'the first dictionary to be compiled with entirely Canadian material'; it has 75,000 entries.

2.4.2 *South Africa*

Most South African dictionaries have been based on British ones. The *Dictionary of South African English on Historical Principles* (1978, with a third edition in 1987) was published by Oxford University Press. It is a dictionary of regionalisms, compiled with the methodology of the *OED* (Delbridge 1983: 31–4; Gold 1989). The *South African Pocket Oxford Dictionary* has 30,000 entries (Allen 1986: 7).

2.4.3 *Australia*

The lexicographical history of Australia began in 1898 with the publication of *Austral English, A Dictionary of Australian Words, Phrases and Usages*, by Edward E. Morris (Delbridge 1983; Görlach 1990: 1486). After that, some minor Australian dictionaries were published, and there was a renewal of interest in things lexicographical in the seventies. All the dictionaries published in Australia were more or less directly inspired by British models at first: the *Australian Pocket Oxford Dictionary* (1976, with a second, revised edition in 1984), the *Australian Concise Oxford Dictionary* (1986), or the *Heinemann Australian Dictionary* (1976, second edition 1978). The most clearly Australian dictionary is the *Macquarie Dictionary* (1981, with a second edition in 1987), 80,000 entries, which was then published in several abridged editions. It was based on the British *EWD*, itself based on *ACD* (see above, 2.3.2.2).

The *Australian National Dictionary, A Dictionary of Australianisms on Historical Principles* was published by OUP in 1989. It has 830 pages, and contains 10,000 Australianisms with 60,000 quotations from 9,000 Australian sources (Ramson 1987). Australia also has a number of slang dictionaries (Görlach 1990: 1487).

2.4.4 *New Zealand*

The *Heinemann New Zealand Dictionary* (1979, with a second edition in 1982) was the first specifically New Zealand dictionary. After that, several others were published: the *New Collins Concise Dictionary of the English Language, New Zealand Edition* in 1982, the *Collins New Zealand Compact English Dictionary* in 1984, and the *New Zealand Pocket Oxford Dictionary* in 1986, published under the direction of Robert Burchfield and based on the seventh edition of the *POD* (1984). All these dictionaries are inspired by the British lexicographical tradition.

2.4.5 *Other countries*

There are many other English-speaking communities where dictionaries are produced or used: Jamaica has a *Dictionary of Jamaican English* (1967, with a second edition in 1980, 15,000 entries), which pioneered the use of spoken material (Ilson 1990*b*: 1967). The Bahamas have a *Dictionary of Bahamian English* (1982), the whole of the Caribbeans a *Dictionary of Caribbean English and Usage* in preparation (Allsopp 1987), etc. All sub-Saharan Africa has a *Dictionary of Africanisms: Contributions of Sub-Saharan Africa to the English Language* also published in 1982, but the projected *Dictionary of West African English* is still dormant (Görlach 1990: 1490).

Some dictionaries are still missing from the scene. India, for example, is very active in the domain of the lexicography of Indian languages, particularly bilingual dictionaries (Singh 1982), but there is no dictionary of Indian English, not even the regional dictionary on historical principles that so many countries now have. This is probably 'because of the lack of local norm' (Görlach 1990: 1490).

2.4.6 *The two types of dictionaries in 'new countries'*

On the whole, the lexicographical production of Australia, New Zealand, Canada, and South Africa is characterized by the presence of two types of dictionaries: dictionaries of regionalisms, and 'local' general-purpose dictionaries. The first type to appear, chronologically, is the dictionary of regionalisms, often preceded by various glossaries or dictionaries compiled in an amateurish way (Görlach 1990: 1476–7). Most dictionaries of regionalisms in English-speaking countries are based on the methodology of the *OED*, with a few variations. They share with the parent dictionary the use of a 'corpus' (sometimes a real one, unlike that of the *OED*), a chronological ordering of senses, a large number of quotations, mostly from literature, etc. But they are much more encyclopedic than the *OED*: they lay more emphasis on the culture, particularly the historical aspects of the rural culture: they are all 'cultural' dictionaries in the particular sense of historical, nationalist dictionaries.

All these dictionaries had to establish a working definition for the notion of regionalism. Walter Avis, in the preface to the *Dictionary of Canadianisms*, defines *canadianism* as 'a word, expression, or meaning which is native to Canada or which is distinctively characteristic of Canadian usage though not necessarily exclusive to Canada; *Winnipeg couch* falls into the first category, *chesterfield* ("sofa") into the second' (preface: xiii). This is a much broader definition than the one used for *americanism* by Mitford M. Mathews in the *Dictionary of Americanisms*: words and meanings that were first used in the United States—which excludes words and meanings current in the USA but that did not first appear there.

Such dictionaries are scholarly records of the state of a language and of a culture. They belong to a category of their own, which may be becoming extinct, because with their historical, *OED*-inspired methodology, and the field-studies that they imply, they are extremely costly ventures, and few people or institutions now have enough money—not even the richest universities—or energy to carry them out any more. They had to be done, but they might never be done again.

The general-purpose dictionaries of all the 'new' countries were normally preceded by the inclusion of some regionalisms in imported dictionaries. The communities soon realized that those dictionaries, imported from the USA or Great Britain, could not do justice to their particular variety of English. The simple addition of a few colourful regionalisms is not enough, when the two varieties differ in more subtle ways (Delbridge 1983: 39). This no doubt was one of the reasons why many English-speaking communities started to create their own dictionaries. But there is more: the compilation of a native dictionary is a symbolical act of independence from the 'mother country', it is a necessary step to assert the cultural identity of the country (see below, 4.2.7): 'For New Zealanders . . . the publication of specifically New Zealand dictionaries is part of a continuing development of national awareness, a process that has been underway from about the beginning of the century and that has slowly gathered momentum' (Scott 1986: 319). And this applies to other countries as well. It is a powerful movement that will no doubt continue, and might eventually extend to regional as well as national entities.

2.5 NEW TRENDS AND OLD TRADITIONS IN ENGLISH-LANGUAGE LEXICOGRAPHY

2.5.1 *New dictionaries and new developments*

2.5.1.1 *Dictionaries for encoding*

There have been several noteworthy developments in English-language lexicography over the last few decades: new types of dictionaries, like the dictionaries of new words or the dictionaries for foreign learners; new techniques for the explanation of meaning, like *LDOCE*'s restricted defining vocabulary, or *COB*'s contextualized definitions, etc. The most important development is probably the publication of all sorts of dictionaries that are more or less exclusively designed to facilitate encoding operations.

This 'lexicography of encoding' is flourishing in the United States as well as in Great Britain. The Americans have a long tradition of dictionaries of synonyms, a remarkable dictionary of collocations (Rodale's *Word Finder*), and endless variations on the theme of *Roget's Thesaurus*,[33] which are more or less innovative. The British lexicography of encoding is more recent: it includes a few dictionaries of synonyms (not many), some dictionaries of collocations, many dictionaries of idioms. The learners' general dictionaries, with their indications of syntactic patterns, also exemplify the same trend.

The *Oxford Dictionary of Current Idiomatic English (ODCIE)* lists idiomatic expressions (volume 1: *Verbs with Prepositions and*

[33] 'Roget' is not a registered trade mark any more than 'Webster'.

Particles, and volume 2: *Phrase, Clause and Sentence Idioms*), with definitions, examples of use, and also the preferred or obligatory collocates of each entry-phrase. For example:

catch up (with): S: *runner; cyclist; driver; car; student; worker*. O: *pack, main body (of runners); (main) party; column; rest of the class*. [S stands for subject and O for object]

ODCIE is a splendid piece of work. It may be too much in places for the consultation skills of many dictionary users, but it provides information that was not available before, in a way that provides food for thought for the metalexicographer.

The *BBI Combinatory Dictionary of English* (*BBI*, from the names of its authors, Morton Benson, Evelyn Benson, and Robert Ilson; 1986) was compiled by American authors, but seems to be commercialized mostly in Great Britain. It is basically meant for foreign students of English, but could be useful to any native speaker. It gives the preferred and the obligatory collocates of about 12,000 entry-words. *BBI* distinguishes grammatical collocations and lexical collocations—the former being already fairly well treated in learners' dictionaries like *ALD* or *LDOCE*.

BBI has several innovative points. It is the first dictionary to indicate clearly those words that cannot be used without any complementation ('*I am fond', '*to base something', '*to fare', '*to carry oneself', etc.). It also makes it possible to find a verb if one starts from the collocating noun, subject or object. For example, *trim* can be found if one looks up *sail*, or *wield* can be found in the entry for *sword*. General-purpose dictionaries, when they do indicate collocations, usually do the reverse: they give the object nouns in the entries for the verbs, simply because the verb cannot be defined otherwise. For example, *ALD* defines *trim* as 'set (sails) to suit the wind', but does not mention *trim* in the entry for *sail*.

The concept of 'collocation' is a difficult concept to define and to work with (see below, 7.1.1.2). Any lexicographer compiling a dictionary of collocations is bound to suffer from this imprecision, and *BBI* is no exception. Its choice of collocations is, naturally, debatable, and the classification of the information in each entry does not follow any meaningful order. Some guidelines have been indicated by recent research (Benson 1990), but clearly the problems inherent in the compilation of a dictionary of collocations have not yet all been satisfactorily solved (Hausmann 1989*e*).

In a category of its own among dictionaries for encoding is Henry Burger's *The Wordtree* (1985), a highly original American dictionary that gives 24,600 English transitive verbs, organized in a strict hierarchy. The author worked for 27 years on his own on this dictionary, which is designed to provide ways to master the world and impose one's point of view on others. It is a fascinating construction, but proves difficult to use: the system is so complicated as to baffle even the most sophisticated user. Yet it is another—admittedly original—aspect of the lexicography of encoding.

There is not yet a 'perfect' dictionary for encoding, and there may never be. Any dictionary attempting to be exhaustive, like Mel'čuk's *Dictionnaire explicatif et combinatoire* (*DEC*), is bound to be so huge and complicated that it will be impossible to use—except, perhaps, if the information is eventually fed into a computer that will simplify the search process (Knowles 1990: 1665). Clearly, a dictionary for encoding will have to use a semantic, not an alphabetical arrangement, or the users will be unable to find a word or phrase when they just have the concept. This is particularly important for idiomatic expressions. A phrase like *to flog a dead horse*, in any alphabetically arranged dictionary, will be at the entry for *flog* (that is the case of *BBI*), or possibly at the entry for *horse*, or at both. This is all right for decoding purposes, but how can the users find the phrase in the macrostructure if they are encoding? What the new lexicography for encoding needs is a new concept of dictionaries, something along the lines of the Robert analogies, with a network of cross-references that allow multiple entries into the data.

Even in general-purpose dictionaries for native speakers, the trend seems to be towards the inclusion of more encoding information. The precursors were some American dictionaries with their usage notes and the Robert dictionaries in France (*GR* was published between 1953 and 1964), and now even the British dictionaries exhibit the same tendency. The reasons are not totally clear. Is it a reaction against dictionaries like *OED*, with their bias towards the decoding of literary texts? Is it that the dictionary publishers are trying to find new ideas to persuade the public to buy more dictionaries? Is it that the public needs more encoding information because the art of expressing oneself is felt to be socially more important than ever, and because it is less consistently taught in schools than it used to be? An interesting aspect of the question is that encoding information does not actually seem to be much used (see below, 5.1.4): why should the dictionary users as a whole want information that they do not use as individuals?

2.5.1.2 *Semantic 'dictionaries'*

The dictionary of synonyms continues to be produced in the USA, and is becoming more important in Britain—the latest British example being L. Urdang's *Oxford Thesaurus: An A–Z Dictionary of Synonyms*, published in 1991. The methodology of these dictionaries has changed very little over the years, but they seem to sell well. It is all the more surprising that they have never been studied in metalexicography. They are usually presented as the lineage of *Roget's Thesaurus*, but in fact the genre goes back much further than that in history. In some countries, they may even be the first ever to have been produced (Boisson *et al.* 1991). Some are semantically arranged, some use the alphabetical order in one way or another. All are probably used mostly for encoding, but perhaps also by people who want to enlarge their vocabulary. Certainly many people buy them, but they are often found disappointing because they are usually just lists of words, without any comments, whereas the public wants an explanatory text, some discursive explanation of the differences in meaning, etc.

A noteworthy recent example of such dictionaries is the *Longman Lexicon of Contemporary English* (*LLCE*), published in 1981 and compiled by Tom McArthur. Its great originality is that it brings together, on the same page, the definitions of words that are semantically related: thus section M52, **Sending and transporting** (verbs), has *send, transfer, transport, convey, deliver, ship,* and *dispatch*. The dictionary is divided into fourteen broad categories, themselves subdivided so that the whole vocabulary is organized in three tiers. *LLCE* is a small dictionary designed for foreign students: all the entries come from *LDOCE*, but *LLCE* has only 15,000 entries—the selection criteria are not explained. The definitions have been adopted from *LDOCE* without any major modifications, unfortunately, and particularly without any attempt at making them contrastive. For example:

tremble: to shake uncontrollably as from fear, cold, excitement, etc.
shiver: to shake, esp. (of people) from cold or fear
shudder: to shake uncontrollably for a moment, as from fear, cold, or strong dislike.

The idea is a wonderful one, which has enormous potentialities for foreign students, but one feels that it could have been taken somewhat further.

The dictionary of synonyms and related words in general is in need of research. As it is, it does not really come up to the expectations of the public, but it is not totally clear what could be done to make it more effective, or more user-friendly, or both.

2.5.1.3 *Monolingual–bilingual dictionaries*

Among the dictionaries for foreign students, one interesting recent development is the monolingual–bilingual dictionary with its source-language definitions and its equivalents in the target language added to each meaning. These dictionaries are important, because they go beyond the traditional distinction between monolingual and bilingual dictionaries. No study of their effectiveness has been carried out yet, but it will be interesting to see how they perform, particularly in the comparative study of the effectiveness of various means of indicating meaning in a foreign language, such as definitions and equivalents (see Tono 1984). These dictionaries deserve more study than they have received so far.

2.5.1.4 *Dictionaries of new words*

The dictionary of new words, a recent development, can be considered as the continuation of pre-eighteenth-century dictionaries of hard words (see below, 3.2.2.1). The trend began in the USA and is now developing in Britain as well, for reasons that are not totally clear: the dictionaries of new words are no doubt useful as complements to dictionaries that tend to become outdated more and more quickly, but such use is so episodic that one may marvel that there is indeed a market for them (Barnhart and Barnhart 1990; Algeo 1990*a*).

2.5.1.5 *Dictionaries of World English*

Another interesting development in modern English-language lexicography is the fact that more and more local varieties of English are represented in dictionaries. Not only do more and more countries produce their own dictionaries (see above, 2.4), but the general-purpose dictionaries of Britain and the USA tend to be more and more hospitable to regionalisms.

This is a recent development, not specific to English-language dictionaries. French lexicographers, Rey notes, were experiencing the same problems in 1977:

Le problème de l'introduction dans les nomenclatures générales de dictionnaires de langue française, conçus en France (à Paris, en général) de termes usités dans une zone géographique précise (régionalismes français, belges, suisses, africanismes, canadianismes, etc.) mériterait une étude, car il commence à se poser pratiquement.[34] (Rey 1977: 144)

French dictionaries, up to a very recent period, had very few regionalisms. British dictionaries did not do very well either; they only had those words that happened to be used by renowned authors (Wakelin 1987). The treatment of varietal words in general-purpose dictionaries is still somewhat erratic. At the end of a study of the inclusion of Americanisms in some British dictionaries in 1981 (*ALD, COD, LDOCE, OPD*, and a few others), I came to the conclusion that the treatment was highly unequal and often inexplicable, but the more recent dictionaries were better than the older ones (Béjoint 1981*b*).

Ilson (1986*b*) compares British and American dictionaries for their coverage of twelve pairs of words, one British and one American: *silencer—muffler, courgette—zucchini, nappy—diaper, torch—flashlight*, etc. His conclusion is that American dictionaries are poor in their indication of Briticisms, and that British dictionaries are clearly more generous in their treatment of Americanisms:

There is a vast difference in coverage. Of the American dictionaries W9 [i.e. *NCD9*] is the only one that comes anywhere near a respectable score: it gets seven out of the twelve. . . . CED gets all twelve right. COD . . . and GID each get eleven, LDEL gets ten, *Chambers*[35] gets ten. Clearly, the British dictionaries are much more aware of American English than the American dictionaries are of British English. (Ilson 1986*b*: 62)

On the whole, all the studies of different editions of the same dictionary, or of different generations of dictionaries, demonstrate that dictionaries are more and more open to regionalisms, even though the coverage may still be patchy and the choices sometimes inexplicable. Some British dictionaries have even started labelling

[34] 'The issue of the introduction into the word-lists of general dictionaries of French produced in France (usually in Paris) of terms used in precise geographical areas (French regionalisms, words specific to Belgium, Switzerland, Africa, or Canada, etc.) deserves serious study, because it is beginning to be a practical problem.'

[35] *Chambers* here means *CTD*.

Brit those words or usages that are specifically British, like *nappy* or *pavement*—American dictionaries always leave the American variant unlabelled (Ilson 1990*b*: 1974).

The ultimate step in a 'lexicography of World English' would be the realization of a dictionary, or at least a lexical database, that would contain all the variants of the English language throughout the world, that 'dictionary of the English-speaking peoples' that David Crystal dreams of (Crystal 1986: 72). This is exactly what the *OED* team at Waterloo eventually hope to constitute (Weiner 1986). The task is staggering, but the use of computers for the production and consultation of lexical databases makes that goal less inaccessible than it has ever been.

2.5.1.6 *Corpus-based and computerized lexicography*

Dictionaries are becoming 'computerized' all over the world, and particularly in Britain and the USA because of the relative prosperity of the market. Computers are more and more used in the preparation, printing, and consultation of dictionaries (Knowles 1990). The first dictionary to be available on magnetic tape was Merrian's *Collegiate* in the sixties (*NCD7*), and many others have now followed suit, including *AHD* and *LDOCE*. More and more dictionaries use corpora managed by computers, for the constitution of lemmatized concordances. Some have begun to implement lexical databases that can be put to a variety of uses—an idea that Quemada expressed several years ago by differentiating between *lexicographie* and *dictionnairique*. The best example is no doubt the work done for the *New Oxford English Dictionary* at Waterloo. Also, a consortium of British publishers is compiling a 'British National Corpus' that will contain '100 million words of contemporary spoken and written British English', says the leaflet, and will be completed by January 1994.

The field of the use of computers in lexicographical work is expanding rapidly, and further developments can be expected. Many more changes would have taken place already, Knowles says, if the publishers had been more willing to invest in the field (Knowles 1990: 1665).

2.5.2 *Differences and similarities in general-purpose dictionaries*

The general-purpose dictionaries of Britain, the USA, and other English-speaking countries exhibit interesting differences. American lexicographers continue to produce encyclopedic general-purpose dictionaries, and there is no sign of imminent change; the reaction to *W3* was a clear enough indication that modifications in the traditional appearance of the general-purpose dictionary were not welcome, at least by a certain proportion of fairly influential people like teachers and journalists.

The British scene is more complex: beside the traditional language dictionaries, the two new types of the encyclopedic dictionary modelled on the American college dictionary, and of the dictionary for foreign students, are commercially successful and represent a certain lexicographical innovation. Besides, the more traditional dictionaries still seem to be prosperous enough. The only type that might be on its way out is the dictionary of regionalisms.

Despite the differences between individual dictionaries and between the national lexicographical scenes, and despite the innovations that have taken place over the last thirty years or so, there are still many striking similarities between all the general-purpose dictionaries of English-speaking countries. Those similarities are more difficult to pinpoint than the differences, because we tend to associate them with the dictionary as a genre. It is hard to imagine that things could have been different.

If the differences between dictionaries are traceable to certain characteristics of each society, and more particularly to the social role of the dictionary, what has caused the dictionaries to be so fundamentally similar? Why should the dictionaries of Britain, the USA, and elsewhere share so many features? This cannot be traced back to any characteristic of the English language, since French dictionaries are the same, *mutatis mutandis*. Nor is it possible to attribute the similarities to research on the lexicon, lexicology, or lexicography, theoretical or practical, since in many respects the dictionaries have not changed very much over the centuries.

The similarities between dictionaries can only be traced to a tradition that is common, with minor differences, to Britain, the USA, France, and many other countries, and that has solidified over the centuries. This tradition is the result of a complex interplay between what the dictionary users have wanted and what the lexicographers have wanted, or tried, to produce and been able to offer.

What goes into the dictionary has depended in the past (and still rightly depends) on factors social and historical, as much as theoretical and linguistic. We are right, in the 20th century, to see if we cannot establish scholarly principles upon which the lexicographer may be expected to proceed; but the lexicographical tradition we have inherited will serve to remind us that the user is as much entitled as the linguist to his vision of what a good English dictionary should be. (Osselton 1983: 13)

In all societies, the users have wanted similar dictionaries because they needed them to solve similar everyday problems of communication, and also for more obscure reasons, because everywhere dictionaries are much more than just linguistic tools: they are emblems of learning, symbols of social success. And in all societies, the lexicographers have offered similar dictionaries because they have made use of the views on language that were available to them, which were naturally very much alike in all Western countries.

The interplay between the lexicographers and the users has created the general-purpose dictionaries as we know them. It explains the demand and supply of dictionaries, and also why they are what they are, both different and similar:

une étude comparée des dictionnaires monolingues de plusieurs langues présenterait des constantes dans l'approche métalinguistique naïve d'un système, mais aussi probablement des points de vue propres aux sociétés et indépendants du système lui-même. Le sentiment métalinguistique dans les sociétés devrait faire l'objet de travaux sociolinguistiques.[36] (Rey-Debove 1971: 316)

Dictionaries are bought because they satisfy some popular ideas that are partly specific to each society and partly common to all, and lexicographers naturally tend to reproduce age-old patterns because there is a demand for them.

[36] 'a comparative study of the monolingual dictionaries of several languages would reveal similarities in the naïve metalinguistic grasp of the linguistic systems, as well as—probably—points of view that vary according to the society and are independent of the system itself. The metalinguistics of societies should be studied by sociolinguists.'

3
The Historical Origins of the General-Purpose Dictionary

3.1 PRE-HISTORY: THE FIRST DICTIONARIES

Dictionaries are probably much older than is generally said.[1] Sumerian lists dating back to the third millennium BC have been found that can be considered as the ancestors of our dictionaries (Boisson *et al.* 1991: 263). There may even have been 'oral' dictionaries, before the development of writing systems: at least one contemporary society that does not have a writing system has been shown to have, among its oral records used in the traditional village recitations, lists of words, either bilingual or monolingual, sometimes with sorts of definitions, half poetry and half lexicography (Boisson *et al.* 1991: 292). Many other societies could have had similar traditions. Of course, all societies with writing systems have produced dictionaries, of various kinds and for various reasons.

The incentive for the creation of dictionaries is not the same in all societies. In some, 'proto-dictionaries' seem to have been used for the instruction of future administrators (Sumer); in others they were designed for commercial or administrative relations with other communities (Egypt), for poetry (as for some early dictionaries of Arabic), or for priests. And it is not unreasonable to think that in some cases the need actually came from the compilers, not from the public. Some dictionaries have been scholarly lists of the things that make up the world more than books about words. They were not

[1] The following pages are only a brief sketch aimed at pointing out some of the most striking features in the historical evolution of dictionaries that help us to understand why our modern dictionaries are what they are. On the history of dictionaries in general, see Rey (1982), McArthur (1986*b*), and Hausmann *et al.* On the history of British dictionaries, see Starnes and Noyes (1946/1991), Sledd and Kolb (1955), Collison (1971), Hayashi (1978), Osselton (1983), Stein (1984*a*), Stein (1985), Read (1986), Osselton (1989), Simpson (1990), Stein (1990). For the history of dictionaries in the USA, see Friend (1967), Wells (1973), Burkett (1979).

simple linguistic tools, but attempts at embracing the world, at imposing some apparent order on the chaos. In societies where words and things were thought to be naturally related, the dictionary and the encyclopedia were indistinguishable.

In many non-European societies, the first dictionaries were not bilingual, contrary to what has been said by many European-centred metalexicographers, but monolingual (Boisson *et al.* 1991), or at most 'bi-varietal' (see above, 1.2.1.4). In Europe, it is customary to consider that the ancestors of dictionaries were the 'glosses' that were compiled to help monks read important texts written in languages that they could no longer understand—Latin or Greek. The 'true' dictionaries appeared when societies began to have commercial or cultural relations with communities that used different languages, and to need translations. The pedagogical nature of those early bilingual dictionaries is often clearly stated in their titles: *The Introductory to Wryte and to Pronounce French* (Barclay, 1521), *Dictionary of the French and English Tongues: Brief Directions for such as desire to learne the French Tongue* (Cotgrave, 1611), etc. (see Hayashi 1978).

3.2 MONOLINGUAL DICTIONARIES FROM THE RENAISSANCE TO THE TWENTIETH CENTURY

3.2.1 *The first monolingual dictionaries*

The first monolingual dictionaries, from the late sixteenth century and down to Johnson, seem to have been dictionaries of hard words (Osselton 1990: 1944),[2] which were clearly designed to educate the public.

> The cultural and educational function of the earliest English dictionaries—down to 1750 at least—was to enable a wider, unlatined, reading public to understand and to learn to use the new technical and abstract vocabulary of learned words, which in many cases thus became less 'hard' and were assimilated into the language. (Osselton 1983: 16)

Monolingual dictionaries, in spite of the relative poverty of their word-list at the beginning compared to the bilingual dictionaries that

[2] Though see Dolezal (1986), who observes that some of the earliest dictionaries had 'easy' words right from the start.

had preceded them (Osselton 1983: 14; Hayashi 1978: 41), thus had the same function: they were instruments for self-teaching. Again, this is clearly expressed for English dictionaries by the long titles that often occupied all of the front page: *A General English Dictionary . . . very necessary for Strangers, as well as our own Countrymen; or for all persons that would rightly understand what they discourse, Write, or Read* (E(dward) P(hillips),[3] 1671), *A Dictionary Interpreting the Hard Words . . . very usefull for all such as desire to understand what they read* (Blount, 1681), etc. (see Starnes and Noyes 1991). The users of such dictionaries were people who suffered from a linguistic—and often social—handicap.

> In a situation where the standard language, as these languages developed in Europe in the centuries that preceded the Dictionary of the French Academy, is not the native dialect of many of its users, many seemingly 'easy words' of such a standard language are 'hard words' for such non-native users of it, so that many of the users seek advice in the dictionary. . . . Even a native speaker of a colloquial variety of the standard language or of a dialect closely related to it will occasionally need advice as to some details of its literary variety. (Zgusta 1986*b*: 75–6)

This was particularly true of children, women, foreigners, etc., and generally speaking of all the categories of people who had no access to the more traditional means of education. Women, for example, were often not admitted into schools and universities: 'Motivated girls lacked even a basic tool to use in teaching themselves until dictionaries were available' (Miller and Swift 1979: 108). The categories were often named clearly, in terms that no lexicographer would dare to use nowadays: 'the unskilful persons' (Cawdrey, 1604), 'the ignorant' (Bullokar, 1616), '[persons of] the capacity of the meanest' (Cockeram, 1623), etc. Whether dictionaries were efficient or not in that respect is another story (see below, 4.2.6).

3.2.2 *The turning-point of the eighteenth century*

During the eighteenth century, the general-purpose dictionaries in Europe, and particularly in France and in England, changed in many ways. The evolution was undoubtedly related to a series of changes

[3] The title-pages were extremely copious, but often did not indicate the name of the author, perhaps because the contents were more often than not simply copied from other dictionaries. Phillips's dictionary is only signed E.P.

in society that were taking place at the same time and that have often been described. It did not take place suddenly, nor at the same time in all societies; it was sometimes slow and erratic, sometimes quick and decisive. Yet the net result is clear: nineteenth-century dictionaries were definitely different from what they had been in the seventeenth century. And the consequences of the changes are still felt nowadays. Osselton sees four main aspects in the turning-point of the eighteenth century:

> The century down to 1850 saw great changes in the notion of what a dictionary should be: it came to be seen as a scholarly record of the whole language; in method, it became inductive—that is, based on or derived from a corpus; the emphasis came to lie far more than hitherto on the literary rather than the technical language; and the dictionary now assumed an authoritarian or normative function. (Osselton 1983: 17)

3.2.2.1 *The dictionary as a 'scholarly record of the whole language'*

Early monolingual dictionaries soon started to try and outdo their competitors by increasing the contents of their word-list, since quantity was, already, a commercial asset. This is probably one of the reasons why dictionaries included more and more frequent words. But why in the eighteenth century, and not earlier, or later? The reasons are more than purely commercial. The general feeling in the intelligentsia of the time, in Britain as well as in France and other countries, that the language had reached a degree of perfection and could henceforth only deteriorate has often been mentioned. It was therefore necessary to act as soon and as effectively as possible, in order to prevent the deterioration from going any further. The language had to be recorded, so that the record would serve as a firm basis for teaching and conservation; in short, the language needed a grammar and a dictionary, but a dictionary of a new type: one that would record all the language, not only a few hard words.

From a humble reference book for occasional use, the dictionary then became the repository of the language as a whole, a thesaurus recording the language in a state that was not amenable to change. The public of dictionary users changed accordingly: the titles no longer mentioned specially handicapped categories. The dictionaries were designed for the whole linguistic community.

Zgusta (1986*b*: 74) argues that the change was initiated by the first *Dictionnaire de l'Académie* in France (1694). For England, the dates given by Collison (1982) or Osselton (1983) are very similar: 1702 and 1708, which are the dates of publication of Kersey's dictionaries. Apparently the English wanted to emulate the French and the Italians in their desire to fix the language in a state that would never change again (Read 1986: 32).

In the earliest dictionaries of that kind, the frequent words were treated with an economy of style that looks strange to our modern eyes. For example, K(ersey)'s *New Dictionary* (1702) defines *dog* as 'a beast', and Kersey's *Dictionnarium Anglo-Britannicum* (1708) defines it as 'a well-known creature' (Moon 1989: 71). Samuel Johnson himself would use such definitions: for example, *fish* is defined as 'an animal that inhabits the water', whereas *armadillo* has a long paragraph of several sentences. Such extremely terse definitions can only be explained by the fact that the frequent words were included for the sake of exhaustiveness, but the lexicographer felt that they did not really have to be defined.

The new dictionaries became increasingly 'linguistic', and the skills required of the lexicographer were of a different nature: the treatment of hard words (our modern *terms*) in dictionaries does not pose the same problems as the treatment of the more frequent words. The dictionary now had to 'define' function words, it had to devise solutions for the treatment of polysemy, etc. And it had to fix the boundaries of the language of reference, to decide what was part of it and what was not, what words should be recorded and what words should not.

In the eighteenth century, dictionaries became records of the whole language only up to a point: the lexicographers recorded only the words of one very special variety of the language, the literary language used by certain authors (see below, 3.2.2.3). After that, in the nineteenth and twentieth centuries, the expansion of the word-list of general-purpose dictionaries continued. It went through a historical phase with dictionaries of the *OED* tradition, when exhaustiveness was understood in its temporal sense: roughly speaking, all the words of one variety of English from its inception to the present day. Then there was a stage when exhaustiveness was social: dictionaries had to have all the words of all the social varieties of the language—hence the inclusion of more and more technical, scientific, and specialized words (Zgusta 1986*b*: 77),[4] and also of more

[4] On this tendency in French dictionaries, see Mazière (1981) and Beaujot (1989: 80). For English dictionaries, see also Landau (1984) and Béjoint (1988).

and more familiar, vulgar, even taboo words (see below, 4.2.5). And all modern dictionaries, in Britain and the USA as well as in France, are now moving towards a spatial interpretation of exhaustiveness—hence the tendency to include more and more regionalisms.

The desire to record the whole language has also had some effects on the microstructure: the more frequent words are now defined in the same way as the more infrequent ones, so that dictionary compilers make great efforts to define words that no user ever looks up (see below, 5.1.4).

3.2.2.2 *The dictionary 'derived from a corpus'*

From the middle of the eighteenth century onwards, Osselton says, lexicographers started using a 'corpus'. At that time, this meant a collection of authentic texts from which, to a certain extent, they extracted their entry-words and also, though in a still less direct way, their microstructural information. Osselton calls the method *inductive*. In fact, the texts used in that way did not constitute a corpus as we understand it today, that is to say a closed set of texts composed prior to its study so as to be representative of the variety of linguistic usage in the community. In modern corpus-based lexicography, all the words in the word-list, all their meanings, and all the quotations that illustrate them come exclusively from the corpus. The 'corpus' of eighteenth-century lexicographers was not closed or in any way meant to be representative of all the varieties of the language. The method is inductive only in the sense that authentic texts were observed and used in the process of the compilation of the dictionary. But the corpus was adapted by the lexicographers to suit their needs. It was there to illustrate what they wanted to say in the first place. It was in fact often used *a posteriori*, to find confirmation of the lexicographers' intuitions.

The eighteenth-century corpus was used, among other things, to provide quotations. Quotations in dictionaries had been used before, but the practice was far from systematic (Read 1986: 32). From then on they became indispensable, at least in all the fairly large dictionaries, for the illustration of the 'good' uses of every word. Johnson had quotations for almost every single word and meaning, from major writers, that he arranged in chronological order when there was more than one (Osselton 1990: 1949; Simpson 1990: 1954). He used them 'to illustrate the meaning of words in context, to establish that a word had been used by a reputable authority, to display how words were used by the best authors, to show the language as it was at an earlier era before it was contaminated by foreign influences, and to impart useful lessons and moral instruction' (Morton 1989: 154–5). Later authors had slightly different motivations—for Littré, it was mostly aesthetic: 'ce sont des lambeaux de pourpre', he said (see Leschiera 1990: 85)—but the idea was always to lend authority to the dictionary.

The desire to draw every word and sense from authentic texts and to use those texts as a source of quotations was a capital innovation in lexicography. The consequences can be felt to the present day, but the whole philosophy has been reversed: where eighteenth-century lexicographers, and many of their later followers, wanted a highly selective collection of 'good' texts to help them indicate good usage, modern dictionary makers have wanted to use texts as the basis for a non-selective, or at least more objective description. There was an intermediate stage in the late nineteenth and early twentieth centuries, when the new lexicographical methods were called 'le principe philologique': 'La philologie et la lexicographie qui s'y réfère . . . reposent sur l'observation des faits de discours; le dictionnaire "philologique" prétend donc construire un modèle linguistique à partir de la pure observation'[5] (Rey and Delesalle 1979: 16). This was the method used by the compilers of the *OED*, who set out to select their entries from an open collection of texts, defined by qualitative criteria. The authors of the *OED* wanted to observe usage, not to sanction it: 'Il faut admettre au moins que le "principe philologique" (honnêtement appliqué) rend impossible une attitude normative par exclusion'[6] (Rey and Delesalle 1979: 18). Yet the documents in the corpus had been chosen by specific criteria, and they were exploited in a non-systematic way. The *OED* 'corpus' was less selective than the texts used by eighteenth-century lexicographers, but it was not as fully encompassing as a modern corpus. It was also used differently: for example, the definitions were often prepared intuitively, and only then did the compilers try to find citations in the corpus to illustrate every meaning they had prepared —an easier method than analysing the corpus in search of meanings.

[5] 'Philology and the lexicography that is attached to it . . . rest on the observation of discourse; the "philological" dictionary aims at constructing a linguistic model purely based on observation.'

[6] 'It must be admitted that the "philological principle" (if it is scrupulously respected) makes it impossible to prescribe by excluding information.'

Corpus-based lexicography was born in the eighteenth century, but it is now very different from what it was then. The use of corpora in modern dictionaries is symptomatic of a desire among the public and the lexicographers for a 'scientific', objective description of linguistic usage.

3.2.2.3 *A dictionary of the 'literary language'*

In the eighteenth century, because they wanted their dictionaries to record the best linguistic usage, lexicographers restricted their search to the literary language, and particularly the language used by the best authors. They selected only those words that had been used in good literature, and illustrated their use with literary quotations.

The exclusive and systematic use of literary quotations in a dictionary that includes all the more frequent words naturally has consequences that some—including Samuel Johnson himself (Read 1986: 38)—have found absurd:

> Le préjugé littéraire pèse sur la lexicographie depuis le XVIIIe siècle; au point qu'il paraîtrait sacrilège en France qu'un grand dictionnaire (et cela vaut pour le G.L.L.F.[7] comme pour le T.L.F.) n'illustrât point la valeur d'emploi la plus commune du verbe le plus usuel par une citation de Hugo, de Huysmans, de Claudel ou de Malraux.[8] (Wagner 1975: 94)

The effects of the new emphasis on literary language were felt for a long time, with a culmination represented by the *OED*, and they can still be felt today, to a certain extent, on the most traditional type of dictionaries. The inclusion of non-literary varieties of English is fairly recent. Technical terms came first, with a tradition in France going back to Furetière (1690), and a progressive acceleration from the nineteenth century to the present in the USA first and eventually in Britain. The more familiar varieties took more time, although very familiar words had been recorded in dictionaries of the Renaissance. The broadening of the scope was no doubt helped by the fact that literary works also began, at the same time, to use other varieties of English, including the colloquial. Some dictionaries, like *LDOCE* and *COB*, now use corpora that contain oral documents.

[7] G.L.L.F. = *Grand Larousse de la langue française*.

[8] 'The literary bias has marked lexicography since the eighteenth century; so much so that it would seem sacrilegious in France for a large dictionary (and this is true of the *GLLF* as well as the *TLF*) not to illustrate the most common use of the most frequent verb by a quotation from Victor Hugo, J. K. Huysmans, Paul Claudel or André Malraux.'

3.2.2.4 *The 'authoritarian, or normative function' of the dictionary*

The aim of the very first monolingual dictionaries was to describe lexical usage, but in the eighteenth century lexicographers felt it was their duty to indicate—and in some cases decide—what was good and what was bad usage. They recommended some forms and banned others. Such an attitude has been called *prescriptive*, the reverse being called *descriptive*.

Prescriptiveness and descriptiveness are based on two different norms: a 'qualitative' norm and a 'quantitative' norm (Rey 1972). The qualitative norm is based on the usage and on the opinion of the 'best' language users, as determined by a more or less clear consensus—often, in fact, only educators and well-known writers. The main difficulty in the implementation of such a norm is the determination of who is qualified to say what. In the case of disputed usages in the eighteenth century, the grammarians and lexicographers based their recommendations on 'rules' which made use of etymology and 'logic', and of descriptions of Latin and Greek: what was true of Greek and Latin, it was thought, also had to be true of modern languages. The qualitative norm corresponds to an eighteenth-century type of 'corpus', which lexicographers used to support their observations rather than to establish usage.

The quantitative norm is based on the observation of the linguistic usage of all the reasonably fluent users of the community. Any form is good as long as it is used by a certain number of speakers. The difficulty here is to determine the minimum number of speakers, or of recorded uses, required to make a usage acceptable. The quantitative norm corresponds to the modern corpus, which can be studied with statistical methods in order to determine frequencies. The dictionary is prescriptive if it uses a qualitative norm, descriptive if it uses the quantitative.

The aim of prescriptive dictionaries is to fix the language, to try to prevent it from changing, change usually being equated with deterioration (Zgusta 1989*a*: 75). The language that the dictionaries tried to stabilize was the variety used, or at least admired, by a certain élite. It was the language used by the best writers, typically some time before the date of publication of the dictionary.

Prescriptive dictionaries use a variety of methods to indicate good usage. One is to omit words, meanings, or phrases: the absence of a word from the macrostructure is often—though not always—an indication that the word is not a 'good' word (Matoré 1968: 200).

Also, usage labels can be attached to certain words to indicate that they are not recommended, and are only included as a warning against their use.

It has been said that all dictionaries are prescriptive. This is partly true, since a dictionary is a book that one consults, in which one tries to find answers. But it would be more exact to say that a dictionary is 'normative', like all didactic books: it cannot help proposing a linguistic model to its users (Zgusta 1971: 210–11; Zgusta 1980: 8; Rey 1982: 30). 'Le dictionnaire de langue peut être caractérisé comme le dictionnaire de "bon usage", le dictionnaire auquel on a recours pour trouver des informations sur la langue des gens cultivés. Sa visée n'est pas purement descriptive'[9] (Guilbert 1969: 19).

The normative, codifying aspect of dictionaries is best seen in the indication of spelling. The dictionary, even if it gives different possible spellings, has to choose a preferred form for use as an entry-word, and thereby may influence usage, particularly if the form that is chosen happens not to be that which is used with more frequency or by the best speakers. Noah Webster saw clearly that spelling was an area where his *Dictionary* could influence usage, and that is why he used it to launch his proposed modifications (see Laird 1970).

> His spelling triumphed in American usage, at least in many words ending in *-our* in British usage, along with *theater* as against *theatre, center* as against *centre*, he cut *musick* and *publick* down to *music* and *public*, although he failed in his equally sensible *imagin, primitiv*, and *thum*. (Laird 1970: 278)

But the distinction between descriptive dictionaries and prescriptive dictionaries is much clearer in the declarations of lexicographers and of some of their public than in the reality of the dictionaries themselves. Total descriptiveness is impossible, because the lexicographer cannot avoid making choices, and total prescriptiveness does not work if it is estranged from the realities of usage, as the difficulties of the dictionaries compiled by the French Academy show quite clearly.

Even Samuel Johnson was not equal to the task of carrying out his prescriptive ambitions. In the earlier stages of the realization of his dictionary, his intentions were clearly prescriptive. This is what

9 'The "dictionnaire de langue" can be characterized as the dictionary of "good usage", the dictionary that one opens in order to find information on the language of educated users. It is not purely descriptive.'

he was writing in 1747 to his protector Lord Chesterfield: 'This, my Lord, is my idea of an English dictionary; a dictionary by which the pronunciation of our language may be fixed, and its attainment facilitated; by which its purity may be preserved, its use ascertained, and its duration lengthened.' But in 1755, when his *Dictionary* was published, he had abandoned some of his hopes of curbing the flow of linguistic change:

> Those who have been persuaded to think well of my design, require that it should fix our language, and put a stop to those alterations which time and chance have hitherto been suffered to make in it without opposition. With this consequence I will confess that I flattered myself for a while; but now begin to fear that I have indulged expectation which neither reason nor experience can justify . . . And with equal justice may the lexicographer be derided, who being able to produce no example of a nation that has preserved their words and phrases from mutability, shall imagine that his dictionary can embalm his language, and secure it from corruption and decay, that it is in his power to change sublunary nature, or clear the world at once from folly, vanity, and affectation. (Johnson, 1755)[10]

His pessimism was later confirmed by the fact, in spite of his personal aura, the words that he had condemned in his *Dictionary* did not all suffer from the anathema: some disappeared from usage, but neither more nor less than other words that he had not condemned, and some (*abominable, antiquity*, etc.) have survived (Sledd and Kolb 1955: 37; Dykema 1967: 44; Wells 1973: 88–9).

Even in such relatively simple domains as spelling, the power of the dictionary maker is only limited. Sir James Murray, the compiler of *OED*, had insisted on the spelling *ax*, without a final 'e', to be used first, with *axe* in second position. But the preferred British spelling never changed, despite the influence of the *OED*. And the same happened to Noah Webster: his desire to change the spelling of English through the earlier editions of his *Dictionary* was clearly prescriptive, but he later became a descriptivist when he realized how hopeless the task was (Laird 1970: 263–90; Görlach 1990: 1481).

3.2.3 *The general-purpose dictionary down to the present*

3.2.3.1 *The democratization of knowledge*

The general-purpose dictionary as it developed in the eighteenth century appeared at the same time as the middle classes emerged in

[10] Preface to the *Dictionary*. See McAdam and Milne (1963: 24).

our societies. The new bourgeoisie had social and cultural ambitions: 'As the bourgeoisie increased their wealth and power, they began to wish to talk like their betters' (McDavid 1979: 24). And the dictionary was one readily available means to help them reach that goal. It was an object that they could buy and study as they wanted. It was, McDavid says, a

> response to the rise of the middle classes, the dissemination of knowledge and literacy, and the general ferment of intellectual curiosity arising from the Renaissance and the Reformation—to say nothing of the perhaps less admirable but thoroughly comprehensible ambitions of the newly risen and affluent to use without stumbling the kind of language to which the traditional upper classes had been accustomed. The need to provide information about language for the uninformed and socially insecure underlies all subsequent lexicography. (McDavid 1973*a*: 5)

The social aspirations of the bourgeoisie coincided with the conservation of the language: 'Since its inception English lexicography has had two goals: to educate the middle class and to protect the language' (Smith 1979: 47). It would have been pointless to try to imitate a language that would keep changing: the language was seen as something fixed that one could get access to and master once and for all. Of course there was a gap between real everyday usage, even 'good' usage, and the literary model that was proposed (the *bourgeois gentilhomme* is an eternal theme), and that gap later increased, if only because the dictionary was becoming accessible to an ever increasing proportion of the population: 'Sur la fin du XVIIIe siècle, l'augmentation de la clientèle correspond à la diminution du format, de l'*in-folio* de prestige aux in-8° et in-12'[11] (Meschonnic 1991: 22). Several dictionaries were sold in cheap fascicles, from the early nineteenth century onwards. The gap between the model and the public could only be reduced by a change in the language recorded by the dictionary, and this is what is happening now.

Towards the end of the eighteenth century, and in the nineteenth, some lexicographers started compiling yet other types of dictionaries: they set out to fight ignorance and its social consequences, to liberate the 'masses'. In Great Britain in the middle of the eighteenth century, John Wesley, founder of the Methodist movement, compiled

11 'Towards the end of the eighteenth century, the increase in the number of potential buyers is accompanied by a reduction of the format, from the prestigious in-folio to the in-8vo and in-12mo.'

a small dictionary explicitly aimed at educating the working classes (McArthur 1986*b*: 134). A few years later, the Chambers brothers had much the same ideal: 'When they set up in business, the brothers called themselves "publishers for the people", expressing through their slogan a particularly Scottish and Presbyterian desire to spread learning to all men and women' (McArthur 1986*b*: 134). The same attitude was found in Germany with the Grimm brothers (Mellor 1979: 70). Pierre Larousse also had clear political ambitions:

> en même temps qu'il désirait vulgariser sainement et, pour être utile au peuple, rester simple à tout prix, Larousse travaillait. . . à réaliser une œuvre qui, par sa science, fût digne du public de bourgeois modestes, d'instituteurs, de petits fonctionnaires qui s'adressaient à elle pour enrichir leurs connaissances et leur permettre de travailler plus efficacement à l'instauration d'une société démocratique et laïque. Le premier Larousse a donc joué, toutes proportions gardées, et dans un tout autre style, un rôle voisin de celui qu'avait assumé l'*Encyclopédie* du XVIIIe siècle: comme celle-ci, il présente une sorte de mise au point des connaissances, en même temps qu'il est un instrument de libération.[12] (Matoré 1968: 127)

Those dictionaries did not propose radical changes in social values; they merely tried to give a large number of people access to the cultural heritage of their societies. Dictionaries have never been revolutionary, in spite of the *bonnet rouge* that Victor Hugo wanted to put on them. Together with grammar-books, obligatory schooling, language academies, and more recently the mass media, they have been part of an arsenal of regulating instruments used by modern societies to ensure the smooth functioning of the linguistic code, to prevent it from becoming a myriad of subcodes, in spite of the division of the population into numerous subgroups, and eventually to maintain a sort of social cohesion. 'Les dictionnaires participaient, avec la centralisation administrative, le développement de l'instruction publique et une certaine standardisation des genres de vie et formes d'activités, à l'unification du français sur la base du

[12] 'while he wanted sensible popularization and simplicity at all costs in order to better serve the people, Larousse worked . . . towards the accomplishment of a work whose scientificity would be worthy of the public of lower middle-class people, schoolteachers, and petty "fonctionnaires" who used it to improve their education and to help them work more efficiently towards a democratic and secular society. Thus, *mutatis mutandis*, the role of the first Larousse dictionary was similar to that played by the *Encyclopédie* in the eighteenth century: both were sorts of summations of human knowledge, as well as instruments for the liberation of mankind.'

parler parisien'[13] (Collignon and Glatigny 1978: 85). Dictionaries have been partners in the maintenance of societies, in the consolidation of social relations and the stigmatization of the marginal (Buzon 1979: 44; Beaujot 1989).

American dictionaries, with their encyclopedicity, are particularly good examples of the dictionary as an instrument of acculturation. They play the same part in social cohesion as other pedagogical instruments, but they are by far the most popular:

> the real goals of language teaching and criticism are not now and were not in the 19th century, protecting the language and teaching linguistic skills to ordinary men. The real achievement of education—especially American education—is perhaps more impressive; its real achievement has been to engineer the maintenance of the social classes as they solidified in the 19th century. It would surely be naive not to see that English language studies have contributed to this end, and it would be worse than naive not to see that much of what passes for education in American schools has, whatever the intention, even now the same result. (Smith 1979: 56)

The dictionary is the best, the most compact, the most economical compendium of knowledge, for anyone who wants to—or cannot do better than—study on their own.

3.2.3.2 *The collective and the individual*

The work of the lexicographer, as Johnson remarked, is a humble one, if it consists in culling words from texts and listing them in alphabetical order with some explanation of their meanings. There is little inventiveness, let alone genius, at play. Yet many dictionaries, particularly in the nineteenth and early twentieth centuries, were compiled by people with strong personalities, who produced highly idiosyncratic dictionaries (Rey and Delesalle 1979: 11): Samuel Johnson, Emile Littré, Pierre Larousse, the idealists, the visionaries, those who used their dictionaries to scold, to preach, to mock, to fight not only ignorance but fatuity, with little respect for the ideal of objectivity as we understand it. The paradox is that their dictionaries are those that are best remembered. Dictionaries aim at being faithful, objective, exact, unimaginative records, and yet they

[13] 'Together with the centralization of government, the development of public education, and a certain standardization of modes of existence and types of activities, dictionaries were instrumental in the unification of the French language after the model of Parisian French.'

are clearly better if they are produced by a powerful, independent mind. Or is it that we love some dictionaries and use others? Or, again, is it that this *we* is wrong, that lexicographers, linguists, and the like love those dictionaries for reasons that are not those of the general public? Is it not the case that many people used their Larousse exactly as they would have any other, 'ordinary' dictionary, without even seeing that it was exceptional?

Times have changed. Dictionary-making is no longer an individual enterprise. The team of lexicographers is not a modern invention, but as in many other areas of human activity, the name game is now played differently: 'old dictionaries were named after their writers, whereas modern dictionaries are named after their publishers' (Flexner, quoted by Algeo 1990*b*: 2004). Many people regret the old days, when dictionaries were much worse, and also much better.

4

General-Purpose Dictionaries and Society

4.1 THE FUNCTIONS OF THE GENERAL-PURPOSE DICTIONARY

4.1.1 *What are dictionaries for?*

Lexicographers have always determined the form and contents of dictionaries by posing as dictionary users themselves (Rey 1977: 96). But lexicographers and linguists are probably the least representative of all dictionary users: they both share the same peculiar interest for the more frequent words, because they know that those are the more difficult to describe; lexicographers may tend to excuse all mistakes because they know how difficult it is to write a dictionary, whereas linguists will typically find fault with everything (see below, 6.1.2.2).

The front matter[1] of dictionaries is a fair enough indication of what their authors were trying to achieve. Dubois and Dubois (1971: 15–17), after having examined the front matter of French dictionaries published in the sixties, came to conclusions that were not particularly surprising: some dictionaries introduce themselves as 'portraits' of the language, and others as instruments for its acquisition—and the distinction is not always very clear. A similar investigation on modern English-language dictionaries would reach the same conclusions, even though many of them say little—and some absolutely nothing—of their aims: there are also 'portrait dictionaries' and 'instrument dictionaries':

The aim of the PDE[2] is to capture and record Modern English and to present a selection of its vocabulary (*PED*)
A treasury of information about every aspect of words (*AHD*)

[1] The compound *front matter* refers to all sorts of text that are usually placed at the beginning of a dictionary, before the first entry. It covers introductions, prefaces, etc. Oddly enough, in modern dictionaries, some of the front matter is actually at the end of the dictionary.

[2] PDE = *Penguin English Dictionary*.

gives information about the meaning, spelling and pronunciation of the most important and most frequently used words and phrases in the English language (*WBD*)

The . . . aim is to provide . . . a comprehensive vocabulary aid for the present-day reader, speaker and writer of English (*CTD*)

[A] guide to the English of today (*OPD*)

to meet the needs of students and others (*WNW*)

Barnhart clearly sums up the function of the 'instrument dictionary': 'the function of a commercial general-purpose dictionary—college dictionaries are the best examples—is to answer questions about words for users of different levels of ability' (Barnhart 1962: 175). More generally, the dictionary aims at answering all sorts of questions about everything in the culture: 'It is the function of a popular dictionary to answer the questions that the user of the dictionary asks, and dictionaries on the commercial market will be successful in proportion to the extent to which they answer these questions of the buyer' (Barnhart 1962: 161).

The way dictionaries are really used, as opposed to the way lexicographers would like them to be used, has been the object of much conjecture. It is logical to imagine that there are different possible uses even for the same dictionary, according to who the users are. McDavid distinguished three types of user, and four types of use.

1. To scholars, in all probability, the most important function of a dictionary is that of a record of the language, whether a diachronic statement of the development of words and their meanings from their earliest records to the present, or the ordering of them in a contemporary context, by frequency or centrality of meaning . . .

2. Another function of the dictionary is that of acquainting a user with a language, or a variety of language, other than his own . . .

3. A third function is to supply incidental information, linguistic or otherwise, for the casual user . . .

4. Finally, there is the role of a conduct book, . . . a guide to what one should do and especially to what one should not do. (McDavid 1979: 19–20)

Hartmann, a few years later, substantially enlarged the list, though without distinguishing between categories of users: he saw seven functions of the general-purpose dictionary.

(a) the dictionary as an authority on usage;
(b) the dictionary as a store of (difficult) vocabulary;

(c) the dictionary as a tool for improving communication;
(d) the dictionary as a means of strengthening the language;
(e) the dictionary as a stimulus to reflection on language;
(f) the dictionary as an aid to foreign-language learning;
(g) the dictionary as an ideological weapon. (Hartmann 1985: 5)

Obviously, no single dictionary can pretend to be equally useful in all of this, and the lexicographer has to decide what the dictionary will be for, and for what sort of people: 'The decision concerning the purpose or the combination of purposes of a planned dictionary is one of the most important ones. A good part of both the scientific and the commercial success of the dictionary will be the result of how reasonably this decision was made and how adroitly it was carried out' (Zgusta 1971: 216).

4.1.2 *How are dictionaries really used?*

4.1.2.1 *Who uses dictionaries?*

Some dictionaries indicate with more or less precision what sort of user they intend to address. Littré's *Dictionnaire*, for example, was meant for the learned people of the time: 'érudits, philologues, médecins et en général intellectuels';[3] the *Grand Larousse de la langue française* is for users 'd'un niveau culturel au-dessus de la moyenne, enseignants, étudiants, lecteurs éclairés'.[4] The *Trésor de la langue française* is for

> l'homme cultivé qui s'incarne dans ce que naguère on nommait les élites, mais qu'on préfère aujourd'hui appeler les cadres supérieurs ou moyens de la société, c'est-à-dire les éléments moteurs des principaux secteurs de la vie moderne, entourés de leurs coéquipiers associés, sans en exclure, en les privilégiant même quelque peu, ni les écrivants et écrivains de toute espèce qui tiennent la plume de notre culture, ni les enseignants de tous degrés qui la mettent en forme didactique en vue de la translation des études à des masses de plus en plus étendues.[5] (Preface to the *TLF* 1971: xviii)

[3] 'erudites, philologists, physicians, and intellectuals in general'.

[4] 'whose education is above average, students, teachers, well-read individuals'.

[5] 'the educated person who is part of what was until fairly recently called the élite, but is now preferably referred to as the upper middle or middle middle class, that is to say the most active elements of the main sectors of modern life, and all the people who work with them, not excluding—in fact even giving some special consideration to—all those who write for work or pleasure, those who hold the pens of our culture, or the teachers of all levels who transform all their writings into didactic language so that they can be transmitted to an ever broader section of the masses.'

All this is fairly vague, because it would not be commercially sound to restrict the public to only one category. The Preface of *LDOCE* is typical of this attitude: 'Although the dictionary is intended primarily for the foreign student, its design and the new features it contains make it particularly suitable as a small reference dictionary for any person—whether teacher, student, linguist, or writer' (*LDOCE*: viii). 'Manifestement, ce discours ne veut oublier personne',[6] writes Meschonnic (1991: 60), though of course the simple, non-educated public is never explicitly referred to.

The usage labels in a particular dictionary or set of dictionaries tell us something of the users, since any deviation from the norm is signalled by a label. Labels stigmatize the deviations from the portrait of the average user (Rey and Delesalle 1979: 22). The conclusions, if one examines modern general-purpose English-language dictionaries, are vague, and very similar for all dictionaries: the average user tends to belong to the middle classes and to be fairly well educated, in Britain and the USA (Béjoint 1981*c*), just as in France (Rey and Delesalle 1979: 22). But such observations are not only vague; they can also be deceptive: they allow conclusions about the dictionary users as the lexicographers see them, not necessarily as they are.

Some metalexicographers, particularly in Britain and in Germany, have recently been asking for a sociological type of study of lexicography that would provide better answers to questions like: Who buys general-purpose dictionaries? What social class are the users? What age and sex? Are the buyers and the users the same persons? In France, Matoré had formulated similar questions in 1968:

> Une étude sociologique préalable, menée conjointement à une étude du "marché", permettrait de déterminer de manière plus précise la nature du public auquel on s'adresse et de le satisfaire davantage en répondant à ses besoins de manière adéquate: on pourrait ainsi adapter le principe de classification, le choix des mots, le type de définitions, etc., à une certaine classe sociale, ou plutôt à une catégorie technologique.[7] (Matoré 1968: 19)

[6] 'The lexicographer is obviously trying hard not to forget anyone.'

[7] 'A preparatory sociological study, carried out jointly with a "market" study, would make it possible to determine more precisely the nature of the public and to cater to their needs more adequately: thus the arrangement of entries, the choice of words, the type of definition, etc. could be adapted to a certain social class, or rather to a certain technological category.'

The idea had been pervasive in the work of Thorndike in the thirties, and may have been expressed by others before. The argument is that studying the population of dictionary users is important because the results could determine the contents and layout of the dictionary. 'The choice of linguistic information in a dictionary, and the means of access provided to it, will vary with the class of user for whom the dictionary is intended' (Dubois 1981: 236). This is often repeated in modern metalexicography. One of the conclusions of the Bloomington conference on lexicography in 1960 was that it was necessary to design different dictionaries for different categories of users. 'Dictionaries should be designed with a special set of users in mind and for their specific needs' (Householder and Saporta 1962: 279). Rey has expressed a belief that a sociological study of the public would explain why linguistic theory is not more satisfactorily implemented in general-purpose dictionaries (see below, 6.1):

> De même qu'une sociologie de la littérature s'édifie à côté de la critique littéraire, une étude sociologique de l'attitude métalinguistique, rendant compte des besoins de la société en matière d'acquisition de la langue, de son attitude libérale ou normative, des niveaux de maîtrise lexicale, etc. pourrait expliquer les retards dans l'application de la théorie.[8] (Rey 1968: 72)

Yet no metalexicographer has come up with any practical hints on how the users could be better known. None of the general books of lexicography published over the last thirty years (Hulbert 1955; Rey-Debove 1971; Zgusta 1971; McDavid and Duckert 1973; Rey 1977; Landau 1984) has anything to say about the question. Hartmann (1979), despite its title, *Dictionaries and their Users*, says little about it.

The expected difficulty is not enough to explain why the repeated appeals for research on the public of dictionary users have never been answered in practice. Of course, the study would be difficult, but neither more nor less than any other sociological research. In fact, there clearly is a lack of enthusiasm: many people doubt that anything of any use can be achieved through such a study. It would

[8] 'In the same way as a sociology of literature is developing alongside literary criticism, a sociological study of metalinguistic attitudes that would account for the needs of the society in the domain of the acquisition of the language, for its liberal or normative attitude to usage, for the different levels of lexical competence, etc. would explain the delays in the application of linguistic theory.'

obviously be a huge enterprise, and could turn out not to have been worth the effort. The conclusions, it is thought, would be that the public of dictionaries is too diverse, its use of dictionaries too varied and inconsistent, its motivations too confused.

4.1.2.2 *What do the dictionary users want?*

What people want with dictionaries is to a certain extent indicated by the commercial success—or absence thereof—of dictionaries. Lexicographers must give to the public what the public expects, or at least what they think the public expects, at the expense if necessary of what a truly scientific description of the language would require. No lexicographers can escape these social pressures, whether they like it or not:

> quand bien même le lexicographe voudrait être relativement indépendant et objectif, quand bien même, conscient de l'image culturelle qu'il impose, cherche-t-il à s'en défendre, il est amené par les types de questions posées et de réponses attendues à céder à une pression sociale: il y a une *attente du lecteur* qu'il ne peut décevoir.[9] (Dubois and Dubois 1971: 100)

A dictionary that sells well is not necessarily a good dictionary from the point of view of the metalexicographer, who may have entirely different criteria; but it is certainly a dictionary that responds to a social need.

General-purpose dictionaries are needed more than any other type, and their success in different societies seems to rest on particular features: American users want encyclopedic facts, usage notes, and information such as word-division and etymologies, while British users want short definitions, no pictures, etc. Everywhere, the typical user has changed, because the culture has changed. The interest in classical history and literature—hence, in France, for example, the pink pages of the *Petit Larousse*, with their Latin quotations translated and explained—is being replaced by an interest in science and technology. Dictionaries reflect the changes in society.

[9] 'even though the lexicographer would like to be relatively independent and objective, even though, conscious as he is of the cultural image that he transmits, he may try to protect himself, he is forced to give in to social pressures through the types of questions asked by the public and the types of answers that the public expects: he just cannot afford to disappoint his readers by not giving them what he is expected to provide'.

But the commercial success of dictionaries should be regarded with caution as well. Dictionary users cannot buy what is not offered for sale. If they buy the dictionaries that are on offer, it may be because they like them and find them useful, or it may be because they have no choice. Dictionaries, as Samuel Johnson said, are 'like watches, the worst is better than none', even if 'the best cannot be expected to go quite true'.[10]

Also, it may well be that the expectations of the public are created by the dictionaries themselves, since the same lexicographical traditions, over the centuries, have created habits in the users, however unconscious of them the users may be.

Another means of access to who uses dictionaries, and for what purpose, is the examination of 'popular' reviews of dictionaries, that is the critical reviews published in popular newspapers and magazines aimed at a public of non-specialists, as opposed to what is published in linguistics journals or the like (see below, 6.1.2.2).

Popular reviews are specific to the general-purpose dictionary among all other kinds of dictionaries and reference books. The bilingual dictionary, for example (Tomaszczyk 1988: 289), and all the other types of dictionaries—as well as grammar-books and encyclopedias—are only reviewed by specialists for specialists.

Many of these popular reviews of general-purpose dictionaries are useless from the point of view of lexicographical method. Rey and Delesalle note about the review articles published in popular magazines about Littré's *Dictionary*:

> Quant à la critique concrète des dictionnaires, qui aurait pu et dû préparer les voies à cette théorie (i.e. la théorie lexicographique), elle est d'abord muette: le dictionnaire sert, c'est quasiment un objet technique et on ne le commente guère. Lorsqu'elle s'exprime, cette critique est débile. Etudiant le sort du Littré dans la presse, depuis sa parution et jusqu'à nos jours, on constate aisément que, dans et entre les lignes de centaines d'articles révérencieux, plats ou pompeux, à peu près rien n'est dit.[11] (Rey and Delesalle 1979: 4)

[10] This may have been based on lines 9 and 10 of Pope's *An Essay on Criticism*: ''Tis with our judgments as our watches, none / Go just alike, yet each believes his own.'

[11] 'As for the concrete criticism of dictionaries, which should have paved the way for this theory (i.e. lexicographical theory), in the beginning it is silent: the dictionary is an object that is used, almost an artefact, and it is hardly commented upon. When the criticism does speak out, it is primitive. If one studies how Littré's dictionary was evaluated in the press, from the day of its publication, one can easily see that, in and between the lines of hundreds of reverential articles, nondescript or pompous, virtually nothing is said.'

But the fact is that such review articles are written and published, and probably read. This is an indication of the importance of the general-purpose dictionary in a given society. In addition, the reviews reflect more or less precisely what the public—or at least a portion of the public, identifiable with the readers of the paper or magazine—want from their dictionaries: they are 'at least partly reliable gauges of that opinion' (Algeo 1989*a*: 30). Rey had expressed similar ideas about popular reviewers of dictionaries in France: 'La critique journalistique sait poser de vraies questions comme celle de l'utilité sociale des ouvrages de référence, ou du reflet des idéologies qui président à leur élaboration'[12] (Rey 1982: 3).

Most popular reviewers everywhere seem to be very much preoccupied by the number of entry-words in dictionaries, and to a lesser extent by the type of entry-words that are included or omitted, and by the use of usage labels. The number of words in the word-list is by far the biggest preoccupation of most popular reviewers. Typical examples are the articles published every year in the French press about the annual edition of the *Petit Larousse*: most of the text is about the new words that have been added, or the words that have been omitted; nothing is ever said of the methodology. All dictionaries are berated for not having included a given word, even if the dictionary is small, even if the word in question is fairly rare, or ephemeral, provided it happens to seem important to the reviewer. Generally speaking, for such critics, the more copious a dictionary is the better it is, however mediocre it could be in its general methodology or its microstructural treatment. The American federal government, before officially recommending a dictionary for adoption in schools and colleges, submits it to a test in which the inclusion of a certain number of words is verified. This way of assessing the quality of a dictionary has infuriated some people: 'The federal government's standards for selecting dictionaries are laughable. For over 30 years the government has selected dictionaries primarily by the number of entries in them, regardless of the quality of definitions' (Barnhart 1962: 177).

The number of words in a dictionary is not unimportant, contrary to what some linguists said, mainly in the sixties.[13] But it is only one

[12] 'The journalistic criticism of dictionaries can confront real issues, like that of the social importance of works of reference, or that of the reflection of the ideologies which have presided over their design and realization.'

[13] See Matoré (1968: 194): 'le nombre de mots ne saurait être considéré comme un critère pour juger de la valeur d'un dictionnaire' ('the number of words simply cannot be used as a criterion to evaluate a dictionary').

aspect, and the quality of a dictionary should be evaluated on other aspects as well.

Popular reviews also concentrate on the inclusion of certain types of word. Most of the time, dictionaries are judged severely because they include words that are deemed to be 'shocking' ('ces mots d'emportement qui blessent la pudeur', as the French Academy said; see below, 4.2.5), or words that are too new to deserve inclusion—in the eyes of the reviewer—or again because the warnings against the use of such words are not explicit enough.

On the whole, the ideal general-purpose dictionary as it appears in the popular reviews is a dictionary that contains as many entry-words as possible, particularly all the 'good' words, but omits taboo words, neologisms, and other 'undesirable' words that do not fit into the popular image of the language; that defines all entry-words with undisputable authority; and that indicates clearly how far each word is acceptable or unacceptable. General-purpose dictionaries are seen everywhere as storehouses of the best language, undisputable sources of word meanings, and authorities on usage in general. In all societies, though the degree may vary according to place and time, they are seen as the guardians of the purity of language, as thesauri of the totality of the lexicon and of all the collective knowledge of the society, as repositories of the truth as well as of the moral and ideological values of the society. They are even, sometimes, seen as patriotic emblems.[14]

This is how the general-purpose dictionary is seen by the public at large, not necessarily as it is used. Those are naïve visions, but they are not to be neglected, because after all the dictionary that people buy *is* this imaginary dictionary rather than the real dictionaries that the lexicographers produce.

4.2 THE POPULAR IMAGE OF THE GENERAL-PURPOSE DICTIONARY

The general-purpose dictionary is much more than an instrument providing answers to linguistic questions, however complex, even for a fairly well-educated public of users.

[14] For another discussion of the different myths attached to the general-purpose dictionary, see Boulanger (1986: 95–101).

4.2.1 *The dictionary as guardian of the purity of language*

The prescriptivism that appeared in the eighteenth century as a result of a number of social changes (see above, 3.2.2.4) is still present in modern general-purpose dictionaries, to a certain extent, particularly in the United States.

4.2.1.1 *The battle over* W3

Lexicographical prescriptivism in the United States is exactly as old as the making of dictionaries, because of the role played by the dictionary in a society characterized by a great deal of linguistic insecurity (Wells 1973). It has always had only one objective: not so much to preserve the language from change, as was the case in other countries, but firmly to indicate good usage—which, for all the earlier period of American history, was British usage.

The agitation that followed the publication of *W3* in 1961 is undoubtedly the most spectacular episode of the recent history of prescriptivism in the USA. Innumerable reviews, comments, and even books have been published about it.[15] The partisans of the descriptive dictionary were represented, in the popular imagination as much as in reality, by the compilers of *W3* and by some academic linguists. Those of the prescriptive dictionary were the others, the teachers, journalists, and a few lexicographers, among whom the compilers of the *American Heritage Dictionary*. It was, to a certain extent, a *querelle des anciens et des modernes*, with the specialists of dictionaries, lexicographers, and linguists mostly on the side of the *modernes*, and the others, those that Bolinger called—with perhaps excessive malice—the 'shamans' (Bolinger 1980: 164) playing the *anciens*.[16] Public opinion in general was massively behind the latter.

What precisely caused the agitation around *W3* remains partly mysterious. It seems reasonable to think that long-standing oppositions suddenly crystallized, perhaps because of other things that were happening at the same time in American society, some Americans

[15] The whole affair has been summed up several times: see Sledd and Ebbitt (1962), Marckwardt (1963/1967), McArthur (1986*b*: 138–40), or, for a more recent and more detached view of the events, Gold (1985). For a bibliography on the subject, see Haebler (1989).

[16] It is excessively simplistic to consider that the specialists, the descriptivists, were right while the others, the prescriptivists, were wrong. The frontier between the two attitudes, as we have seen, is fuzzy enough to make one guard against such blunt judgements.

feeling that authority in general, and not only linguistic, was being excessively challenged in all sorts of ways and all sorts of places.

W3, as we have seen, had a certain number of new features compared to its predecessors: the omission of archaic words and of proper names, the absence of the traditional encyclopedic supplements, the absence of about three-fourths of the pictorial illustrations of *W2*, the indication of so many pronunciation variants that some entries are confusing, etc. But all this occupied a tiny place in the torrent of reproach that all but carried away *W3*. What the prescriptivists could not admit was that the new dictionary, in their eyes, had forfeited its role as an indicator of good usage. The critics were infuriated most by the quotations from certain authors that were not particularly good literary models: Mickey Spillane, Harry Truman, Richard Nixon, etc.; by the modification of the traditional list of usage labels (see above, 2.2.1.1); and by the 'objective' treatment of some objectionable words and phrases. The most discussed case was the entry for *ain't*, which said:

> though disapproved by many and more common in less educated speech, used orally in most parts of the United States by many cultivated speakers . . .

The comment, which merely describes current usage, was judged excessively permissive, and was interpreted as the pernicious influence of structuralist linguists.

The descriptive attitude of the compilers of *W3* had been deliberate: 'For us to attempt to prescribe the language would be like *Life* reporting the news as its editors would prefer it to happen', said Gove, the editor-in-chief (Gove 1961). And, a few years later, he had not changed, despite what had happened: 'Lexicography should have no traffic with guesswork, prejudice, or bias or with artificial notions of correctness and superiority. It must be descriptive and not prescriptive' (Gove 1967*a*: 7).

Still, the torrent of abuse that was poured on *W3* was partly inexplicable, for two reasons. First, *W3* was not particularly permissive when compared with similar dictionaries, even if the front matter made the descriptivist stance of its compilers clear enough. The language proposed as a model was not 'anything goes', it was 'general cultivated conversational usage, both formal and informal'.[17]

[17] Part of the problem was precisely that: *W3* described *conversational*, everyday, not 'literary' English.

And *W3* was certainly not the first dictionary to proclaim its desire to represent the language as it was really used. Some reviewers at the time pointed out that *W2*, in 1934, had been at least as clearly descriptive as *W3*—though of course this remark did not pacify the opponents. Even before that, for the 1864 edition of Webster's *Dictionary*, Chauncey A. Goodrich pointed out that a dictionary can only describe usage (Marckwardt 1963/1967: 33). And Isaac Funk, in his Preface to the *Standard Dictionary of the English Language* published in 1913, had said much the same thing.

In spite of this, the battle was extremely violent, with much acrimony on either side.

> The rock-bottom practical truth is that the lexicographer cannot abrogate his authority if he wants to. He may think of himself as a detached scientist reporting the facts of language, declining to recommend use of anything or abstention from anything; but the myriad consultants of his work are not going to see him so . . . The fact that the compilers disclaim authority and piously refrain from judgments is meaningless; the work itself, by virtue of its inclusions and exclusions, its mere existence, is a whole universe of judgments received by millions as the Word from on high. (Follett 1962: 77)

It is a matter of metalexicographical interest that a new dictionary can arouse almost as much passion as, if not more than, apparently far weightier issues. The quarrel soon became so violent that it was out of proportion with the situation, prompting some wry comments:

> In 1961 there was far more newspaper concern, editorial and otherwise, with the Merriam-Webster's *Third New International Dictionary* than with American policy toward Southeast Asia, and the good grey *New York Times* objected far more strenuously to the real or imagined defects of the *Third* than it did to Mr. Kennedy's taking what turned out to be irretrievable commitments to South Viet Nam. (McDavid 1979: 18)

Two dictionaries, the *American Heritage* and to a lesser extent the *Random House*, jumped with a consummate sense of timing on the lexicographical bandwagon and advertised themselves as the champions of prescriptivism—whether this was an accurate description or not—thus multiplying their chances of commercial success. The editor-in-chief of *AHD* made the point rather forcefully in the front matter of *AHD*: the new dictionary would, he said,

> faithfully record our language, the duty of any lexicographer, but it would not, like so many others in these permissive times, rest there. On the contrary, it would add the essential dimension of guidance, that sensible

guidance toward grace and precision which intelligent people seek in a dictionary. (W. Morris, *AHD*, p. vi)

It took a few years for things to calm down and for *W3* to be accepted as a great dictionary by almost everybody in the USA, after many other countries. But the battle, however unreal, has left traces: according to the latest research published on the subject, the American public still considers that one of the major roles of the general-purpose dictionary is to indicate good usage (Algeo 1990*b*: 2006). This may explain the unwillingness of American lexicographers to embark upon innovations in dictionary techniques or design.

4.2.1.2 *The descriptivism of modern dictionaries*

On the British side, dictionaries have been more descriptive than prescriptive, true to the heritage of Samuel Johnson. The compilers of the *OED* made it clear right from the start that they intended their dictionary to be descriptive:

A Dictionary, then, according to that idea of it which seems to me alone capable of being logically maintained, is an inventory of the language . . . It is no task of the maker of it to select the *good* words of a language . . . The business which he has undertaken is to collect and arrange all words . . . whether they do or do not commend themselves to his judgment . . . He is an historian . . . not a critic. (Trench 1857)[18]

This position was later reasserted very clearly in the Preface to the *OED* itself. The British public was never really interested in the opposition between prescriptivism and descriptivism—which is probably why they considered *W3* as a good dictionary right from the start. The quarrel now seems a thing of the past in modern British dictionaries[19] or metalexicography.[20]

In France, where the Académie française and its *Dictionnaire* were for a long time opposed to more descriptivist lexicographers—like Vaugelas in his *Remarques sur la langue française* (1647), or Richelet

[18] The passage is drawn from Dixon (1967: 20).

[19] The last traces of prescriptivism are to be found, oddly enough, in the most innovative dictionaries of our times: the dictionaries for foreign learners.

[20] Algeo (1989*a*: 29) attributes the need of the American public for prescriptivism to the lack of an academy as in France or Italy. But the example of Britain clearly shows that this is not enough. Probably colonialism was a factor (Algeo 1989*a*: 30).

and his 1680 *Dictionnaire françois*[21]—the distinction does not arouse as much passion as in the United States. Littré even managed to reconcile the two attitudes: for him, contemporary usage is the first and main object of study of a dictionary, but this contemporary usage is 'contained' in the language of the past (Rey 1970*c*: 318–19). Yet the normative ideal is still very present among the public, and it is one of the main reasons why people buy general-purpose dictionaries.

> Si le dictionnaire me renvoie, mêlée à mille autres, l'image exacte de mon parler, il ne me paraît pas utile. J'y veux trouver des exemples, des interdictions, des règles dont le respect me rendra plus respectable. Les amateurs d'ouvrages puristes, en 1694[22] comme au XXème siècle, n'ont pas d'autre mobile; ceux de tout dictionnaire de langue ont cette raison avec d'autres.[23] (Rey 1970*c*: 24)

4.2.2 *The dictionary as thesaurus of the whole lexicon*

The general-purpose dictionary is often considered as a book that contains all the words of a lexicon. There is in our societies a naïve view according to which the only thing the lexicographer has to do is bend down, so to speak, and pick up the words that are there, ready to be harvested: 'le lexicographe n'a rien d'autre à faire qu'à répertorier par ordre alphabétique ce qu'il lit et ce qu'il entend. . . Cette conception est profondément enracinée, même parmi les classes cultivées et chez les enseignants'[24] (Rey-Debove 1971: 39). This is encouraged by the dictionary publishers, who all too often use statements to the effect that their dictionary has 'all the words of the language'.

[21] Richelet, for example, at his entry for *langue*, says: 'il est autant possible de fixer la LANGUE Françoise qu'il est possible de fixer l'humeur des François'('it is no more possible to fix the French language than it is to fix the humour of the French'); and at the entry for *gens*: 'ce qu'il y a donc à faire là dessus c'est de consulter l'oreille & les hommes habiles dans la langue' ('what one must do is consult the ear and those who are skilled in the language') (Corneri 1990: 48).

[22] Date of publication of the first *Dictionnaire de l'Académie française*.

[23] 'If the dictionary reflects exactly my own language, mixed up with thousands of others, I shall find it useless. What I want is examples of what to say, what not to say, rules that will make me more respectable if I follow them. Lovers of purist works, in 1694 as well as in the twentieth century, have no other motivation; lovers of all "dictionnaires de langue" have this motivation as well, among others.'

[24] 'the lexicographer has nothing to do but arrange what he reads and hears in alphabetical order . . . This idea is deeply rooted, even among the educated classes and the teaching professions.'

The claim is particularly problematic for the English language, which has so many, partly incompatible, varieties—social, regional, situational, modal, etc. (see below, 6.2.1). The question of how far the lexicographer should go in the inclusion of 'varietal' words has a clear practical answer: any word is potentially useful to the users. But there is a conflict between the inclusion of as many words as possible, including 'eccentric' ones, and the need of the users for an authoritative portrait of the language. Anybody for whom 'The word X is not in the dictionary' is synonymous with 'The word X is not English', or 'There is no such word' (Algeo 1989*a*: 32), and who wants the dictionary to have 'all the words' that can be useful finds himself caught in this dilemma.

4.2.3 *The dictionary as thesaurus of all the collective knowledge of the society*

The general-purpose dictionary is seen not only as a thesaurus of the whole lexicon of a language, but also as a repository of the whole culture, even of all human knowledge—hence the phrase 'a walking dictionary', used of someone who 'knows everything' (Algeo 1989*a*: 29). A good dictionary, some people say, is 'almost like a little encyclopedia'! Because of the alphabetical arrangement of its entries, the general-purpose dictionary is really the world from A to Z (Rey 1982: 22). It is a compendium in a format that can be manipulated; dictionary users can hold human knowledge in their hands[25] and then put it back on their bookshelves and enjoy having it.

The nature and quantity of information that could be given in a dictionary is theoretically endless. The American public seems to require more encyclopedic information than the British (see above, 2.2.1.2), and particularly the sort of information that contributes to the acculturation of the individual: when reviewers regretted the elimination from *W3* of a certain number of proper names, they mostly deplored such omissions as the names of characters in the Bible, or the names of places in the USA or in American history—those facts that help to integrate the dictionary user into American society. Beyond that, not much is known of a possible hierarchy of

[25] This trait would explain, in Wierzbicka's terms, why people have a totally different relation to dictionaries, at least fairly small ones, than to encyclopedias, which are usually huge multi-volume works. See Wierzbicka (1985) for the importance of size and shape of objects.

different types of information required in different societies and at different periods. Dictionaries tend to copy one another too much. The dictionary-cum-encyclopedia-cum-almanac tradition may be on its way out (see above, 2.2.1.2), as there are now many sources of encyclopedic information that are much more readily available than they used to be.

4.2.4 *The dictionary as guardian of absolute and eternal truth*

In spite of the decline of the strictly prescriptivist tradition, the general-purpose dictionary is still often seen as the repository of linguistic 'truth', as opposed to actual usage (Sledd and Ebbitt 1962: 268). For many users, even well-educated ones—as the numerous letters sent by readers to the daily papers testify—what the dictionary contains is more divine than human in essence, as if the lexicographer had access in a mysterious way to sources of information that are not available to ordinary human beings (Cook 1959: 21).

That is why the word *dictionary* is often used in the singular, and with a definite article (present writer included), as if there was only one dictionary per language, which would come in different formats and types of presentation but would contain exactly the same information (Dolezal 1986; Moon 1989: 63). Thus, if a word or phrase is not in the word-list of the dictionary, the conclusion is that it does not belong to the lexis of the language, or even that, somehow, it does not exist. Even people who use such a word every day have been known to draw those conclusions.

In addition, many people do not understand the transience of the information contained in the dictionary. They tend to think that the information given by the dictionary is timeless, that it will eternally be true. Thus, in some families, the tendency to keep the same dictionaries for decades. 'Pour une bonne partie des gens le dictionnaire est un livre qui ne viellit pas, qui n'en a pas le droit, dont les mots et les définitions restent les mêmes'[26] (Boulanger 1986: 96).

This total trust in the dictionary explains its role in courts of justice in all countries. 'The dictionary comes to be looked on as a legislative organ, to which one turns for a standard of "good" as opposed to "bad" usage. This attitude is indeed encouraged by the phrase "the

[26] 'For a large number of people the dictionary is a book that does not age, that has no right to age, whose words and definitions remain the same for ever.'

dictionary" with its misleading similarity to "the Bible"' (Leech 1974: 204). J. Robinson (1982) mentions some interesting cases where dictionaries were used as evidence in a court of justice. In 1893, for example, in the United States Supreme Court, dictionary definitions were presented as evidence to determine whether a tomato was a fruit or a vegetable 'in order to determine tariff' (J. Robinson 1982: 112). Other words were submitted to similar tests in other cases: *oleomargarine, vaccine, snuff, rags, junk*, etc. Typically, they are nouns for things that can be sold, exchanged, or rented, though there must have been other cases hinging around adjectives or verbs. Robinson mentions the case of a certain gentleman who was sued by a lady who accused him of having called her *chicken*: 'The man claimed no wrong and called as his witness "Webster's dictionary". The judge then consulted "an antiquated copy of Webster", found the word did refer to a young woman, and subsequently released the defendant' (J. Robinson 1982: 110).[27]

Moon (1989: 60–1) mentions other British cases: in July 1988 a tenant was suing his landlord, who had promised 'board and lodging'. *SOED* was used to determine the meaning of *board and lodging* in a text issued by the House of Lords. Does a continental breakfast count as *board*? In another case the word to define was *souvenir*. Can a tee-shirt be a souvenir? If so, then a shop can sell tee-shirts on Sundays (Harris 1981: 190–1). In many of those cases, the exact nature of the dictionary that was used is not even disclosed; it is what Moon calls 'the UAD: the Unidentified Authorizing Dictionary' (Moon 1989: 63), a mythical object that nobody has ever seen but that everybody uses.

That sort of blind faith in the dictionary varies somewhat from country to country; in the USA, it amounts to 'lexicographicolatry' (Algeo 1989*a*: 29). It may also vary according to social class. That more-educated users are less likely to treat their dictionary as the 'UAD' is confirmed by at least one experimental study: 'Les basses qualifications (BQ) plus que les cadres moyens et supérieurs (CMS) et que les enseignants (E) ont tendance à faire confiance au dictionnaire'[28] (Descamps and Vaunaize 1983: 99–100).

[27] The appellation 'Webster's dictionary', though referentially vague, seems to function as a magical one in many cases in the USA, like a guarantee of the quality of the contents.

[28] 'The working classes (BQ) tend to trust the dictionary more than the middle or lower middle classes (CMS) and more than the teaching profession (E).'

There may be a gradual but general improvement of the sophistication of all dictionary users, who now know more about the principles of lexicography than they ever did before (Quemada 1987: 242). But the increased cautiousness that Quemada detects and that he interprets as less naïvety could also be due to a distrust of authority in general. This would deserve a thorough study.

4.2.5 *The dictionary as guardian of the moral and ideological values of the society*

If it is to be commercially successful, the general-purpose dictionary must reflect the ideological values of the public that is supposed to buy it—not what is practised, but what is seen as an ideal.

The ideology of a society shows through in some aspects of the macrostructure and of the microstructure, particularly the choice of words, the wording of the definitions, and the choice of examples, so that the dictionary can be used, in reverse, as a means of access to the values of a society: it can give a reasonably accurate idea of what is valued, or on the contrary stigmatized, by the more prestigious social groups (Algeo 1990*b*: 2006–7).[29] 'Dictionnaires, encyclopédies, grammaires sont donc à merveille les lieux où lire entre les lignes, où reconnaître, plus facilement qu'ailleurs, les conflits, les masquages des conflits, les clichés qui font l'album de famille d'une culture'[30] (Meschonnic 1991: 16).

In the choice between inclusion and exclusion, as well as of the type of definition, lexicographers are caught between their desire to be truly descriptive, which prompts them to record all the reasonably frequent words and to say exactly how they are used, and the fear that the simple fact of including and defining 'nasty' or generally objectionable words might result in giving them a semblance of respectability.

[29] Yet the conclusions to be drawn from such a study must be considered with caution: between the society and the observer there is the 'filter' of the lexis and the filter of the dictionary. The relations between the four elements are complex: the lexis gives an 'imperfect' image of the society, for various reasons, and the dictionary can only give an 'imperfect' image of the lexis: it does not list all of it, and it does not fully describe the elements that it does give, etc.

[30] 'Thus, dictionaries, encyclopedias, and grammars are the best examples of texts that one should read between the lines, where the conflicts, the hidden and ignored oppositions, the clichés that make up the family album of a culture can be detected more easily than anywhere else.'

4.2.5.1 *The treatment of difficult words*

The words of sex and excretion are taboo in all Western societies (Sagarin 1963), but their exclusion from dictionaries is a relatively recent phenomenon. Before the lexicographical revolution of the eighteenth century, most dictionaries gave them with no particular qualms.[31] 'In a polyglot dictionary published in 1548 by Pasquier Le Tellier of Paris, words are supplied for intimate functions of the human body, in eight languages' (Steiner 1980: 23–4). Bailey, in his *Universal Etymological English Dictionary*, seventh edition, published in 1735,[32] gave all those words, which he called 'canting words', and John Ash's dictionary, published in 1775, still had 'vulgar words'. Johnson has a six-line poem (by Swift) to illustrate *fart*, and Noah Webster criticized him for having retained too many 'low words' (*Letters*, to David Ramsay, 286–7).

The change, again, was initiated by the French *Dictionnaire de l'Académie* in 1694, which refused to include any shocking words: the dictionary was a 'record of the whole language' (to use Osselton's words again) only to a certain extent. The exclusion or inclusion of taboo words in French dictionaries has been studied by several authors (Girardin 1979; Feldman 1981; Lehmann 1984; Boulanger 1986). Feldman studies several editions of the *Petit Larousse* from 1906 to 1980. She shows that the dictionary became gradually less and less puritanical, but that the change was slow and somewhat erratic. *PL* started by recording the words of female sexuality, and only then the male vocabulary, probably because the social taboo was stronger on male sexuality. The whole process was slow, and was only completed in the eighties: the word *phallus* appeared only in the 1974 edition, and *masturbation* in 1976. *Infibulation* and *excision* were still absent in 1980.

But, those are 'scientific' words. When the words themselves are 'dirty', the lexicographer finds them even more difficult to include, even though most may be extremely frequent in everyday conversation: *chier* appears in 1978 in *PL*, and *baiser* (the verb) was still absent in 1980 (Feldman 1981: 3, 133). *Con* in its anatomical sense appeared for the first time in *PR* in 1970 (Girardin 1979: 93). The study by Boulanger is a more general overview of all kinds of exclusions in modern French-language dictionaries. The conclusions

[31] For Old and Middle English vocabularies (before 1548), see Stein (1985: 69–71).

[32] Bailey's dictionary went through thirty editions, from 1721 to 1802.

are similar to Feldman's: puritanism is still strong at the end of the twentieth century, even though there is a noticeable evolution over the last few years (Boulanger 1986: 30).

There is no book-length study of English-language dictionaries from that angle. The information is disseminated in papers dealing with particular words or particular dictionaries (Read 1934; Burchfield 1973, 1980; Steiner 1980; Aman 1985; etc.). The conclusions of those papers are that all dictionaries have tended to be puritanical and that they are slowly changing.

In the USA, the omission of embarrassing words in some dictionaries is due to the fact that dictionaries need official approval to be listed among the books recommended for purchase by state and federal governments to various educational establishments. *AHD*, for example, had to have a special edition for the state of Texas which had no taboo words. The word *fuck*, which is obviously extremely frequent in many types of discourse,[33] was thus eliminated from the Texan edition, even though, as one reviewer observed with unconcealed amusement, it could still be found in the etymology for the word *snafu* ('s(ituation) n(ormal) a(ll) f(ucked) u(p)'), where it had obviously been overlooked by the lexicographers in charge of the bowdlerization (Hoss 1974: 36). *Fuck* is still not listed in *W3*.

The exclusion of words that are obviously frequent in discourse but are incompatible with the commercial ambitions of the dictionary sometimes leads to embarrassed explanations from lexicographers caught between their desire to be descriptive and the impossibility of disregarding powerful social forces. One well-known example of this kind is the following declaration by David Guralnik, in the Preface to *WNW*, whose obviously faulty argumentation is relieved by humour:

> The absence from this dictionary of a handful of old, well-known vulgate terms for sexual and excretory organs and functions is not due to a lack of citations for these words from current literature. On the contrary, the profusion of such citations in recent years would suggest that the terms in question are so well-known as to require no explanation. (Preface to *WNW*, 1970 edition: viii)[34]

[33] With a frequency of 179, it is part of the 15,000 most frequent words in the Birmingham corpus (BCET), which is mostly composed of written documents. With a different corpus, it could be even more frequent. In some films and novels, it seems to represent 50 per cent of the words used.

[34] A similar declaration can be found in the Preface to Eric Partridge's *Dictionary of Slang and Unconventional English* (1937), which is even more surprising in a dictionary of slang.

If the argument had been valid, Guralnik should have excluded all frequent words from *WNW*.

All general-purpose dictionaries in all countries now move towards greater liberalism in the inclusion of taboo words. 'Striving for frankness in lexicography is now an established contemporary practice' (Steiner 1980: 23; see also Algeo 1990*a*: 217). Of course, the evolution is more or less rapid in different societies. Thus, monolingual dictionaries of Russian still did not have any taboo words in 1980, and the bilingual dictionaries published in the USSR gave them only in the foreign language (Kauffman 1980: 267; see also Meschonnic 1991: 21)! Comparing the successive editions of the same dictionary, like *W2* and *W3*, or again the different editions of *NCD*, on this particular point brings the same conclusions. The evolution, for the United States, began in the early sixties.

> For some time past Danish–English dictionaries printed in Denmark have been almost unique in using English 'four-letter' words to translate their Danish counterparts. In 1966 it is possible to state that recent trends in the United States are towards greater liberalization in these matters. Webster's *Third International*, a leading monolingual dictionary, has largely eliminated the omission of such words and bilingual dictionaries will probably follow suit. (Haas 1962/1975: 50)

The first American dictionary ever to record the word *fuck* was—surprisingly enough, considering the prescriptive stance of the compilers—*AHD* (except for the Texan edition), published in 1969. It seems that *NCD8* (1973) was the first general-purpose dictionary ever to admit all these words freely. Other dictionaries now do the same, the only exceptions being those that are aimed at a special public, like the 'family dictionaries' (in the USA) or the children's dictionaries everywhere.

The British public has tended to be less sensitive to the question (see Burchfield 1972 and 1973). The first edition of *POD* (1924) already listed *bumf*[35] (Allen 1986: 5–6), but the compilers of *OED*, when they started working, decided to eliminate all taboo words—Hulbert (1955) does not say a word on the subject. The policy changed somewhat, especially after the letter N, for one reason or another, so that the word *shit* was included, but *fuck* was not. Some people have explained the change in policy by the death of Queen

[35] Oddly enough, *ALD4* lists *bumf* among its 'new' words.

Victoria, but the work of compilation had not reached the letter N in 1901 (it was still doing M in 1906; see Allen 1986: 3).

There are many ways in which the lexicographer can make offensive words appear less offensive. For example, a word can be 'defined' by a synonym, which is usually a more respectable word. For example, *CED*, like most dictionaries, defines *jerk off* as 'masturbate', *piss* as 'urinate', etc. This is a perfectly legitimate treatment, but it amounts to treating those words as one would foreign words in a bilingual dictionary (Girardin 1979: 88). Vulgar words can also be defined 'scientifically', or on the contrary in the vaguest possible way, etc. Lehmann (1990) shows how in French contemporary dictionaries a word like *utérus* has often been defined in such a way that the reader soon gets lost in a maze of confusing cross-references, including *gestation, fruit, enfant, descendant*, etc. The definition for *clitoris* in *WBD*—almost the same as in *CED*—reads:

> a small, erectile organ at the forward part of the vulva of the female of most vertebrates, homologous with the penis of the male.

Such definitions offer the protection of respectable science. Also, there is an implication that the clitoris is to be found only in animals, not in humans, and the reader is sent back to *erectile, homologous*, perhaps even others. Finally, the definition does not say a word of the fact that the clitoris plays a part in sexual pleasure.[36] Similarly, the definitions for *orgasm* in dictionaries like *WBD, WNW*, or *NCD* do not say anything about pleasure, as if this was unimportant, or too dangerous to mention.

It is probably as a reaction against such tendencies that *COB* wrote for *clitoris* the following definition, in its very recognizable style:

> A woman's clitoris is the small sensitive lump above her vagina which, when touched, causes pleasant sexual feelings that can lead to an orgasm.

This definition may be excessively 'anthropocentric', but at least it is clear, and accurate.[37]

[36] The definition has the clearly encyclopedic trait 'homologous with the penis of the male', which does not seem indispensable for a basic understanding of the concept. Perhaps this detail is necessary because *clitoris* had to be defined in connection with *penis*, exactly as *woman* is usually defined through *man* in most dictionaries . . .

[37] One important evolution in modern lexicography may be the fact that dictionaries are more and more often written by women. This may have consequences on the contents and the style.

English, like other languages, has pejorative words to refer to social groups that are disliked because of their ethnic origin, their religion, the colour of their skin, etc. American English examples are *chink, coon, dago, frog, greaser, gu-gu, hunkie, kike, mick, nigger, skibby, spick, squarehead, wop,* etc. Those words, even the more frequent ones, used to be excluded from general-purpose dictionaries because they were offensive. A study of American general-purpose dictionaries of the sixties and seventies suggests that their exclusion is linked with the collective guilt of the American society towards those minority groups (Béjoint 1980). The study used 14 such 'ethnonyms' and six dictionaries (*AHD* 1970, *WNW* 1970, *WBD* 1972, *NCD* 1975, *RHC* 1975, and *FWC* 1977). The results are reproduced in Table 4.1, where the + sign means that the item is included and 0 that it is not, and where dictionaries are ordered by date of publication.

As could have been expected, the general tendency is clear: the more recent a dictionary is, the more liberal it is—the only exception here being *AHD* (Béjoint 1980: 116). At the same time, British dictionaries were more liberal for that sort of lexical item, probably

TABLE 4.1

	AHD 1970	*WNW* 1970	*WBD* 1972	*NCD* 1975	*RHC* 1975	*FWC* 1977
Chink	+	0	+	0	+	+
Coon	+	0	0	0	0	+
Dago	+	0	+	+	+	+
Frog	+	0	0	0	+	+
Greaser	0	0	0	+	+	+
Gu-gu	0	0	0	0	0	0
Hunkie	+	0	0	0	+	+
Kike	+	0	0	+	+	+
Mick	+	0	0	+	+	+
Nigger	+	0	0	+	+	+
Skibby	0	0	0	0	0	0
Spick	+	0	0	0	+	+
Squarehead	0	0	+	0	+	+
Wop	+	0	0	+	+	+
TOTAL	10	0	3	6	11	12

a reflection of different relations with the minority groups.[38] Oddly enough, some of those words that were Americanisms were in British dictionaries much before they were in American ones (Béjoint 1980: 113).

There are also many meanings, compounds or phrases using the names of peoples, that are almost always pejorative, if not downright insulting: *street Arab, to dutch, Dutch courage, Dutch rub, Dutch treat, Dutch uncle, Dutch widow, to English, French kiss, French way, French postcard, Excuse my French, Hungarian, Irish banjo, Irish confetti, Irish fan, Irish grape, Irish turkey, to jew, Spanish athlete, Scotchman, young Turk, welsher*, etc. (Béjoint 1980; see also Tournier 1985: 290).[39] The inclusion of some of these meanings, even if it is accompanied by many precautions, can also stir the fury of the communities in question, and 'the ferocity of such assaults is almost unbelievable' (Burchfield 1980: 15). Many lexicographers have had such problems: Burchfield (1980) mentions protests against the word *Jew* (defined as 'unscrupulous usurer or bargainer') in the twenties in *POD*, against *Palestinian* (defined as '(native or inhabitant) of Palestine; (person) seeking to displace Israelis from Palestine') in 1976 in *COD*,[40] against the fact that 'the definition of the word *American* in some of the Oxford dictionaries failed to allow for the existence of black Americans and of Latin Americans', etc. In *The Wordtree*, the subject proposed for the verb *to hijack* is *Arab*.

Most modern dictionaries try to fend off potential trouble by employing usage labels that will warn the reader against the indiscriminate use of such words or meanings. The label *opprobrious* is now attached to *jew* for the meaning 'unscrupulous usurer or bargainer' in the *OED* (Burchfield 1986). *COD7* uses the letter R (meaning 'racially offensive use'), which is used for about 25 words: *Asiatic, coon, dago, darky, Eyetalian, Jap, jew, Jim Crow, Kaffir,*

[38] Things have not calmed down totally: Burchfield (1980: 19) says that 'toward the end of 1976, Mr. Al Grassby, Australia's commissioner for community relations, called for the withdrawal of the *Australian Pocket Oxford Dictionary* from circulation because it contained . . . words like *wog, wop*, and *dago*'.

[39] On the whole, if one studies such (mostly American) words and phrases, the following pictures emerge: the Germans and Dutch are awkward, cowardly, egoistic, and brutal, Hungarians are peasants, the Scots are stingy, Turks are cruel and pitiless, the Irish are vindictive imbeciles, Greeks are debauchees, the Welsh are hypocrites, and the French are sexual perverts (Béjoint 1980: 109).

[40] Of course, the 'corrected' definition aroused the fury of 'various Jewish organizations' (Burchfield 1980: 20).

kike, mick, munt, nigger, nip, ofay, poor white, sheeny, shine, spade, squarehead, street arab, turk, wog, yid, and *young turk* (the latter for two meanings).[41] Warning labels are now more systematically attached, though the *OED* still trails behind, even in its new edition (McCluskey 1989: 114). *RHD* (1987) has a detailed explanation in its front matter, and uses two special labels: *Disparaging* for the words that are used in order to belittle someone, and *Offensive* for the words that can be resented by the receiver, even if they are not used deliberately to belittle them.

For some of those words, the definitions adopt vague formulae of the kind that has been described by Ayto (1986): 'Of, or pertaining to, X'. The embarrassment of the lexicographer appears clearly when one realizes that, even within the same dictionary, similar words are treated differently: *CED* has

French (adj.): 4. relating to, denoting, or characteristic of France, the French, or their language

but

Irish (adj.): 2. ludicrous or illogical

Does that correspond to a real difference in usage, or is it that the lexicographer's opinion shows through?

In general-purpose dictionaries, many definitions reflect the society's general attitudes on all sorts of ideological, political, or moral issues. This is true not only of taboo words and of ethnonyms, but also of the words used in the description of political systems, and of many others that are difficult to classify.

For words used to refer to social or political values or systems, like *structuralism, marxism, capitalism, imperialism, maoism,* or *democracy,* and also *psychoanalysis, class struggle, comrade,* etc., objective definitions are simply impossible. The definitions given by general-purpose dictionaries are more or less clearly the reflection of the opinions of the lexicographers, or the result of what the lexicographers, for one reason or another, thought they had to write in order to satisfy the dictionary users. And it is difficult for metalexicographers to grasp the inaccuracies or biases of such definitions, especially if they are dealing with contemporary dictionaries of their own society.

[41] Jean Tournier: personal communication. For a detailed discussion of those words, see Stein (1984*b*).

Dubois and Dubois (1971: 102–3) note that the definitions of *marxisme* in French dictionaries are often introduced by 'distancing' formulae such as 'Doctrine qui prétend. . .' that are not used in the definitions for words like *christianisme* or *nationalisme*. But of course the Dubois were not objective in their role as metalexicographers either . . . Similarly, a bias towards Christianity has been found in some modern English-language dictionaries (see Battenburg 1989: 132). In the *Trésor de la Langue Française, comité central* is defined without any reference to the communist political system, and *bureau politique* is simply not included (Girardin 1979: 89).

Some of the definitions of *W3* have been criticized for their lack of objectivity:

> One reviewer found the definitions of *democratic* and *Republican* fair . . . but remarked that the definition of *McCarthyism* gave only the anti-McCarthy view . . . and that the definition of *Stalinism* ('the political, economic and social principles and policies associated with Stalin; *esp.*: the theory and practice of communism developed by Stalin from Marxism-Lenninism') was by contrast lackluster and contained an inaccuracy: the second part of it is 'absurd, since Stalin never had a theory in his life.' (Gold 1985: 233)

The negotiations for the adaptation of *ALD* to the Soviet market —which was completed in the early eighties—went through some difficult times because of the definitions of such words as *capitalism, censorship, democracy,* etc. The original definitions in the English edition were of course unacceptable to the Russian lexicographers, who found them excessively biased, or even blatantly wrong. Here are a few examples (from Moon 1989: 77–8) of the original definitions in the British edition (GB) and of the definitions as they were finally adopted for the Russian edition (USSR):

capitalism (GB): economic system in which a country's trade and industry are organized and controlled by the owners of capital, the chief elements being competition, profit, supply and demand.

(USSR): an economic and social system based on private ownership of the means of production operated for private profit and on the exploitation of man by man.

communism (GB): ideology that proclaims the abolition of class oppression and exploitation, and the foundation of a society based on the common possession of the means of production and the equal distribution of goods.

(USSR): a theory revealing the historical necessity for the revolutionary replacement of capitalism by Communism.[42]

imperialism (GB): belief in the value of colonies; policy of expanding a country's empire and influence.

(USSR): the highest and last stage of capitalism.

internationalism (GB): the doctrine that the common interests of nations are greater and more important than their differences.

(USSR): the solidarity of the working people of different countries in their struggle with capitalism.[43]

The frontier between such definitions and political discourse is flimsy indeed. It will be interesting to see how the definitions in the Russian edition of *ALD* fare with the new political system in what used to be the USSR. No doubt Stalin, as a linguist, would have been interested to see how deeply, and how quickly, the representation of the language in a dictionary can submit to social and political changes.

Even though all dictionaries reflect the dominant values and ideas of the societies that produce them, there are nuances in their political stances. Descriptive and synchronic dictionaries tend to be classified as 'progressive', whereas prescriptive dictionaries and dictionaries that are turned towards the past are usually thought of as conservative, or reactionary. Some, in the United States, in the wake of the dictionary war around *W3*, called *AHD* the 'Joe McCarthy Dictionary' (McDavid 1981: 14) or the 'George C. Wallace Dictionary' (Forgue 1981: 90). In France, some have distinguished between 'radical' and 'liberal' dictionaries—and the distinction was naturally expressed in the traditional terms of 'right' and 'left'. Quoting an article by Guespin in which the author had classified *PR* as a 'bourgeois' dictionary, Rey wrote with wry humour: 'Donc, le petit bourgeois ira tout spontanément au Robert ou au TLF, alors que le syndicaliste et l'intellectuel conscient s'adresseront à la librairie Larousse'[44] (Rey 1977: 129).

Many words in a language can be defined in different ways

[42] A strange example of a circular definition, where *communism* is defined by communism' (see below, 6.2.12).

[43] For other examples, particularly from a Chinese dictionary, see Moon (1989: 79–80).

[44] 'Thus, the *petit bourgeois* will spontaneously turn to the Robert or to the *TLF* while the trade-unionist and the class-conscious intellectual will turn to the Larousse dictionaries.'

according to one's ideological or moral values: *woman, abortion, prostitute, adultery, sin*, etc. In French dictionaries, up until a very recent date (1971 in *PR*), *femme* was always defined in relation to *homme* (typically 'La compagne de l'homme'), but *homme* was never defined in relation to *femme* (Lehmann and Beaujot 1978). The dictionary reflects the ideological biases of the society: 'généralement les dictionnaires définissent par opposition le terme perçu comme sémantiquement négatif dans le système socio-culturel qu'ils décrivent'[45] (Rey-Debove 1971: 244). That is why, for example, *poor* is defined by 'not rich' or *near* by 'not far', and the definition of *woman* via *man* says a lot about the society. A *Sex* usage label for 'sexually discriminatory usage' is needed—and will no doubt appear soon.

In English dictionaries, some nouns that are the feminine forms of other nouns, like *actress, manageress*, or *waitress*, are still often defined as though they were simply the feminine forms of the corresponding masculine words, whereas they sometimes have entirely distinct meanings. A good example is *manageress*, whose real meaning is totally obliterated in the entries for *manager* in *COD5* or *CTD* (1983) (Moon 1989: 84).

Many other definitions could be examined, each betraying some ideological bias. *AHD*, for example, defines *abortion* as:

> induced termination of pregnancy before the fetus is capable of survival as an individual

which implies that the foetus *is* an individual. *WBD* defines the same word as:

> the inducing of premature delivery in order to destroy offspring

which clearly evokes the idea of 'murder', and does not mention that abortion can be decided to save the mother's life in some cases. Finally, *WNW* adds to its definition of *abortion* the remark

> . . . called *criminal abortion* when unlawfully induced.

Modern lexicographers have become much more sensitive to those problems than their ancestors were. Leschiera (1990) shows that from Robert Estienne's *Dictionaire françois–latin* (1549) to the *Grand*

[45] 'dictionaries usually define by antonymy the word that is perceived as semantically negative in the socio-cultural system that they describe'.

Robert (1985), *femme* is defined more and more as a human being in the same way as *homme* is defined, and the same is true of English-language dictionaries. Still, no dictionary can be totally objective in a domain where true objectivity is simply impossible. 'Indeed, how is the lexicographer to deal with such lexemes as *God, abortion, atheism, feminism, Scientology, moral majority, sin, after life,* and *socialism*? If all views are to be presented, the definition turns into an encyclopedia article' (Gold 1985: 233).

4.2.5.2 *The choice of examples*

The choice of the semantic content of examples is relatively free, since examples are mainly meant to illustrate syntactic behaviour or to provide additional semantic information. This relative freedom of the lexicographer makes examples interesting objects of study, particularly for their ideological biases.

> Les exemples, en tant que discours sur le monde, nous restituent les centres d'intérêt et les jugements communs de la société dont la langue est décrite . . . Les exemples non signés dévoilent la société vue par le lexicographe, non pas dans une vue toute personnelle. . . mais dans un type d'évocation préférentielle.[46] (Rey-Debove 1971: 272–3; see also Quemada 1968: 527)

What Rey-Debove says of examples is also true to a large extent of citations: both are chosen by the lexicographer with a certain degree of freedom. 'The examples they [i.e. the lexicographers] choose to illustrate meanings can therefore be especially revealing of cultural expectations' (Miller and Swift 1979: 76). In the *Dictionnaire du français contemporain* (1971), the word *anticléricalisme* is illustrated by the following:

> L'anticléricalisme s'était développé en France au XIXème siècle avec l'aide que l'Eglise avait alors apportée aux pouvoirs absolus.[47] (See Collignon and Glatigny 1978: 150)

In the 1911 edition of *COD*, the entry for *subject* had the example 'The Indians are our subjects', which now seems strange. In the same dictionary, the entry for *good* was illustrated by 'Give her a

[46] 'Since they refer to the world, example sentences constitute a repository of the common values and interests of the society whose language is described . . . Unsigned examples reveal the society as it is seen by the lexicographer, not in a highly idiosyncratic way . . . but in a sort of preferential description.'

[47] 'The development of anticlericalism in France in the nineteenth century had been fuelled by the help given by the Church to authoritarian regimes.'

good beating', and the entry for *spectacle* by 'A drunken woman is a deplorable spectacle' (Allen 1986: 2)—no doubt a reflection of the attitudes of some of the compilers. In the same article, Allen gives examples of entries that, oddly enough, betray a certain taste for the macabre: *minus* is illustrated by 'returned minus an arm' and *wind up* by 'shot his wife and child and wound up by stabbing himself' (Allen 1986: 2). The metalexicography of English still needs a thorough study of examples from the point of view of the ideology that they uphold.

Several metalexicographers have observed that in most American dictionaries until the early eighties, the meliorative adjectives (*brave*, *strong*, etc.) tended to be illustrated by sentences with male subjects, while the subjects tended to be female for the pejorative adjectives like *shy*, *weak*, etc. (see also Gershuny 1977 and Battenburg 1989: 132). Some recent dictionaries have tried to change that: Landau (1985) mentions some of the changes that took place between two editions (1968 and 1983) of a dictionary for children, the *Thorndike Barnhart Beginning Dictionary:*

check: (1968) When we finished eating, Father asked the waitress for the check.
(1983) After we finished eating, the waiter brought the check to our table.
seize: (1968) In fright, she seized his arm.
(1983) In fright, I seized her arm.

Some dictionaries have even been totally revised from a feminist point of view, so that the traditional roles are reversed: the *American Heritage School Dictionary* (see Graham 1975) is an example.

Objectivity in dictionaries is certainly impossible, for obvious reasons. But it is not even certain that it would be advisable. Dictionary users do not necessarily want objectivity: they want their dictionary to transmit what is generally thought to be good or bad in the society in which they live. They want their dictionaries to mirror the likes and dislikes of the society as a whole. The difficulty, for lexicographers, is to disentangle themselves from generally accepted prejudices, and to decide how far the public should be pandered to: 'Two temptations are . . . always present: to pander to irrational prejudices as a merchandizing ploy and to ignore those prejudices because they are messy to deal with' (Algeo 1989*a*: 32).

4.2.6 *The dictionary as a means of social promotion*

Early monolingual dictionaries were instruments for self-teaching (see above, 3.2.1), and after the eighteenth century, lexicographers took their pedagogical role very seriously, whether they wanted to represent authority, or give a complete record of the language, or again present a compendium of human knowledge for the education of the masses. Both users and lexicographers assumed that using a dictionary—some people even learnt it by heart—was conducive to social improvement.

No one can seriously believe today that the dictionary still plays a role in the social promotion of its users, but there is still a vague notion that it could. The very fact of possessing a dictionary—short of using it—seems to be enough to give some users the impression that they belong to the more prestigious social groups. 'Objet emblématique, il [i.e. the dictionary] constitue une marque d'appartenance à la classe des possédants du savoir'[48] (Galisson 1983: 85). But it is an emblem that exists only in the minds of the users, not in reality. The dictionary may be a magical object, 'un lieu d'engendrement de fantasmes, un refuge de l'imaginaire, un recours mythique contre les dures réalités du monde à conquérir'[49] (Galisson 1983: 19).

General-purpose dictionaries occupy a very special position in all the societies that produce them. They are not only tools for more effective linguistic communication, but also quasi-magical instruments for the improvement of the individual, means to gain access to the dominant culture.

> Le dictionnaire fonctionne alors comme un signe de ralliement, un signe de reconnaissance: la possession d'un grand dictionnaire de langue ou sa consultation me permettent, par une relation quasi-amoureuse, quasi-narcissique (me reconnaître moi-même dans le regard de l'autre), de me reconnaître comme appartenant à un certain milieu, à une certaine élite.[50] (Buzon 1979: 44)

[48] 'The dictionary is an emblematic object that testifies to the fact that one belongs to the class of those who possess knowledge.'

[49] 'a locus where fantasies originate, a refuge for the imagination, a mythical bulwark against the hard realities of a world that is there to be conquered'.

[50] 'The dictionary then acts as a rallying signal, a sign of recognition: by owning a large "dictionnaire de langue" or consulting one I can perceive—through a relation that is almost amorous and quasi-narcissistic (I recognize myself in the eyes of somebody else)—that I belong to a certain circle, to a certain élite.'

4.2.7 *The dictionary as a patriotic emblem*

The emblematic power of the general-purpose dictionary is so strong, so real in a way, that the dictionary is felt to be necessary to any nation that wants to be recognized as an independent entity. It is one of the rare objects that can materialize the existence of a language, and hence of a nation, acting as a symbol of the unification of a community. The American dictionaries, particularly—though not only—those of Noah Webster, played a role in the independence of the United States. It was important, more symbolically than practically, for the Americans to stop using the British dictionaries that they had used so far (Laird 1970: 263–90). Webster's declarations on the subject are clear enough:

> As an independent nation our honour requires us to have a system of our own, in language as well as in government. Great Britain, whose children we are, and whose language we speak, should no longer be our standard. For the taste of her writers is already corrupted, and her language is on the decline. But if it were not so, she is at too great a distance to be our model and to instruct us in the principles of our own tongue. (Webster, 1789)

And of course, this language required a specific dictionary. No wonder Webster called his dictionary *Dictionary of the American Language*, and no wonder he went to such pains to differentiate the American lexicon from the British, particularly through a reform of spelling.

More recently, the publication of 'local' dictionaries has also played a part in the cultural independence of some nations. Haugen (1985) explains how the dictionary was important for the Scandinavian countries and their linguistic problems, and we have seen how dictionaries were important for countries like New Zealand (see above, 2.4.6).

4.2.8 *Different dictionaries for different societies*

The naïve ideas of the public about general-purpose dictionaries amount to what Algeo (1989*a*: 32) calls 'misunderstandings', in the sense that what the public needs is at odds with what the lexicographers would like to produce. But the naïvety may not be entirely on the part of the public; the lexicographers themselves may think that the dictionary is more important, more powerful than it actually is.

The attitude of the public towards the general-purpose dictionary is changing everywhere. Modern societies, on the whole, are probably less naïve, more realistic, about the role of dictionaries. This, as we have seen (see above, 4.2.4), is the opinion expressed by Quemada:

> L'image du dictionnaire connaît une sensible démythification dans le grand public (par la vogue des jeux de lettres et de vocabulaire qui l'utilisent comme juge-arbitre auprès des apprenants de français, par la généralisation de son usage en classe où il devient une sorte de manuel de vocabulaire). Devenu au quotidien objet de confrontations, sinon d'appréciations critiques, le dictionnaire n'est plus tenu pour infaillible comme naguère. De plus en plus d'usagers savent aujourd'hui qu'il n'y a pas de dictionnaires à tout faire et qu'il importe de les utiliser avec à propos pour en faire le moins mauvais usage.[51] (Quemada 1987: 242)

If Quemada is right, then one might wonder how that improved lucidity of the public will affect dictionary-making. But it is not obvious that he is right. What he takes for lucidity might only be an evolution of the attitude of the public, a loss of interest in language, a wariness of authority, a manifestation of increased individualism. Clearly, more research is needed on the image of the dictionary for the average educated user (Algeo 1989*a*: 33).

[51] 'The image of the dictionary is now clearly being debunked among the general public—through the language games that use it as an arbiter for the learners of French and through the generalization of its use in schools, where it has become a sort of manual of vocabulary. Having become the object of daily discussion, if not of critical assessment, the dictionary is no longer thought to be infallible, as it was not so long ago. More and more dictionary users now know that there is no such thing as an all-purpose dictionary and that it is important to use dictionaries properly in order to make the most of them.'

5

What are General-Purpose Dictionaries Really For?

5.1 THE STUDY OF REFERENCE NEEDS

Lexicographers in many countries have recently felt the need to go beyond empirical observations on the use of the general-purpose dictionary, seeking to find out what the users really do, as opposed to what they are believed to do, in order to make sure that the dictionary really corresponds to the needs of the public. Some thought right from the start that this was a wild-goose chase: 'What do the prospective users want (a fine exercise in ESP, wishful thinking, and ethnocentric projection)?' (Forgue 1981: 93). The study of user needs is indeed a strange idea if it is considered in the context of the lexicographical tradition. Old-time lexicographers did not ask who the users were and what they wanted: *they* knew what was good for their public, and any potential discrepancy between the dictionary and what the public wanted was irrelevant, since the public simply had to adapt to the dictionary as it was. The trend has now been reversed, with lexicographers trying to find out who their users are and what they need.

The experimental study of the reference needs of dictionary users has become a very active field in the last ten years or so. In 1979, Tomaszczyk could still deplore that the pleas by Wiegand and a few others for a study of the situations of dictionary use (Wiegand 1977: 81) had been vastly ignored by the lexicographical and metalexicographical community: 'Of the main factors determining the shape of popular commercial dictionaries the needs of the audience they are designed for have thus far received very little attention' (Tomaszczyk 1979: 103). But there are now so many studies of the use of general-purpose dictionaries that it is difficult to keep track of all of them.[1] The first were carried out in the early sixties.

The study of the reference needs of the users of general-purpose dictionaries aims at providing answers to such questions as: In what sort of situation do the users feel the need to consult their dictionaries? When do the users use a dictionary rather than other potential sources of information? Why? What sort of lexical item, and what sort of information on these items do the users consult most? Which do they consult least? Are there items or kinds of information that they never use? What are they? Are there language needs that are not satisfied by the general-purpose dictionary? What are they? In a word, the question is, what do people use general-purpose dictionaries for?

Most of the studies were carried out with dictionaries of English, monolingual or bilingual dictionaries or both, and by means of a questionnaire distributed to the subjects. Some used native speakers, adults, adolescents, or children, some used both native and non-native speakers, and many used only non-native speakers, mainly students. Some studies even distinguished between students according to their field of study, for example language specialists as opposed to science or technology students.

The bias towards students is easily explained: most of the research has been carried out by academics and has been concerned with the use of dictionaries in the context of learning English, and the researchers have just tended to use their students—a captive audience. Other populations of users have been less thoroughly studied, and the results of studies by commercial publishers have not been made available to the general public (Summers 1988: 113).

[1] In chronological order, the date given here being the date of publication, not necessarily the date of the study, here is a list of the available studies: Barnhart (1962), Quirk (1973), Bujas (1975), Opitz (1979), Tomaszczyk (1979), Baxter (1980), Béjoint (1981*a*), Bensoussan *et al.* (1981/1984), Ard (1982), Hartmann (1983*b*), MacFarquhar and Richards (1983), Mitchell (1983), Galisson (1983), Greenbaum *et al.* (1984), Hatherall (1984), Nesi (1984), Tono (1984), Griffin (1985), Kharma (1985), Kipfer (1985), Atkins *et al.* (1987), Herbst and Stein (1987), Iqbal (1987), Kipfer (1987), Tono (1987), Bogaards (1988), Neubach and Cohen (1988), Summers (1988), Bareggi (1989), Battenburg (1989), Benbow *et al.* (1990), Diab (1990). Fortunately, most of these studies have their own cumulative bibliography.

5.1.1 *Questionnaire studies*

Barnhart's study (Barnhart 1962) was carried out by sending questionnaires to 108 teachers belonging to 99 higher-education establishments in 27 American states. This was said to represent 56,000 native English-speaking students in freshman year. Despite the size of the work involved, Barnhart sums up his conclusions in only a few lines:

> The teachers were asked to rate six types of information commonly given in college dictionaries according to their importance to the college freshman. Their replies indicate that the college freshman uses his dictionary most frequently for meaning and almost as frequently for spelling. Pronunciation is third with synonym studies and lists, usage notes, and etymologies far behind. (Barnhart 1962: 162–3)

The study was a pioneering piece of work. The postal questionnaire has long been abandoned by dialectologists as a means of collecting information because, though it allows for more questions, it offers less guarantee as to the accuracy of the answers (Greenbaum 1977). Still, the fact that Barnhart's results should have been later confirmed indicates that his methodology was not totally unsound.

Quirk's study (Quirk 1973) used 30 questions and a population of 220 British students (half humanities students and half science), all native speakers, at the University of London. Some questions were about the reasons why the students used their general-purpose dictionary, either at the university or at home with their families. The subjects declared (Quirk 1973: 80) that they used their dictionaries (*COD* 29 per cent, *POD* 15 per cent, *SOED* 10 per cent, and a few others) for:[2]

meanings	67%
spelling	26%
other	13%[3]
games	7%

For their families the uses (as reported by the students) were:

meanings	37%
spelling	26%

[2] The percentages are not given by Quirk. They have been calculated from the figures that he gives.

[3] Among the 'other' uses are etymologies, pronunciation, etc.

other	18%
games	17%[4]

The conclusions are very similar to Barnhart's. But the differences between the use of dictionaries by the students and by their families are interesting: families are characterized by the fact that they use general-purpose dictionaries for word games much more often than students. This indicates that there might be some sense in designing dictionaries for a category of users called *family*, as American lexicographers have done for some time.

Answers given to questions 16 and 17 ('16. Comprehensibility of definitions, 17. Adequacy of definitions in respect of subject's own knowledge') betray a widespread dissatisfaction with the definitions of general-purpose dictionaries. Some subjects find the language used in the definitions too difficult to understand (162, 74 per cent), those who find it most difficult being those who use their dictionaries least often. Others, on the other hand, find the definitions excessively simple (175, almost 80 per cent), the most dissatisfied here being the science students.

Quirk's study was emulated in 1977–8 in the United States by Greenbaum *et al.* (1984) with a population of 240 American students at the University of Wisconsin at Milwaukee. There were 32 questions that were almost exactly the same as Quirk's. The dictionaries most often used were *NCD* (70 per cent), *WNW* (32 per cent), and *AHD* (18 per cent).[5]

On the whole, the results were very similar to Quirk's. In both studies, the general-purpose dictionary is above all seen as an instrument used to find out what words mean, and the users are dissatisfied with the definitions. There were also a few differences: American students seem to use their general-purpose dictionaries more frequently than British students, at least if one believes what they say. Also, American students were more interested than British students in spelling. Finally, there were fewer differences between the use of dictionaries by the students themselves and by their families—oddly enough in the only country where there are family dictionaries.

Tomaszczyk's subjects (Tomaszczyk 1979) were university students

[4] Quirk does not explain why the totals are not 220 and 100%.

[5] Contrary to the British students, the American students seem to own, or at least consult, more than one dictionary each.

specializing in foreign languages (284 persons), and teachers and professional translators in Poland and the United States (165), in all 449 persons representing 16 different languages. The study used a 57-item questionnaire (not published) aimed at exploring the use of bilingual and monolingual dictionaries in the study of a foreign language.

The conclusions: all subjects use bilingual dictionaries for their encoding activities, whatever their level of competence in the foreign language, but the more advanced subjects use monolingual dictionaries more than the less advanced. On the whole, subjects found the monolingual dictionary rather difficult to use, particularly the definitions, which were often found difficult to understand.

Subjects deplored the absence of proper names and of pictorial illustrations. They also wished they could use specialized subject dictionaries, which would be less cumbersome than general-purpose dictionaries. They were generally more satisfied with their monolingual than with their bilingual dictionaries: 'advanced learners and speakers seem to be getting the most out of them' (i.e. the monolingual dictionaries) (Tomaszczyk 1979: 116).

The subjects used their dictionaries for:

meanings (definitions or equivalents)	85%
synonyms	74%
spelling	72%
pronunciation	65%
grammar for encoding	59%
etymology	19%

The types of lexical item most often consulted were:

idioms	72%
taboo words	45%

Tomaszczyk's was the first study to investigate the needs of foreign learners of English. His conclusions are not very different from the conclusions of Barnhart, Quirk, or Greenbaum *et al.*

Baxter studied a population of 342 Japanese students at various levels (Baxter 1980). All used bilingual dictionaries, which they found easier to use. Monolingual dictionaries were virtually never used by students other than those who majored in foreign languages. The definitions of the monolingual dictionaries, again, were thought to be too difficult.

Baxter states in his concluding remarks that the monolingual dictionary is more useful than the bilingual dictionary in the teaching of English as a foreign language, even for relatively elementary learners, but this does not derive directly from his study. The paper is in fact a plea for the use of the monolingual dictionary in the teaching of foreign languages, based on the argument that only the monolingual dictionary allows the acquisition of a lexical element in the context of other words of the same language (the definition and the examples), in contrast with the bilingual dictionary and the word-list, where lexical elements are learned with their equivalents in the other language. This goes against the natural tendency of all students in all languages, who will naturally go for bilingual dictionaries.

In 1980, I investigated the use of dictionaries among a population of 122 students of English at the University of Lyon by means of a 21-question questionnaire (Béjoint 1981*a*). The conclusions partly confirm the findings of previous research, with some new information. Most students (96 per cent) owned, used (40 per cent once a week at least), and appreciated (77 per cent) their monolingual dictionaries. But they only bought those that were recommended by their teachers; in fact, they hardly knew any others.

Students were generally more satisfied with their monolingual than with their bilingual dictionaries—as in Tomaszczyk's study. But monolingual dictionaries were not fully used. Many students were not even aware of the wealth of information they contain. The front matter was hardly ever read (only about 10 per cent read it), and the coding for syntactic patterns was not used at all by more than half of the subjects.

This pessimistic view of the use of dictionaries by foreign students contrasted with Tomaszczyk's optimism but was later confirmed by other studies: Herbst and Stein, for example, noted that most students did not even know that syntactic patterns were coded in their dictionaries: 'It is significant that in a survey carried out amongst 160 students at the universities of Augsburg and Erlangen-Nürnberg only 70 knew that the *OALDCE*[6] (which is the dictionary they used at school) contained syntactic information in the form of verb patterns' (Herbst and Stein 1987: 120).[7]

Monolingual dictionaries were mostly used for the decoding of written text:

[6] OALDCE = *ALD*.

[7] See also Rundell (1988: 127).

translation from English to French (L2 to L1)	86%
decoding of English text	60 %
encoding in English, including translation	58%
decoding of oral English	14%
encoding orally in English	9%

and mostly for finding out the meanings of words:

meaning	87%[8]
syntactic patterns	53%
synonyms	52%
spelling	25%
pronunciation	25%
language varieties	19%
etymology	5%

The types of lexical item for which the monolingual dictionary was consulted confirm that the dictionary was most often used for finding out meanings in the process of decoding: the lexical elements that were most often looked up were the infrequent ones:

68% look for idioms very often
55% look for encyclopedic words sometimes
53% look for culture-specific words sometimes
49% look for abbreviations sometimes
40% look for slang words sometimes

In contrast,

66% never look up common words
47% never look up structural words
45% never look up taboo words[9]
38% never look up proper names. (Béjoint 1981*a*: 217–18)

My subjects deplored the absence of words that are relatively rare: technical and scientific words, slang,[10] Americanisms (in British

[8] The figures represent the number of students who placed the information among the first three when asked which information they looked up most often (Question 8).

[9] The results may have been modified by the reluctance of students to confess—especially to their teachers—that they look up taboo words in their dictionaries.

[10] This finding is not necessarily contradictory with the fact that only '40% look up slang words sometimes'. Perhaps the students often do not even bother to open their dictionaries for such words, because they know in advance that they will not find them. This may be true for taboo words as well.

dictionaries), etc. There was little interest for the more frequent words: the students did not feel the need to consult a dictionary for those words, and whenever they did they found the entries much too long, and divided up according to criteria that they did not understand. Finally, the students did not particularly feel the need for extra microstructural information like word frequency, collocations, pictures, etc.

Given those findings, it is not surprising that learners' dictionaries were not found to be much more useful than dictionaries for native speakers: the special information given in learners' dictionaries to help encoding activities was hardly ever used.

5.1.2 *Other types of studies*

Studies based on questionnaires have been criticized—not surprisingly, since dialectologists had been through the same experience a few decades before. There are two arguments: the first is that the researcher can never be sure of how much the subjects understand of the questions, and more generally of what sort of response is expected. Is it reasonable, for example, to ask questions on slang words or taboo words when the subjects might know little of what those categories are for the researcher? The second argument is that the results may represent more what the subjects thought they should answer in the circumstances than their real linguistic usage. Hatherall's reasoning has been mentioned a hundred times by metalexicographers:

> Are subjects saying here what they do, or what they think they do, or what they think they ought to do, or indeed a mixture of all three? . . . Do we not, on this basis, arrive at a consensus on how subjects are likely to behave when faced with a particular questionnaire, rather than authentic data on what they use the dictionary for? (Hatherall 1984: 184)

However, this does not totally invalidate questionnaire studies. After all, it is well known, in linguistics as in other domains, that the thing being observed is modified by the very act of observation. Some have called the phenomenon the 'Observer's Paradox' (see Labov 1972: 90); it applies in biology, anthropology, and even archaeology or palaeontology. Yet some research, however imperfect, is still better than none.

It is clear that more research is needed on ways of investigating the dictionary user's behaviour, in order to eliminate as much as possible the effects of the observer's paradox. This can be achieved in several ways. One is, using the model of dialectologists and sociolinguists, to devise the study in such a way that what the subjects say they do and what they actually do can be compared. It is also possible to imagine studies in which the behaviour of the subjects is observed rather than reported on, the problem being then that the number of subjects will be far smaller than in traditional studiss: Ard (1982) observes only two. It is also possible to observe the results of the consultation process, if tasks are proposed to the subjects in which they have to consult dictionaries. The results can be compared with those obtained in the same tasks by subjects without dictionaries (Bensoussan *et al.* 1981/1984). Of course this allows conclusions on the results of the consultation process only, not on the different stages and procedure.

The subjects of Bensoussan *et al.*'s study (1981/1984) were several hundred Israeli students of English. They were all given the same tasks, but some had a dictionary to help them and some did not.

Two conclusions emerged. The first was not new: the students preferred using a bilingual rather than a monolingual dictionary. The second was more unexpected: there was no clear correlation between the use of a dictionary and the quality of the results obtained by the students in the tests. Students without a dictionary did just as well as those who used a dictionary. The explanation is not obvious, but it may lie in a better definition of the consultation skills of the users: some users with low proficiency find the dictionary too difficult to use, and others with high proficiency find it useless because they more or less know the answers anyway (see also Neubach and Cohen 1988).

The study by Atkins, Lewis, Summers, and Whitcut was a huge undertaking, using about 1,100 students of English in seven countries of Europe, with four native languages, Spanish, Italian, French, and German, in decreasing order of the number of subjects. The subjects received a long questionnaire, and were asked to do a certain number of tasks with or without a dictionary, monolingual or bilingual. The results were: more than half the subjects owned at least one dictionary, but 60 per cent of them had never had any instruction on how to use it, the worst being the French. Bilingual dictionaries were much more often used than monolingual ones (Atkins and Knowles 1990: 385). Monolingual dictionaries were mostly used for decoding text. The study confirmed Bensoussan *et al.*'s conclusion that in some cases students do better without a dictionary than with one. For example, question 3/13 was (in its French version):

Complétez les phrases suivantes en cochant le mot qui convient. . .:
It's a bad . . . . to bite your nails.
behaviour
practice, custom
habit
je ne sais pas

Of non-dictionary users, 73 per cent got the answer right, as against 64 per cent of the students who used a dictionary (Atkins and Knowles 1990: 389). This is bad news, the authors comment, for 'the masochistic lexicographer'! But the results might be due to the same methodological uncertainties as in Bensoussan *et al.*'s study (see above).

Bareggi combined a questionnaire, a test, and an interview (Bareggi 1989). She found that her subjects (70 students of English at the University of Turin) were interested in the syntagmatic information provided by learners' dictionaries: 'Nel LD, infatti, lo studente non ricerca soltanto il significato o lo *spelling*, ma anche informazioni sull'uso o sulla collocazione delle parole'[11] (Bareggi 1989: 176). Whether this signifies a change in the needs of students over time, or a difference between Italian and other students, is not clear.

Galisson (1983) used a 17-question questionnaire, but his questions were designed in such a way that he circumvented some of the pitfalls of other studies. He studied a population of 96 students, in France (Paris) and the United States (Middlebury)—one of the rare studies comparing native speakers and foreign learners. He found that both bilingual and monolingual dictionaries were frequently used and well appreciated, even though they were not fully mastered. Dictionaries were used mostly for decoding text, while encoding activities lagged far behind. The most often sought-after type of information was word meaning, followed by spelling, in the native language as well as in the foreign language. Dictionaries were more often used in the foreign language than in the native language. They were also used more skilfully by the more advanced students.

[11] 'The students used the learners' dictionary not only for meanings and spellings, but also for information on the usage and collocations of words.'

Galisson found evidence for the gap between what the subjects imagined the dictionary to be—the 'image'—and what it actually is—the 'usage'. His subjects were found to have some of the naïve ideas outlined above (see 4.2), and the real usage of dictionaries was shown to be only vaguely related to their image:

> "Image" et "usage" ne se situent donc pas dans un rapport de cause à effet. . ., n'entretiennent pas de relations logiques dans la mesure où l'attachement des informateurs au dictionnaire y apparaît aussi évident (ils l'achètent, le transportent, s'en entourent, le jugent indispensable à l'apprentissage des langues, etc.) que la méconnaissance qu'ils en ont et le mésusage qu'ils en font.[12] (Galisson 1983: 84)

In other words, the dictionary is useful by its presence, by the fact that it *can*, or *could*, be used if necessary, as much as by the fact that it *is* used. It is thought to contain all the answers to all the questions, and knowing that is reassuring enough. The dictionary has a kind of 'magical' power:

> le dictionnaire. . . exerce. . . une sorte d'attrait/fascination que ses utilisateurs subissent mais ne s'expliquent pas. Cela souligne l'aspect "talisman" d'un ouvrage différent de tous les autres, auquel on prête des vertus un peu magiques de protection contre l'inquiétante opacité du monde, et des pouvoirs quasi-mystérieux pour comprendre les autres et se faire comprendre d'eux.[13] (Galisson 1983: 25)

This is no doubt the most original and the most interesting conclusion of Galisson's study, one of the rare experimental studies of how the public, even of educated people, considers general-purpose dictionaries.

5.1.3 *Studies of the needs of other populations of users*

The conclusions reached by the studies of populations of students are confirmed in the rare studies of other kinds of dictionary users,

[12] '"Image" and "usage" are not linked by a cause-and-effect relation . . . they are not related by any logical link, in the sense that the interest that the subjects have in their dictionaries (they buy dictionaries, take them along with them, keep them around, and deem them indispensable to the learning of a foreign language, etc.) is as obvious as the fact that they do not know them very well, and do not use them as well as they could.'

[13] 'the dictionary . . . exerts . . . a kind of attraction/fascination to which the users are submitted but which they do not explain. This underlines the fact that the dictionary is different from all other books, that it is a "charm" which is thought to possess almost magical powers that protect against the disturbing opacity of the world, quasi-mysterious powers that enable one to understand other people and to be understood by them.'

though the two populations have never been precisely compared (Ilson 1990*b*: 1969).

Interestingly, research done by Longman into the use of dictionaries by native speakers in the UK showed that looking up meaning was actually the most frequent use for the dictionary in most households, with checking for correct spelling coming second. Reference to the dictionary for word meanings was not for common words, but 'hard words':

1. words commonly confused or misused (e.g. *aggravate* being used to mean *annoy*, instead of *make worse*; *infer* being used instead of *imply*);
2. encyclopedic words—from science and technology, politics, economics, etc.;
3. new words (e.g. *rate-capping, spreadsheet*);
4. rare or obsolete words (*abigail, pellucid*).

The dictionary, in our research project at least, was more commonly referred to for word games and to settle family arguments than for schoolwork or individual interest. Clarification about word-meaning appears to be the main native-speaker requirement. (Summers 1988: 113–14)

The results are clear: native speakers have the same quasi-exclusive interest for the meaning of hard words as non-native speakers and students in general. The use of dictionaries in households for word games confirms the findings of Barnhart and Quirk, and the fact that special dictionaries for crossword puzzles and Scrabble are needed. But here again the information for encoding does not seem to be consulted, perhaps because it is a type of information that cannot be stated in simple, concrete terms.

5.1.4 *The results of experimental studies of users' needs*

The results of the studies of users' needs should be handled with caution: the number of subjects were usually small, the statistical treatments often sketchy, and the influence of methodology impossible to evaluate. The conclusions were almost totally predictable. They are virtually always the same, and metalexicographers, in 1992, already seem to have lost some of their faith in the study of user needs.

1. Dictionaries are used more competently by the more linguistically sophisticated users. This is particularly clear in the case of foreign learners: the more advanced they are the better users they will be. Fortunately, some of the skills necessary for dictionary consultation (see below, 5.2) can apparently be taught.

2. The monolingual dictionary is mostly used for decoding written text. This is true of all categories of users.

3. The monolingual dictionary is used mostly to find out the meanings of words, particularly rare words. The entries for frequent words, especially function words, are hardly ever consulted, even by the students who could have been expected to need them. Yet many users find the definitions difficult to understand, even in their native language.

4. Information on encoding is used less than the lexicographers hoped—and probably even less than the experimental results indicate, since users probably feel guilty about not using the dictionary as their teachers would like them to. This seems to be particularly true of the information that is presented in coded form.

The finding is important, because the coding of syntactic patterns is precisely the kind of information that lexicographers spend more time with. If the foreign students do not use it, then only the foreign-language teachers will, and one may wonder whether the lexicographers' efforts are justified.

The reasons why encoding information is not used as much as the lexicographers would like are not obvious. Probably the information is too difficult to process, and the benefit gained by accessing it is not enough to justify the effort. The Preface to the *Pan English Dictionary* (1979), for example, says:

> Research has shown that most schoolchildren and many adults are deterred from making full use of the range of information which the majority of dictionaries provide. They are often confused by the density of the text and by the extensive use of symbols and abbreviations characteristic of traditional dictionaries. (*PAD*: vii)

The dictionary continues to be seen as an instrument designed to provide quick and superficial support in case of emergency. Dictionary users do not want the consultation process to be lengthy—'browsing' is a different activity, indulged in only by certain categories. When people consult a dictionary, they are typically engaged in some linguistic activity, usually reading text, and they do not want this activity to be interrupted for too long. Hence everything in the dictionary that takes time because it is difficult to locate or difficult to interpret—like the information on encoding—will tend to be used less than the more easily accessible information.

Still, this does not explain why definitions, which are also found difficult, are so heavily used. This may be because people are much more conscious of gaps in their lexical knowledge than in their grammatical knowledge. It is possible to master all, or virtually all, the syntax of a language, and any gap in this knowledge can remain a long time without being detected or ever hampering communication. Gaps in syntax rarely prevent anyone from decoding text, and for encoding it is always possible to choose a syntactic pattern that will short-circuit the problematic area. Mel'čuk argues that there are '4,374,000 paraphrases' for one given sentence.[14] This may explain why dictionary users are not particularly interested in improving their syntactic skills, and why they do not use the information provided for encoding.

5. Dictionary users on the whole have little imagination: they tend to think that the dictionaries they know are the only sort that exists, even the only sort that is humanly possible to produce, as if there was a relation of direct implication between the linguistic facts and their lexicographical representation. Of course, the answers that they give are influenced by the habits they have acquired over the years —or months—during which they have used particular dictionaries. But, more importantly, the passivity of the users in the face of their dictionaries may be due to the fact that the metalinguistics of the average dictionary user is in fact derived from the dictionary itself (see below, 6.1.2.2).

Thus lexicographers are faced with a paradox: dictionaries are used almost exclusively as collections of definitions, and the information that takes most time to prepare (the entries for frequent, polysemous words and the information for encoding) is hardly ever used. 'Users are apparently not much concerned about the things on which lexicographers devote their attention' (Algeo 1989*a*: 31). Some metalexicographers conclude that lexicography is now totally misguided:

> lexicographers consistently, or perhaps persistently, put into dictionaries certain kinds of information for which the vast majority of users have no need and would not miss if they were not included in dictionaries. Into this category would come grammatical information including part-of-speech labels, etymology, and perhaps pronunciation. (Jackson 1988: 198–9)

[14] The sentence he takes as an example is 'Le style de persécutions policières des gens de lettres en Union Soviétique a évidemment connu, depuis un demi-siècle, des changements sérieux' (Mel'ĉuk 1988*b*: 25).

The solutions are not obvious. Should dictionaries be changed to satisfy the users? Should we produce simple dictionaries that are just collections of easy-to-read definitions? Or should we try to educate the users so that they can use the increasingly sophisticated dictionaries?

5.2 THE SKILLS OF THE DICTIONARY USER

Whether one is trying to improve the dictionaries or to educate the users, the study of the consultation skills of dictionary users is an indispensable preliminary step. The questions to be answered are: How do the users identify the lexical item that they want to look up? How do they find what they need in the macrostructure, particularly for multi-word units and for polysemous entries? How do they find what they want in the microstructure? Do the users of all societies behave in the same way, or not? If not, how do they differ, and why? When do dictionary users consider that the consultation process has been completed? What makes them think that they have found what they needed? How do they choose between homonyms, or between the meanings of a polysemous word? What are the preferences, if any, among the different modes of organization of the lexicographical information, among the different types of definition, etc.?

The study of the skills of dictionary users is less advanced than the study of their needs. Many of the questions still have no answer whatsoever. The complexity of the lexicographical text, the variety of dictionaries, the innumerable individual parameters of the users, and the variety of situations in which dictionaries are consulted make it a very difficult field indeed, drawing on the adjacent fields of sociolinguistics and especially psycholinguistics.

> Personne ne sait comment le dictionnaire latin–français est lu par une classe qui peine sur Tacite, comment le *Littré* servait à l'écrivain, vers 1900, ni comment une famille paysanne peut bien déchiffrer les pages écornées d'une vieille édition du *Larousse*. Aux psychologues, aux sociolinguistes de le dire[15] (Rey 1977: 95)

[15] 'Nobody knows how a Latin–French dictionary is read by a class which is sweating over Tacitus, in what way the *Littré* was useful to a writer around 1900, nor how a peasant family can decipher the dog-eared pages of an old copy of *Larousse*. Only psychologists or sociolinguists can answer those questions.'

The skills of dictionary users probably vary with each category of user, perhaps even with each individual: 'tous les niveaux de compétence sont représentés chez les usagers: ce qui est inconnu de l'un est connu de l'autre'[16] (Rey-Debove 1971: 38). Yet this should not be a deterrent to research. It is possible to study dictionary skills if the number of variables is reduced: one dictionary or type of dictionary, one user or category of user.

5.2.1 *The complexity of the look-up process*

Several metalexicographers have recently underlined the complexity of the psycholinguistic processes involved in dictionary look-up (Scholfield 1982: 185; Whitcut 1986: 112; etc.). This is how Miller and Gildea describe it:

> Recall what happens when you interrupt your reading to look up a word. The continuity of your thought is broken, but the context in which the unfamiliar word occurred must be kept in mind while you search: first you search for the dictionary itself, then you search through the dictionary alphabetically for the word you want. Then, once you have found your word, you may still have to make several decisions: first, you may have to choose among two or three different entries on the basis of part of speech; next, within the chosen entry, you may have to decide among several alternative senses. And, finally, the context of your original passage must be compared with a succession of contexts in the dictionary until a best guess can be made about the intended sense. Context-matching is a high-level cognitive skill. It is hardly surprising that children have trouble finding and understanding the information that they need. (Miller and Gildea 1985: 2)

And yet, Miller and Gildea mention only one situation of dictionary consultation: when the user is reading and needs to find out the meaning of a word. The different operations of dictionary consultation can be listed as follows (see also Scholfield 1982: 186–93):

1. Choosing the appropriate dictionary according to the problem.[17]
2. Identifying the problem area, word or phrase.
3. Determining where in the dictionary the word or phrase is most likely to be treated.

[16] 'the skills of the users vary enormously: what is unknown to some is known to others'.

[17] Kirkpatrick (1985: 7) argues that most dictionary users have no idea of the different kinds of dictionaries available on the market or of what each kind has to offer.

4. Guessing what form the word will be listed under (the lemma).
5. Guessing where the word will be placed in the alphabetical ordering as it is used by that particular dictionary. This might imply choosing among two or more different listings: proper names, geographical words, abbreviations, etc.
6. Finding the word in its place as an entry or sub-entry, or in an entry or sub-entry. This might imply choosing among homographs, using syntactic or semantic information.
7. Interpreting the information given in the entry. This may mean interpreting:
   — information about spelling: derived or conjugated forms, plurals, comparatives, irregular verbs, information about word-division, etc.;
   — information about pronunciation: sounds, position of stress, etc.;
   — information about language varieties: usage labels;
   — information about syntax: part of speech, position of adjectives, countable or uncountable aspect of nouns, choice of preposition, etc.;
   — information about meaning: synonyms and antonyms, hyperonyms and hyponyms in different kinds of definition, other kinds of semantic relations, examples, citations, pictorial illustrations, figurative meanings, etc.;
   — information about word history: etymology.

5.2.2 *What the user must know: evidence from the dictionary*

Dictionary consultation requires a good mastery of the syntactic patterns of the language and of a large part of its lexicon. These skills vary according to the type of dictionary: *LDOCE*, for example, can be consulted—at least in theory—by anyone who knows 2,000 words of English (according to its compilers; 6,000 according to some metalexicographers—still a fairly low figure). The users of the *OED* will need much more than that, and even the users of *COD*, when they encounter definitions such as that for *snake*:

limbless reptile of suborder *Ophidia*

According to Neubauer, the users of some German dictionaries containing 60,000 words have to know a vocabulary of 20,000 (in Hausmann 1990*a*: 227).

Yet the linguistic skills necessary for the successful consultation of a dictionary are only those of the average educated language user. Even the 6,000 words needed for *LDOCE* are not more than what is needed for reading very simple texts—around 5,000 words according to some researchers (Ostyn and Godin 1985). Schelbert convincingly argues that much of what goes on in the everyday use of language is extremely complex but that most language users perform those complex operations adequately without even thinking about them, and that the skills are successfully applied to dictionary consultation.

If there is a sign on the door saying 'Please knock', we do not feel compelled to knock every time we pass the door. The sign is read but not acted on—or only when there is occasion to enter the room. We are familiar with the hierarchy of linguistic functions and we know when a sign acts as a signal or as a symbol. We are also capable of reading and handling meanings dynamically. We can juggle with variations and prototypes (Holenstein 1980: 69);[18] we know how meanings adjust and bow to context. We understand modalities. We can use the whole/part relationship syntactically and rhetorically. We sense what is the same, similar and dissimilar, which is a vital skill for users of a dictionary. And finally, we frequently resort to paraphrase in ordinary discourse. (Schelbert 1988: 63)

Schelbert gives the example of pictorial illustrations for names of animals in certain dictionaries: the dimensions of the different animals do not correspond to reality (the picture of the flea may be as big as the picture of the elephant, even if the two are on the same page), and some are represented in whole whereas for others only the head is shown, etc. Yet this does not seem to pose particular problems to the dictionary users, who are used to interpreting pictorial representations in other circumstances.

There are many similar conventions that operate effortlessly in the everyday use of language. If you see 'Disaster services' on a van of the Red Cross, you know that it is the noun *services* and not the verb, and that the whole thing means 'services in case of disaster'; you know that *entrée des artistes* means 'entrance *for* the artists' and *entrée des vestiaires* means 'entrance *to* the cloakroom'; you know that *yellow* in *yellow dog* is not the same *yellow* as in *yellow dress*; you know that in 'The carrots are better here than in that other field' you are not

[18] E. Holenstein, *Von der Hintergehbarkeit der Sprache* (Frankfurt am Main: Suhrkamp, 1980).

talking about the same carrots; that in 'I need some money, I'll go to the bank', *bank* does not refer to the river's edge. The myriads of things in a dictionary that have to be interpreted are not more complex. The dictionary users who encounter the definition 'one who hawks goods about' for *hawker* (definition from *COD6*) will know that *one* refers to a person, and will draw certain conclusions as to what sort of goods can be hawked.

Some of the information contained in the dictionary could not be understood if the users did not bring to it their knowledge of the world—supposing it can be separated from linguistic knowledge. The need to know something of the world is clear in the case of definitions of culture-specific words: how could a dictionary definition convey the meanings of *olive, double-decker, drugstore,* or *croissant* for someone who knew absolutely nothing of the referents? But world knowledge is also necessary in more subtle cases: if a dictionary defines *cat* as 'domestic animal that catches mice', the user who consults it will need to know that in our societies this refers to the cat. The definition would have pointed to a different animal in a society where it was not the cat that was used for catching mice—as in ancient Egypt, where it was the genet. In fact, since many domestic cats do not catch mice at all, what the user has to know is that in our societies the cat is—as Wierzbicka would have it—thought of as the domestic animal that catches mice (see Wierzbicka 1985; see below, 7.2.3). It is to be noted that such 'definitions' do not define; they just point to the right referent, which the users have to know to a certain extent beforehand if they are to learn something in the consultation.

The knowledge that is necessary for consultation varies greatly from one dictionary to another, according to the way words are defined. Some of the definitions of *W3* (remember the example of *door*: see above, 2.2.1.2) seemed to rest on a minimum of prior cultural knowledge, while making major demands on the linguistic knowledge.

Some definitions rely on a scientific knowledge that is not narrowly cultural, but that nevertheless runs the risk of outwitting the users. *W3* and other American dictionaries define colour-words by wavelengths. For example, the definition for *orange* in *NCD8* is

> any of a group of colors that lie midway between red and yellow in hue and are of medium lightness and moderate to high saturation.

Colour-words are notoriously difficult to define. Some dictionaries, such as *DFC* or other American dictionaries, define them through their position in the rainbow. Many, following the suggestions of linguists (see Wierzbicka 1985), now define them through some prototypical referent, preferably universally known, or at the very least known in the community that the dictionary is designed for: *blue* is defined as the colour of the sky on a nice day, *white* is defined as the colour of snow (not very useful for snow-less countries), or of milk, *red* as the colour of blood, *green* as the colour of leaves in spring, etc. In *LDOCE*'s definition of *brown* ('of the colour of earth, wood, or coffee'), the reference to coffee is more accurate in Britain or the USA than in France or Italy, where coffee is thought of as black.

All language users seem to have at least some metalinguistic skills, like the ability to cut up the string of discourse into units (usually words), to understand the basics of how words can be categorized according to part of speech, and to define words to some extent and process a definition. The latter trait seems to be universal (Mathiot 1979; Manes 1980; Riegel 1987; Iris *et al.* 1988; Markowitz and Franz 1988):[19] folk definitions are used all over the world, particularly by adults talking to children, and they seem to achieve their purpose, which is the transmission of meaning. What is not clear is how far this ability helps dictionary users to understand dictionary definitions. Or, to put it another way, what relations are there between folk definitions and dictionary definitions? (see below, 6.2.13).

In addition to those basic skills, dictionary users must master the alphabet, must be able to read, etc. (G. Gross 1989: 176). None of this exceeds what any normally educated language user will have to know in order to function normally in his social milieu, though again dictionaries vary widely in what they expect their users to know: from *PAD*, or *CULD*, which spell out everything and studiously avoid any sophisticated metalanguage, to *COB*, which for example classifies some of its verbs as V-ERG, for 'ergative'.

Dictionary users also need to master some of the lexicographical conventions: that the entry-words are lemmatized, and what the

[19] Folk definitions have been thoroughly studied by researchers with different backgrounds, linguists, anthropologists, psychologists, etc. French researchers seem not to consult English literature and vice versa. See R. Martin (1990).

rules are, that homonyms are usually distinguished by part of speech, etc. They need to be able to read phonetic notations, abbreviations, etc. Dictionaries differ in their use of 'dictionarese' and in the general clarity of their presentation, American dictionaries being generally more accessible than British dictionaries.

On the whole, the difficulties of consultation should not be overestimated. If millions of people use dictionaries every day with a certain amount of success, it is because the process is somewhat like learning to read, or learning to walk: it is virtually impossible to describe how people do it, yet they do it. The

> dictionary is a social artefact, no doubt with a 'prototype' of its own, whose users become familiar with its conventions unconsciously—just as lexicographers do. The 'secret language' of dictionaries is often better understood, in practice if not in theory, than sophisticated linguists claim. (Ilson 1984: 85)

5.2.3 *What the user must know: experimental studies*

The experimental study of the skills of dictionary users is much less advanced than the study of their needs, no doubt because the field is at the frontier of several disciplines. There are studies of the classification of multi-word units, of the use of context, of definitions, of examples, etc., but many other areas have never been investigated.

5.2.3.1 *The localization of multi-word units*

In Question 19 of my study outlined above (Béjoint 1981*a*; see 5.1.1.), the users were asked where they would look up some multi-word items.

> The results are given in decreasing order of unanimity of response to individual items.
>
> 1. *artificial insemination:* 93% would look it up at *insemination*.
> 2. *boil down to*: 81% would look it up at *boil*.
> 3. *false alarm*: 80% would look it up at *alarm*.
> 4. *magnetic tape*: 79% would look it up at *tape*.
> 5. *come down with*: 71% would look it up at *come*.
> 6. *lose sight of*: 65% would look it up at *sight*.
> 7. *rid of*: 58% would look it up at *rid*.
> 8. *fountain pen*: 58% would look it up at pen. (Béjoint 1981*a*: 218)

In the case of nominal compounds, the tendency is clear: students expect the compound to be explained in the entry for the 'main' word, which in English is usually the last. Two strange results indicate that the reactions of the subjects may depend on their native language: for *ice cream*, the answers were about 50 per cent for *ice* and 50 per cent for *cream*. The hesitation of French-speaking students may be due to the fact that for some *ice cream* is a kind of *glace* (*ice*), and for others it is a kind of *crème* (*cream*). If this is correct, then it means that the categorization of the lexical items of the foreign language may operate according to criteria drawn from the native language. In the case of *living room*, more students said they would look it up under *living* than under *room*, and this may be due to the fact that in French a living room is referred to as *le living*. In general, French speakers have difficulties with English compounds because they are pre-determined.

For verbal compounds, the results are less clear. Subjects seem to proceed by elimination: they eliminate the function words first—perhaps because experience has shown them that the entries for function words are usually inextricably long and complex. Then they tend to choose the noun or the adjective, if there is one (*lose* ***sight*** *of*, *get* ***rid*** *of*). But the intuition of the relative frequency and polysemy of the elements may also play a part in the decision: the more frequent and polysemous a word is the more complex the entry will be, and consequently the more difficult the consultation.

Dictionary users do seem to expect all multi-word units to have one element that is more important than the others, and they seem to prefer to look them up within the entry for this element. This may be because they feel the need to structure their lexical acquisitions by relating every new item to other words that they know. The relations between words, whatever they may be, are probably used as a help to memorization. This would mean that dictionaries like *LDOCE*, for example, are wrong to enter compounds like *artificial insemination* according to the beginning of their first element: users know that artificial insemination is a 'kind of insemination'.

Bogaards (1990), investigating the consultation of multi-word units by French and Dutch speakers, concludes that the French tend to go for the least frequent word whereas the Dutch seem to systematically prefer to use the noun wherever possible. This difference in look-up procedures may be explained by the fact that different lexicographical traditions have adopted different solutions:

for example, in French dictionaries multi-word units tend to be classified at the rarest, the least polysemous word, whereas in the British tradition they tend to be classified at the first content word (Rey-Debove 1989*c*: 933). But, Bogaards says, 'Etant donné la nouveauté du champ de recherche et la valeur restreinte des enquêtes dont nous avons rendu compte dans cet article, les conclusions énumérées ci-dessus ne peuvent être que provisoires. Il reste bien des questions qui attendent une réponse'[20] (Bogaards 1990: 101).

5.2.3.2 *Look-up strategies*

Mitchell's study (Mitchell 1983) aimed at exploring the reading strategies of 94 Scottish schoolchildren using monolingual English dictionaries. The conclusions were rather pessimistic: the children do not use the contexts very well, choose too rapidly, and as a consequence often hit upon the wrong answer. They also often proceed by elimination, choosing what is not explicitly rejected by the dictionary. They are unable to use the distinctions based on part of speech, choose the wrong homonym, etc.

Tono (1984) used 402 Japanese students picked at random, who were given texts in English that they had to translate into Japanese. Those texts contained words that had been invented by the investigator, who had designed special dictionary pages containing explanations for those invented words. He had prepared different kinds of dictionaries for the same words, which he gave to different groups of subjects. Some dictionaries contained equivalents with examples, some equivalents without examples, some only examples, all those in varying order.

Tono noticed that the students had a strong tendency to choose the first solution that their dictionary proposed, as long as it was not too obviously wrong—the same 'negative choice strategy' as had been noticed by Mitchell. Subjects tended to avoid reading the whole entry if they could, and to stop reading as soon as they saw something that might be what they were looking for, especially in the case of long entries. The qualities of a dictionary that the subjects seemed to value most were clarity and brevity.

However, Tono also showed that English majors were better

[20] 'Given that this is a new area for research, and that the surveys described in the present article are only valid up to a point, the preceding conclusions can only be provisional. Many questions remain that await an answer.'

dictionary users than non-specialists—further evidence that the skills of dictionary users are directly related to their general linguistic skills. Also, those students that had been taught how to use the dictionary obtained better results than those who had not.

In another study, Tono (1987) found that Japanese 15-year-old and 17-year-old students who had received training in dictionary use fared better in linguistic tests with dictionaries than when they had none, thus contradicting Bensoussan *et al.*'s as well as Atkins *et al.*'s results.

Kipfer (1985) investigated the use of monolingual English dictionaries by some 292 American high-school students. Her subjects used dictionaries more for encoding (writing) than for decoding (reading), and many of them were poor dictionary users, not knowing what the dictionary had to offer. However, Kipfer noticed some clear improvements after the subjects had been instructed in the use of dictionaries.

Herbst and Stein (1987) examined the use of dictionaries in the context of foreign-language learning by 160 first-year university students specializing in English and 60 teachers of English in Germany. Subjects found it particularly difficult to use the encoding information in their dictionaries, and the investigators blamed the students and their lack of motivation and interest rather than the dictionaries. The solution suggested, here again, was that more systematic instruction in the use of dictionaries be given in schools and universities.

5.2.3.3 *Understanding meaning*

Miller and Gildea's paper (1985) is an account of several experimental studies carried out mostly with young children in the USA. In one of those, children were given words that they did not know together with their dictionary definitions, and were then asked to use the words in sentences of their own. The results showed that the dictionary definitions were unable to convey the meanings of the unknown words—whether because the definitions were faulty or because the children lacked the skills necessary to interpret them. Miller and Gildea (1985: 3) give the example of *chaste*:

> 1. innocent of unlawful sexual intercourse 2. celibate 3. pure in thought and act, modest 4. severely simple in design or execution, austere

The 7-year-old subjects then produced sentences like 'The amoeba is a chaste animal', perhaps based on 1, or 4, and 'The plates were still chaste after much use', probably based on an imperfect reading of 3, *pure* being associated with *unspoilt* or *intact*. Another example was *repudiate*:

1. cast off; disown: 'to repudiate a son' 2. refuse to accept: 'to repudiate a doctrine' 3. refuse to acknowledge or pay: 'to repudiate a debt'

One child produced the sentence 'The rocket repudiate [*sic*] into the sky', probably as a result of reading only the first two words of the first definition, *cast off*. The experimenters explained that the children in such a situation will seize anything that they know and thus bring the consultation process to an end as soon as possible.

Yet the experiment was somewhat unfair on the subjects: first, a 7-year-old child is not normally capable of using a dictionary designed for adults; secondly, the definitions chosen (in some unnamed American dictionary) were particularly difficult, because they used some very infrequent words like *celibate, austere, disown, doctrine*, or *acknowledge*, and even difficult concepts for a 7-year-old, like 'sexual intercourse'; the same words proposed with definitions from *LDOCE* or *COB* would probably have produced different results, and other words would have changed things completely. In any case, the study does not reveal much that was not known before. It is generally accepted that reading a dictionary definition is not enough for anyone to grasp the full meaning of a word, with all the connotative and collocative information necessary in order to use it properly. It may be enough for the word to enter the passive vocabulary, but certainly not the active vocabulary.

Another experiment of Miller and Gildea's took place with 12-year-olds. The children were asked to guess the meanings of words for which they were given dictionary definitions, or example sentences drawn from dictionaries, or again sentences drawn from the *New York Times*. The results are shown in Table 5.1.

TABLE 5.1

Rating	Definition only	Dictionary sentence	NY Times sentence
Acceptable	36	55	52
Marginal	33	22	19
Unacceptable	31	23	26

Source: Miller and Gildea 1985: 8.

Apparently, the dictionary definition was the least efficient means of conveying meaning, at least for the chosen words and for that population of 12-year-olds. The dictionary example was the best and the ordinary context was second best. This should be handled with caution, since it is not clearly confirmed by other findings (see below). However, the experimenters concluded that dictionaries can only help the users to remember some meanings that they have temporarily forgotten, but certainly not to acquire new meanings from scratch (Miller *et al.* 1990: 240).

Black's study (1985) has not been published, but it is briefly described in Maingay and Rundell (1987: 132–3) and evoked in Summers (1988: 118–23). It also aimed at investigating the relative efficacy of different techniques for the explanation of meaning. For decoding text, example sentences were found to be slightly more effective than definitions without examples, although the difference was statistically of dubious value: see Table 5.2.

TABLE 5.2

	Definitions only	Examples only	Definitions plus examples	Control
Experiment 1	74	82	75	55
Experiment 2	67	67	64	48

Source: Summers 1988: 120.

For encoding activities, the results were even less clear: 'the mix of definition plus example would be seen as the most successful, being equal to the examples-only entry style in producing correct . . . sentences, but producing fewer incorrect sentences (28) than examples only (44)' (Summers 1988: 122). The conclusion, apparently, was that the present organization of dictionaries (definition plus example) is the best possible technique for the explanation of meaning. This contradicts Tono's and Miller and Gildea's results.

The results of experimental studies are much more sketchy for users' skills than for their needs. They indicate that dictionary users have difficulties at some stages of the consultation process, such as the location of multi-word units and the exploitation of the definition. There is no doubt that users derive some benefit from the use of dictionaries—otherwise they would not consult them, nor even buy them. But the profit may be less than lexicographers have tended to imagine.

5.2.3.4 *Towards a 'psycholexicography'*

Dictionaries play a minor part in the whole process of lexical and linguistic acquisition. They can only provide some information that has been temporarily forgotten, or that fits into a well-mastered whole. Yet the work of psychologists and psycholinguists in the domain of the acquisition, management, and use of lexical meaning is certainly relevant to lexicography.

Little is known of how lexical elements are acquired, and even less about what takes place when someone uses a dictionary. Apparently, the way a lexical element is acquired can influence the quality of the acquisition (Carey 1978: 267; O'Rourke 1974: 61). Do we go first for a prototype and only then distinguish the features, or do we 'accumulate' features to form concepts? Can some words, concrete words for example, be more easily and quickly acquired than others (Hamers and Blanc 1983: 144)? How do we integrate the newly acquired information into the pre-existing lexicon? What sort of structure, or structures, do we use? How can the more frequent words be easily and rapidly accessible (Fodor 1983)?

Lexicographers in general have ignored all this domain for too long. Such a 'psycholexicography', or 'psycholexicology' (Miller *et al.* 1990: 236), could make dictionaries more effective by modelling their organization and metalanguage on what is known of the mental lexicon. Lexicographers now realize that this is an important area for potential improvement, but they have not done much about it.[21]

5.2.3.5 *Better dictionary users*

The gap between how the lexicographers would like their dictionaries to be used and the way they are really used is likely to widen in the future: 'the EFL dictionary becomes an increasingly sophisticated reference tool, consciously adapted to specific study needs, but in danger with each innovation of outstripping the often rudimentary reference skills of those it is designed to serve' (Cowie 1983: 136). Two solutions are possible (Crystal 1986; Zgusta 1986*a*: 143): the first is to train the users so that they become more competent, and

[21] Apparently, Longman have recently asked a psychologist—Philip Johnson-Laird—to participate in the preparation of dictionaries (Summers 1988: 118).

the second is to try and produce dictionaries that are easier to use (Whitcut 1986: 111). The study of the needs and skills of the users should be seen as an effort to produce more user-friendly dictionaries, but not everyone agrees that this is the right thing to do:

> it is not at all clear to me why we ought to make dictionaries more user friendly by changing them to be more in accord with users' needs. No other book caters to its users in such a way—least of all a reference book—and I am not yet convinced that such changes will increase the 'usability': for instance, one of the most difficult, but interesting and useful, dictionaries to read is the *Oxford–Duden Pictorial English Dictionary*, one whose format is arguably the way it is because it is 'user-friendlier' since it is entirely visual. (Frawley 1988: 208)

The two solutions of the improvement of the dictionary and of the education of the dictionary user are not necessarily incompatible (Rossner 1985: 99; Whitcut 1986: 111; Rundell 1988: 127), but some are pessimistic about the chances of either solution:

> Like most lexicographers, I meet many serious and dedicated users who have not discovered half of what the dictionary entry contains for them. This is a chastening experience for both them and me. They go off to read the Introduction (but they won't), and I go off to cut down the content and improve the accessibility of the next dictionary (but regularly gang agley at the proof stage). (Atkins 1985: 23)

The improvement of the consultation skills of dictionary users has been undertaken recently by lexicographers themselves, particularly in the case of learners' dictionaries, which contain extensive front matter explaining how to use the dictionary. Also, many dictionaries now come with little booklets of explanations and exercises: Whitcut (1979) for *LDOCE*, Underhill (1980) for *ALD*, etc. (Stark 1990). But these texts, with a few exceptions (Hausmann 1977; Collignon and Glatigny 1978; and Kipfer 1984, which are more likely to be used by teachers or even potential lexicographers than by the average user), are designed to be used with only one dictionary. This may in some cases be detrimental to the genuine education of the user, if the dictionary in question happens to use highly idiosyncratic solutions. The prefaces and brochures always underplay the weaknesses of the dictionary they are designed for.

What is more, such texts are not normally read by the users, as experimental studies have shown. Crystal expresses the dilemma of the lexicographers with characteristic humour: 'should they attempt to educate the consumer into new ways of behaving—at the very least, a national campaign to persuade dictionary users to read their prefaces?' (Crystal 1986: 78–9).

The most efficient way to educate dictionary users is no doubt through the educational system, in class, as part of the normal curriculum. This is not much practised in educational establishments, but some experimental results indicate that it works (Tono 1984, 1987; Griffin 1985, etc.). Crystal portrays the ideal dictionary users that would result:

> Such users have been taught to understand dictionary conventions . . . in junior school, where they were given a nice-looking dictionary, . . . and not . . . a book which looks boring, is falling apart, and which is written in a language well above what would be expected of them in other aspects of the curriculum. During school, they have taken part in several of the national dictionary-using competitions which have been sponsored by national academic bodies and publishers . . . As adults, they have continued to go in for such competitions, and have probably subscribed to *English Today*. (Crystal 1986: 79)

Hausmann sees a further benefit in the improvement of the dictionary skills of the public. He thinks that the more enlightened the public is the better dictionaries will be:

> many dictionary users—even those with a higher level of education—are lacking in lexicographic knowledge and cannot tell the difference between a superior and an inferior dictionary. As a result they fail to see why they should pay more for a better dictionary. . . . Only when the public knows as much—if not more—about dictionaries as the publishers will the market be able to exert pressure on the publishers to improve dictionary quality. (Hausmann 1986: 109)

The education of dictionary users will be modified when computerized dictionaries become widely available and used. A computerized dictionary is at the same time easier and more difficult to use than a paper dictionary. It is easier in the sense that it has multiple keys to access the information, but more difficult in the sense that it does not allow discontinuous reading (browsing) or diagonal reading (scanning), which every practised dictionary user knows so well.

One question remains unanswered: should the users be taught to use the dictionaries that the lexicographical community has prepared for them, or should they be educated to imagine dictionaries that would be different? In other words, are we not actually trying to force our dictionaries down the users' throats?

6

The Linguistic Traditions of Lexicography

DICTIONARIES have always been shaped by the needs of their users, or at least by what lexicographers knew, or imagined, of those needs, and by what lexicographers knew about language in general and about words in particular; not only by what the users wanted, but also by what the lexicographers could offer. The fundamental similarities between the general-purpose dictionaries of many societies can partly be explained by the similarities in the linguistic knowledge of the lexicographers.

6.1 LEXICOGRAPHY AND LINGUISTICS

6.1.1 *Lexicographers and linguists*

Lexicographers have always been linguists of a sort, but they have tended to be considered as non-linguists, and to be rejected by the academic world of linguistics. Until well into the twentieth century, in France and to a lesser extent in Britain, most linguists were not interested in dictionaries at all, except as easily accessible sources for their studies of language, or as records of exotic languages and dialects. The general-purpose dictionary was found uninteresting for two reasons. First, it was regarded as a commercial product, an artefact that had not changed much since its origins and that had often been produced without the help of any linguistic theory. The dictionary was seen as too unscientific to be worthy of academic interest; it was only an impure by-product of linguistics (Rey 1982: 17). Also, as a book about words, it shared the relative absence of prestige of lexis and semantics in the linguistics of the nineteenth and first three-quarters of the twentieth century. Lexicology was not a recognized branch of linguistics; in fact, it is still not a central discipline anywhere, even if there are recognized experts in some countries (Lipka, Tournier, etc.).

The situation in the USA changed before it did in Europe, partly because dictionaries were different and partly because the linguists were different. H. C. Wyld, the editor of the *Universal Dictionary of the English Language*, was also a famous and successful linguist, and the editor of *The Century Dictionary*, W. D. Whitney, was 'a well-known Sanskrit scholar and linguist'[1] (Landau 1984: 72). Still, the feeling that dictionaries had been unduly neglected by the academic world was expressed by some Americans as late as the sixties: 'Certainly we descriptive linguists tend to be contemptuous of vocabulary. It is almost a dogma among us that vocabulary is the least significant part of language (save for a group among us who even doubt that vocabulary is really a part of language after all)' (Gleason 1962: 86). Perhaps money also played a part in the gulf that divided the two worlds:

> the interplay and tension between ivory-tower academic lexicography and clearcut commercial lexicography (as for example in Oxford) has tended to sustain a kind of scholarly suspicion of the commercial, whether in terms of dictionaries or encyclopedias. Something that might be sold in a dimestore or hawked from door to door did not necessarily appeal to the cultural aesthetics of university men. Although such men might be capitalists, they did not want to be seen as hucksters, and often their academic susceptibilities and principles were at odds with the marketplace interests of the publishers who more and more went to them for advice and information. (McArthur 1986*b*: 137)

Lexicographers and dictionary publishers did not particularly want the contribution of linguists in the compilation of dictionaries either. They failed to see what linguists could contribute to the practical task of dictionary-making: they thought that academics would be of little use in lexicographical work, with all its practical and social constraints, to which linguistic theory is ill-adapted. The following, though expressed as late as 1963, is typical: 'although more theoreticians would be a welcome addition to the field, they must remember that their theories should be interpretable above all in terms of practicality' (Urdang 1963: 594).

In the forties and fifties, the interest of linguists in the general-purpose dictionary began to increase everywhere. It became less and less unusual then to study dictionaries, to write about them, and

[1] He was 'the only person of this origin to be cited and celebrated by Saussure' (R. Bailey, personal communication).

even to co-operate in lexicographical, or pre-lexicographical, work. Again, the process took a long time, and in 1958 the examination of dictionaries from the point of view of linguistics was still presented as something to be undertaken: 'I think it is time to take up a systematic study of the lexicological principles which ought to be followed. . . . Curiously enough, this question seems to have interested few linguists' (Knudsen and Sommerfelt 1958: 98). At the same time, some publishers began to go to linguists 'for advice and information' (in McArthur's terms), and some lexicographers started being interested in linguistic theory. They had become conscious that linguistics could play an important role in the improvement of dictionaries. The first contacts seem to have been difficult, at least in Britain and France.

Apparaissent enfin dans les dernières décennies—surtout après 1950—des intérêts explicites pour l'objet dictionnaire. Ils sont d'abord le fait des lexicographes eux-mêmes, mais ceux-ci ont du mal à considérer une pratique qui les absorbe par ses multiples difficultés quotidiennes. Plus rarement, des linguistes envisagent avec quelque condescendance les procédés et procédures de la description, qu'ils évaluent à l'aune des théories les plus récentes, et souvent les plus fragiles, les moins assimilées, de la linguistique.[2] (Rey and Delesalle 1979: 4–5)

American publishers, or at least some of them, had had linguists working for them much before that, as we have seen: Leonard Bloomfield, Charles C. Fries, Albert C. Baugh, Sir William Craigie, Mitford M. Mathews, and Allen Walker Read all sat on the editorial committee of *ACD*, and the supervisory board of *FWC* had A. H. Marckwardt, F. G. Cassidy, S. Hayakawa, and J. B. Macmillan. Yet the participation of linguists in lexicographical projects was not entirely unproblematic: when Merriam-Webster attempted to persuade a famous linguist to chair the editorial committee of what was to become *W3*, their efforts failed. All the linguists that were contacted refused, perhaps because they were afraid to see their theories put to the test by the practical work of compiling a

[2] 'Then, over the past few decades—particularly since 1950—an explicit interest in the dictionary as an object has become manifest. First, it was the lexicographers themselves, but they found it difficult to evaluate a practice which absorbed them in its multiple daily difficulties. Sometimes, though not as often, linguists envisaged with some condescension the procedures and processes of description, which they evaluated from the point of view of the most up-to-date, often the most fragile and the least well-assimilated theories of linguistics.'

dictionary. This did not detract the popular reviewers of *W3* from denouncing the influence of structuralist linguists, who were accused of being descriptivists (Marckwardt 1963/1967: 37) (see above, 4.2.1.1).

The relations between the linguists of the academic world and the lexicographers are now intense in the English-speaking world, and go both directions. The many conferences on lexicography are attended by linguists as well as lexicographers: the first was held in Bloomington, Indiana, in 1960, and it was followed by many others. The first to be held on English territory was organized by R. Hartmann in 1979 at Exeter. Several well-known linguists (William Labov, Uriel Weinreich, James McCawley, Charles Fillmore, Dwight Bolinger, Randolph Quirk, Anna Wierzbicka, etc.) have published papers or books on dictionaries. Some have even been closely involved in the compilation of dictionaries: David Crystal, A. C. Gimson, John Sinclair, Igor Mel'čuk, etc. At the same time, many practising lexicographers are also expert metalexicographers or linguists: Patrick Hanks, Robert Ilson, etc., and McArthur's humorous description of the relations between linguists and lexicographers may already be *passé*:

> Although commercial works of reference have inevitably benefited in terms of quality from their academic connections, and although academics have also benefited financially from their commercial connections, a certain (sometimes incompletely stated) resentment is still detectable on the part of scholars, in that they seem to wish they did not have to sully themselves in this way. (McArthur 1986*b*: 137)

In fact, we may already have entered the next phase: while British dictionary publishers compete to secure the help and advice of linguists, in the context of their 'dictionary war' (see above, 2.3.3), the linguists-cum-lexicographers-cum-metalexicographers who established the French tradition (Marcel Cohen, Jean Dubois, Louis Guilbert, Paul Imbs, Bernard Quemada, Alain Rey, Josette Rey-Debove, and a few others) may be hard to replace when the time comes, and there is a distinct lack of enthusiasm on the part of French publishers. The general feeling seems to be that the data on which current dictionaries are based are good enough for the almost mechanical production of derived dictionaries for a long time, without the assistance of linguists.

6.1.2 *Linguistics and the dictionary*

6.1.2.1 *Dictionaries and linguistic schools*

Dictionaries developed at a time when linguistics was little taught and practised. It is a common observation that dictionaries can be compiled by authors who are not linguists at all, but this does not mean that there is no linguistic knowledge in a dictionary. All dictionaries necessarily adopt and transmit some points of view on language, even if the lexicographers are not aware of any (Dubois and Dubois 1971: 15; Rey 1982: 17–18). 'Each lexicographical work reflects a linguistic theory which the author more or less consciously applies' (Quemada 1972: 427).

The main currents of theoretical linguistics have had echoes in practical lexicography, but mostly faint ones, as if the rumours had taken a long time to reach the quiet studies of working lexicographers, and as if they had been weakened by the time they finally arrived. This is because theoretical linguistics is not easily applied to lexicography, particularly new approaches, which are typically ill-fitted for a general-purpose dictionary that is meant to be used by the man in the street. Also, lexicographers have always been wary of linguistic bandwagons.

> De curieux décalages se produisent: alors même que la linguistique, après Saussure, abandonne le comparatisme et l'histoire pour la description immédiate des fonctions de la langue, la philologie classique restant d'ailleurs vivante et active, les dictionnaires développent leur tradition, hors des doctrines ou avec celles du passé.[3] (Rey 1970*c*: 22)

All early twentieth-century dictionaries were based on the great tradition of historical linguistics that was reborn in the latter part of the nineteenth century. This is not finished yet: the *OED* has been described as a pre-Saussurean dictionary, and it surely is in the sense that it focuses on the individual word and its existence as a discrete unit rather than on the lexical and linguistic system (Rey and Delesalle 1979: 15; see below, 6.2.3). From that point of view, *OED2* is not much different.

[3] 'Strange delays can be observed: just when linguistics, after de Saussure, was leaving comparativism and historicism and taking up the immediate description of the functions of the language—classical philology remaining alive and active in itself—dictionaries developed their own tradition out of the reach of doctrines, or with the help of those of the past.'

Some of Saussure's views have filtered through, little by little, without causing any great revolution. But his idea that a word should be considered in the multi-faceted contexts of its paradigmatic and syntagmatic associations is just beginning to be implemented: 'we are far from having attained a (truly) Saussurean lexicography. Too many dictionaries make do with definitions and neglect verb patterns, collocations, synonyms, and antonyms, not to mention morphosemantic paradigms' (Hausmann 1989*c*: 342).

In the sixties, some dictionaries were clearly influenced by structuralist linguistics, particularly in France, several decades after structuralism hit the academic world. French lexicographers were trying to treat the lexicon as a 'structure', and thought that the role of the dictionary was to clarify the relations between words. Mitterand described what structuralist dictionary makers were trying to achieve:

> ils refusent de mêler la diachronie à la synchronie, tendent à diminuer le rôle de la définition. Ils lui substituent, ou au moins lui ajoutent une énumération raisonnée, et exhaustive chaque fois que cela est possible, des réseaux d'opposition et de contrastes fondamentaux dans lesquels s'inscrit le mot, pour un état donné de la langue. Ils usent avec prudence de la citation littéraire, à laquelle ils préfèrent des témoignages empruntés à la conversation, à la presse, ou aux textes didactiques, et ils excluent les citations relevant d'un état de langue étranger à la période de référence. Ils s'efforcent de distinguer avec rigueur les différents systèmes de distribution dans lesquels s'inscrivent ces réseaux contextuels, et qui coïncident soit avec des oppositions homonymiques, soit avec des cloisonnements socio-professionnels. . . Enfin ils attribuent aux constructions syntaxiques du mot une importance primordiale et qui gouverne la disposition interne de l'article.[4] (Mitterand 1963: 111–12)

[4] 'they refuse to mix up diachrony and synchrony and tend to give less importance to the definition. Instead of the latter, or at least in addition to it, they give a reasoned —and exhaustive, whenever possible—list of the networks of opposition and fundamental contrasts which the word enters into, for a particular state of the language. They use literary citations only cautiously, preferring extracts from conversations, the press, or didactic texts, and they exclude citations from a language variety that is not the language of reference. They do their best to distinguish rigorously the various systems of distribution that those contextual networks constitute, and that coincide either with homonymic oppositions, or with socio-professional distinctions . . . Lastly, they give primary importance to the syntactic constructions of each word, using them as the governing principle for the internal organization of the entry.'

This was implemented most clearly in the *Dictionnaire du français contemporain* (*DFC*), edited under the direction of Jean Dubois, certainly one of the most remarkable achievements of French lexicography in the twentieth century, almost amounting to a lexicographical revolution. Yet a strict implementation of structuralism as the French saw it was bound to produce a dictionary that was more interesting for the specialist than it would be easy to use for the average user. Among other things, the desire not to mix different varieties of the same language makes sense only if the dictionary is used for encoding, not for decoding.

In the USA, the views of structuralist linguists on lexis were different, at least if Bloomfield is taken as the main influence. His brief, well-known description of lexis as a 'list of basic irregularities' (Bloomfield 1933: 274) should have led to dictionaries dealing exclusively with what is specific to each word, as opposed to what applies to more than one and belongs to the grammar, but this was never implemented, not even envisaged. *W3*, despite what its critics said, can hardly be said to be a structuralist dictionary, except perhaps for its (relative) synchronicity. As for British lexicographers, they were characteristically restrained in their adherence to the structuralist dogma.

The influence of transformational and generative grammar on dictionary-making has been even more limited, and this comes as no surprise, since many transformationalists said that their theory had little to offer to lexicography. 'The Chomskyan revolution . . . passed by pretty well unnoticed, at least as far as lexicography in English is concerned' (Hanks 1990: 31). A generative dictionary could have challenged the accepted notion that a dictionary should be a record of the language; it would have had to be a record of the *potentialities* of the language. There have been suggestions that lexical units should be split up into morphemes or 'parts', and that only those should be used as entry-elements (for example, *de-* and *-fuse* instead of *defuse*), in order to produce a truly generative dictionary. But most linguists and lexicographers thought that this was impossible: 'I think that if we imagine 100 tomes of the size of the unabridged *Oxford English Dictionary*, we may get through a third of the English alphabet in that kind of a notation. I consequently rather doubt if a fully specified TG dictionary of any natural language will ever be written' (Makkai 1976: 53).[5]

[5] There is no 'abridged *Oxford English Dictionary*'.

The interest of linguists for lexis was renewed a few decades ago as a reaction against those theories that had little to say about lexis and semantics (see below, Chapter 7). The most promising aspect of modern semantics for lexicography—though it has not had any impact on practical dictionary-making yet—is probably prototype theory and the ensuing discussion of the modes of categorization, of word meaning, and of the nature of semantic features (see below, 7.2).

When the compilers of dictionaries were not trained linguists, they made use of what was available to them, which was the general socially accepted linguistic knowledge of the public they were writing for. This 'popular metalinguistics' was in turn influenced by the leading schools of linguistics, so that the generations of general-purpose dictionaries have accumulated the traces of linguistic thought over the centuries.

6.1.2.2 *What linguists think of dictionaries*

While the critical reviews of dictionaries published in the more popular newspapers and magazines tend to concentrate on the contents of the word-list and on the authority of the dictionary (see above, 4.1.2.2), the reviews written by linguists have tended to focus on the contents of the microstructure, especially on the entries for polysemous words and their organization, and on the definitions.

Most linguists writing about general-purpose dictionaries since the fifties have been dissatisfied with the definitions: they do not take into account folk definitions (Weinreich 1962: 30), they are circular (Wierzbicka 1980: 81), they mix up information about the world and information about the sign (Weinreich 1964), they do not indicate obligatory syntactic patterns (McCawley 1973: 167), they use terms that are not kept constant throughout the dictionary (Gleason 1962: 100), they do not distinguish between meaning and context-bound 'applications' (Weinreich 1962: 29), they do not indicate connotative values (G. Lakoff 1973: 151), they are too vague to allow encoding (Apresjan *et al.* 1969), they do not rest on any solid theoretical foundations (Pottier 1965), they do not identify which of the meanings of polysemous words they use (Mel'čuk 1988*a*: 172), etc. Hausmann (1990*a*), after summing up some of these arguments, concludes that dictionary definitions might be useful in many cases, and are probably less useful than is usually assumed, particularly for certain categories of words.

The criticism of dictionaries by linguists has become less severe over the last few years, a sign that linguists now know more about dictonaries and the difficulties of their compilation than they did in the past. 'Dictionary-bashing', an easy sport for whoever does not have to solve the everyday problems of lexicography, is still practised (Rey 1982: 17; Frawley 1988: 189), but it is less common and less fierce than it used to be. Weinreich, who was one of those linguists who *were* interested in dictionaries, nevertheless expressed himself with the severity that is typical of the period when he was reviewing *W3* in 1964: 'It is disconcerting that a mountain of lexicographic practice such as an unabridged dictionary of English should yield no more than a paragraph-sized molehill of lexicological theory' (Weinreich 1964: 408). Weinreich obviously assumed that a dictionary should be a basis for lexicological theory. But his pronouncement could have been reversed: any lexicographer could have deplored that so many mountains of linguistic theory should have yielded so little in terms of practical application to lexicography.

Lexicography and linguistics are now inextricably mixed. No modern lexicographer can afford to ignore what linguistics has to offer. Linguistic research cannot be ignored, even if it certainly does not have all the answers: 'lexicography is a purposeful human activity for which the principles of language are merely one among a number of parameters that determine the actual shape dictionaries take' (Geeraerts 1989: 287). Lexicography is not applied linguistics (Rey and Delesalle 1979: 10); it is less than that and also much more: 'The relationship of linguistic theory to lexicography . . . must be highly indirect if the lexicographer and the pedagogue are to accomplish anything' (McCawley 1973: 165). Linguists enjoy a luxury that lexicographers do not have: time, which makes it possible for them to think, to try out solutions, to make mistakes and start all over again, so that lexicographers can ask them to concentrate on particularly tricky points (Atkins *et al.* 1988: 111).

The relations between linguistics and lexicography may be even more complex than is usually imagined. Hudson (1988) argues from the point of view of a linguist that some of the accepted principles of 'mainstream linguistics'[6] may actually have been imposed by the lexicographical traditions of our societies.

[6] Hudson explains what he means by 'mainstream linguistics': 'the theories which are heavily influenced by Chomsky . . . They are:

a. EST—the Extended Standard Theory of transformational grammar . . .;
b. GB—Chomsky's current theory, called the Government and Binding theory . . .;
c. GPSG—Generalised Phrase Structure Grammar . . .;
d. LFG—Lexical Functional Grammar' (Hudson 1988: 290).

> The basic problem is that any of us linguists is also a citizen, with the same experiences as any other typical citizen. We all have dictionaries on our shelves, and have grown up in a society where dictionaries are standard items of furniture. These dictionaries are of course the traditional commercial ones, which have various structural characteristics. . . . What I am suggesting, then, is that folk linguistics contains various ideas about the lexicon, alias dictionary, which are at least in part founded on the traditional practice of lexicographers. Any linguist brought up in a culture where these folk ideas are prevalent is likely to be infected by them in early life and must beware of building them, without critical examination, into their professional thinking. (Hudson 1988: 287–8)

If Hudson is right, then the lexicographers who turn to linguistics for help may actually be given ideas that in fact originated in their own lexicographical traditions.

> And forward-looking lexicographers must be even more careful not to mistake ideas which originated in traditional lexicography for carefully considered and researched tenets of scientific linguistics. I applaud any attempt by a lexicographer to learn from linguistics (or from any other relevant discipline), in the hope of being able to move towards radically new and better kinds of dictionary; but it would be tragic if the effect of this contact with linguistics was just to tie lexicographers even more firmly to their own tradition. (Hudson 1988: 288)

Of course lexicographers will accept these ideas all the more readily as they confirm age-old practices and now have the additional aura of 'science'. If this is true, then dictionaries are what they are partly because of linguistics, and linguistics is what it is partly because of dictionaries.

6.2 LEXICOGRAPHICAL TRADITIONS

Our general-purpose dictionaries as we know them are the result of a complex interaction between several factors that have solidified over the centuries and are now deeply ingrained in our societies. Meschonnic wonders at 'ces étranges collections de termes isolés les uns des autres. Nous y sommes si habitués, tant ils nous semblent nécessaires, petits meubles commodes dont les tiroirs contiennent la réponse aux questions qu'on leur pose, que nous n'en voyons plus la monstruosité et l'archaïsme'[7] (Meschonnic 1991: 10). Dictionaries have changed relatively little over time:

> Zgusta's (1971) handbook remains a seminal work in lexicography not only because it is well done in and of itself and therefore deserves praise, but also because little has changed over the years in lexicographic practice: for example, current definitional practice is not that different from Aristotle's. Similar comments may be made about Landau's (1984) book, which is an excellent, synoptic study of dictionaries, but which is also an affirmation of distinguished PAST practice rather than a book of new ideas. It is therefore understandable that Bailey (1986) should remark that it is difficult to find a 'new idea' in lexicography since what evolution there has been in lexicographic practice has been slow indeed: '. . . we will agree, I think, that there is no abrupt or revolutionary change in the more than 250 years of English lexicography' (p. 124). (Frawley 1988: 189–90)

Makkai goes even further: 'Nothing significantly new has happened in lexicography since the first printed dictionaries after Gutenberg invented the printing of books' (Makkai 1976: 55).

Dictionary-making in our societies has traditionally been based on ideas such as:

the lexicon is a list of discrete units,
words have only one meaning,
words all have the same type of meaning,
all words can be defined, etc.,

all of which may not be as obvious as they are made to appear by the solidity of the tradition. Some metalexicographers think that lexicographers generally tend to submit to tradition without questioning it: 'when lexicographic practice is raised for scrutiny, the very deeply foundational questions are rarely asked, and if such questions are asked, the answers infrequently conflict with established, conservative practice' (Frawley 1988: 190).

It is certainly not easy to question the bases upon which dictionaries have been designed and compiled for several centuries. It may turn out to be a totally useless exercise if dictionaries cannot be changed because of social pressures and commercial necessities. It may be misguided in some particular cases, or downright wrong

[7] 'those strange collections of unconnected terms. We are so used to them, they look so necessary to us, those small chests of drawers containing the answers to the questions we ask them, that we can no longer see how monstrous and archaic they are.'

because there is no other way things can be done. But it is the only way to look at dictionaries non-descriptively, to go beyond the traditional message of metalexicographers to lexicographers: 'This is not how it should have been done' or 'This is how it should have been done', or again, all too often, 'This is how you did it'. It is more interesting, and probably more useful eventually, to wonder why things were done that way and not any other way, and what the decisions were based on: solid research, or just pure compliance with the traditional way of doing things. And it may also turn out to be important if, as Hudson (1988) says, much of linguistics is in fact based on what the dictionaries have said, and how they have said it, for centuries.

6.2.1 *A dictionary can be representative*

Oddly enough, the ideal of exhaustiveness appeared in the history of lexicography when the dictionary began to be normative; the two ideals are contradictory if they are applied scrupulously (see above, 3.2.2.1). Every lexicographer knows that true exhaustiveness is impossible, but the desire of many publishers, more than lexicographers, to include as many words as possible—the only exceptions being the dictionaries for children, or for foreign learners—is dangerously close to the popular image of lexis as a closed set, something like a pre-scientific vision of the world, with sharp edges: 'there is ample evidence, from lexicographic theory and practice to publishers' promotional literature, to suggest that the provision of the maximum possible number of word-meanings is—whether implicitly or explicitly—the central aim of lexicographers working in the NSD [i.e. Native-Speaker Dictionary] tradition' (Rundell 1988: 128).

The objective of representativity that we have mentioned (see above, 1.1.2.8) is more reasonable, but it raises two questions: the first is whether a dictionary can really be representative, and the second is whether the users need a representative dictionary. The lexis of a language is sometimes represented graphically by a circle whose contents become increasingly fuzzy as one moves from the centre to the outer edges, or by a sort of planetary system, with a nucleus around which satellites of various sizes gravitate (see Rey-Debove 1971: 66).

The English vocabulary contains a nucleus or central mass of many thousand words whose 'Anglicity' is unquestioned; some of them only literary, some of them only colloquial, the great majority at once literary and colloquial, —they are the *Common Words* of the language. But they are linked on every side with other words which are less and less entitled to this appellation, and which pertain ever more and more distinctly to the domain of local dialect, of the slang and cant of 'sets' and classes, of the peculiar technicalities of trades and processes, of the scientific terminology common to all civilized nations, of the actual languages of other lands and peoples. And there is absolutely no defining line in any direction: the circle of the English language has a well-defined centre but no discernible circumference. (*OED*: xxvii)

If the lexicon of a language is indeed something like that circle or that planetary system, then it should be possible to draw up a word-list that would be representative of the whole. If one moves away from the centre in concentric circles, the result should be a faithful image of the total lexicon. This is what is sometimes called the 'reduction' of the word-list (see above, 1.1.2.8). But the fact that this is not totally realistic comes out clearly if one examines . . . dictionaries. Rey-Debove, having analysed three French dictionaries (*PL*, *PR*, and *DFC*), concludes that the word-lists of the bigger dictionaries never completely include those of the smaller ones: 'aucune nomenclature n'en contient une autre, elles ont toutes des entrées propres quelle que soit leur taille. Ce fait reflète des divergences dans l'appréciation de l'importance des mots assez courants, et non seulement des mots rares'[8] (Rey-Debove 1971: 79–80). She gives examples of fairly frequent words that are absent from one or two of the dictionaries: *balai-brosse*, *bikini*, *chocolaté*, *coquillettes*, *cure-pipe*, *déodorant*, *faux-filet*, *golden*, *jupe-culotte*, *nougatine*, *ouvre-bouteille*, *porte-jarretelles*, *saucissonner*, *yéyé*, for example, are not in *PL*, which nevertheless has words like *macfarlane* (Rey-Debove 1971: 108). The words that are omitted are often names for everyday things, household artefacts which lexicographers tend to overlook: Forgue (1979) has argued that some potential sources, like mail-order catalogues, often go unexplored, because they are felt not to be prestigious enough. The conclusion to be drawn from Rey-Debove's study is that although lexicographers would agree on a

[8] 'no word-list is totally contained in another. Each, however small, has entries that no other has. This reflects the differences in the assessment of the importance of relatively common words, and not only of the rarer ones.'

large proportion of what words are central, there would still be some hesitation about some words.

The larger the dictionary the more one has to move away from the central core.

Dans un vaste dictionnaire général de nature "culturelle", comme le *Grand Robert*, la nomenclature—environ 80,000 entrées—suppose qu'à côté de 40,000 mots courants ou semi-courants (environ) de nombreux aspects spécifiques, voire marginaux du lexique sont abordés. Parmi ceux-ci, des archaïsmes, des formes littéraires assez rares, des régionalismes, des mots propres à des milieux—ou même au Milieu: argotismes—, mais aussi des mots scientifiques, techniques, juridiques, professionnels, didactiques.[9] (Rey 1985: 5)

The choice of those rarer words is even more problematic, because there is no firm basis one can build on, no point of comparison, there are no solid criteria. The compilers of *W3* confessed several years after publication that the dictionary was particularly poor in words of mathematics, simply because the 'marking and reading program was fairly weak' (Preface to *6,000 Words*: 17a). Finkenstaedt and Wolff (1973: 24), having studied the word-list of *SOED*, observed that some of the choices of the compilers were inexplicable. They also compared the representation of specialized words in *SOED* and *ALD*, counting the number of times that field labels were used. Some of their results are shown in Table 6.1.[10] No doubt some of the variations can be attributed to the imprecision in the use of usage labels, but it is surely significant that *ALD* has so many words from music and that *SOED* has so many words from mineralogy. According to the authors, 'the reason why can easily be discovered: W. Whewell, one of the founders of the OED, was a mineralogist himself' (Finkenstaedt and Wolff 1973: 105).[11] This certainly *explains*

[9] 'In a large "cultural" dictionary like the *Grand Robert*, the word-list—roughly 80,000 entries—is such that, beside the 40,000 or so common or fairly common words, many specific, even marginal, aspects of the lexis are drawn upon. Among those, archaisms, fairly rare literary forms, regionalisms, words specific to some circles—even the slang of criminals—and also scientific, technical, legal, professional, didactic words.'

[10] Given the different sizes of the two dictionaries, only the proportions of the various fields in each dictionary can be interpreted. The question is not what the figures are in the absolute—since there is no way anyone can tell what would be an 'adequate' figure—but how the proportions of each field vary in the different dictionaries.

[11] Some metalexicographers say that the amateur mineralogist was James Murray himself.

TABLE 6.1

	SOED	*ALD*
Mineralogy	619	9
Historical use	613	25
Pathology	423	51
Heraldry	205	4
Music	152	42
Poetical	124	31

Source: Finkenstaedt and Wolff 1973: 103.

why the proportions of the different fields vary so much, but the fact remains: it is difficult to contend that dictionaries are representative of the lexicon, if the representation can vary so much.

The image of the lexicon as a circle is a convenient device, which looks comforting in its simplicity. But reality is not as simple as that; the lexicon is a complex entity, with many subgroups of words whose frontiers are unclear and which stand in some kind of unspecifiable relation to one another; it is 'un conglomérat de plusieurs entités, c'est-à-dire des lexiques des langues "fonctionnelles" (langues des groupes de gens ayant une même profession ou appartenant à une seule classe sociale, etc.). . . Et les langues fonctionnelles, à leur tour, ont-elles une existence réelle? Leur lexique ne se compose-t-il pas d'innombrables vocabulaires individuels?'[12] (Ducháček 1959: 98). That is why a truly functional dictionary, like the ideal dictionary of the structuralists, could only be very small, like a dictionary for children.

The juxtaposition of non-compatible elements in a dictionary is not a bad thing for the user—provided usage labels indicate clearly in what circumstances each lexical element is typically used, especially if the dictionary is to be used for encoding—but it raises the question of the representativity of the dictionary. What does the dictionary represent? What is the language, where does it begin and where does it end? The reduction of the lexicon is not a totally impossible task, or different dictionaries would have completely

[12] 'a conglomerate of several entities, that is to say of the lexicons of "functional" languages (languages of groups of people sharing the same professional activity or belonging to the same social class, etc.) . . . And what about each of these functional languages? Do they exist as such? Isn't their lexicon composed of innumerable individual lexicons?'

different word-lists; but it is not a neat, precise operation either. The reason is as simple as the solution is difficult: the lexicon of a language does not exist as such, apart from the dictionaries and the minds of the language users, and it is impossible to draw a faithful portrait of something that does not exist. Representativity is impossible in theory and possible in practice only if a margin of uncertainty is accepted.

6.2.2 *The more frequent words are also the more useful*

When the lexicographers reduce the available lexicon to a manageable size to obtain their word-list, they normally select the most frequent words, those that in the traditional view would lie around the centre of the circle. This used to be done intuitively, and is now made easier by the use of frequency lists, which partly confirm the lexicographers' intuitions: they show, for example, that the most frequent words—in any language—are the function words. But those lists—this is now well known—have proved to be of less use than was expected, because of the difficulties of lemmatization, because there are so many multi-word units that the computer fails to recognize, because of the imprecision of the notion of 'word', because of polysemy, because of the coexistence of so many more or less incompatible subcodes, and because some words that are obviously important have been found to have relatively low frequencies. In fact, the specialists of the statistical study of language came long ago to the conclusion that it is impossible to speak of the

TABLE 6.2

Frequency of occurrence	No. of types
1	131,298
2	28,838
3	13,964
4–9	29,389
10–99	33,058
100–999	8,796
1 000–9999	1,550
10 000–99 999	156
100 000 or more	19

Source: Hanks 1989: 9. Renouf (1987: 121) has slightly different figures.

frequency of a word in the absolute. One can only say that a particular form is frequent in one type of discourse, or even in a precise corpus (Muller 1975: 5).

If a corpus is divided into 'slices' according to the number of occurrences of types (not tokens), the figures are as shown in Table 6.2 (these are for the Birmingham corpus).

This means that, for example, if the dictionary contains 43,579 words (19+156+1,550+8,796+33,058), it will list words whose frequency is only ten in a corpus of 18 million words (tokens), and an average-sized dictionary of, say, 75,000 words will have to list many words with very low frequency (three occurrences), but not all the words with that frequency. To list all the words with three occurrences, it would have to have 86,932 words (19+156+1,550+8,796+33,058+29,389+13,964). Of course. No one expected the figures to divide into neat slices ready for use in lexicography.

But this is not all. For all modern lexicographers, the more frequent words are also the more important. 'Les ensembles de mots sont structurés par une notion d'importance. . . fondée essentiellement sur la fréquence des occurrences dans le discours (plus précisément la fréquence et la répartition). Grosso modo, les mots les plus souvent prononcés ou écrits sont les plus importants'[13] (Rey-Debove 1971: 30). It is not totally clear whether Rey-Debove is talking about importance in the language or in the dictionary, but the two are probably thought to coincide. Frequency lists are also considered as lists of words according to their importance—hence the frustration when it was discovered that things were not as simple as that.

'Importance' is generally not defined otherwise than via frequency, but the following reveals what lexicographers mean by it: 'Beyond a certain point, each new noun we add has a decreasing usefulness' (S. E. Martin 1962: 155). The most frequent words are the most important and also the most useful. This is clear in all modern dictionaries, and the 'simplified' dictionaries of modern times—like the dictionaries for foreign students or for children—are the best illustrations. It is hard to imagine, at the end of the twentieth

[13] 'The sets of words are structured by the notion of importance . . . which is essentially based on frequency of occurrence in discourse (more precisely, frequency and distribution). Roughly, the words that are pronounced and written most often are the most important.'

century, a general-purpose dictionary that would have rare words but not the frequent ones.[14]

Yet the idea that the more frequent words are also the more useful rests on a shaky definition of 'usefulness'. The surveys that have been carried out on the use of dictionaries indicate that the more frequent words are hardly ever consulted: 'The frustration stems partly from the fact that by selecting the more common words and meanings the lexicographers have left out the ones on which we need help most' (Burrill and Bonsack 1962: 192). How can an entry be useful if it is never used? Also, from the point of view of information theory, the rarer a word is the more information it carries when it is used in discourse, and the more useful it is when it is consulted in a dictionary. It is not unreasonable to argue that the more useful words in a dictionary are not the more frequent, but on the contrary the rarer ones, or at least the most 'difficult'[15] (Geeraerts 1989: 292).

One may wonder whether the space occupied by the painstaking explanation of frequent words would not be better used if a greater number of rare words were included. Quine himself toyed with the idea: 'It has long seemed odd to me to clutter a popular domestic dictionary with idly compulsive definitions of words that all speakers of the language know' (Quine 1973: 249). The omission, or cursory treatment, of frequent words would certainly make dictionaries more useful in a way.[16] Any denial of this is bound to evoke the notion of exhaustivity, of the role of the dictionary as a complete record of the language, and simply of tradition: 'The fact that in our peculiar culture there is great demand for unilingual defining dictionaries, which include definitions of words so common that no one would conceivably want to look them up, is itself an interesting ethnographic datum' (Weinreich 1962: 26–7). But there is clearly a contradiction between the role of the dictionary as a record of the language and as an instrument for providing solutions to linguistic problems.

[14] There are 'dictionaries' of rare words, archaisms, foreign words and phrases, etc., but they are certainly not perceived as general-purpose dictionaries.

[15] The rarer words are often also the more difficult to acquire, those that the learner, whether a child or a foreign student, acquires last. But some rare words may be easy because of their morphology (e.g. *freezable* or *panful*).

[16] Such a recommendation, Hausmann (1989*b*: 219–20) remarks, was made a long time ago by Ponsonby A. Lyons in the entry for *dictionary* for the *Encyclopaedia Britannica*, 1877 edition.

The tradition of including 'all' the words of a lexicon, even the more frequent ones, was born in social circumstances where it made sense, but it does not necessarily make as much sense now. Even if it is admitted that the lexicon is a system, does it follow naturally that the dictionary must try to be a faithful representation of this system? The words that are 'important' in the lexicon and the language are not necessarily those that are the more important in the dictionary, for the user. In other words, even supposing the dictionary could be representative, the question is whether the users need a representative dictionary, and the answer to that question is not as simple as one would have thought.

6.2.3 *Words are discrete units*

The discreteness of lexical units—*word*, *lexical item*, *lexical element*, *lexeme*, *vocable*, etc.—is rarely questioned in linguistics. Every grapheme used in discourse is attached to a 'unit', which is a potential candidate for inclusion as an entry-word in the dictionary.

> L'enchaînement de l'énoncé peut être scindé en certains segments constituant les entrées du dictionnaire et. . . , à chacun de ces segments, correspond un contenu qui fait l'objet de l'élaboration de l'article du dictionnaire. . . l'énoncé est considéré comme une combinaison d'éléments qui ont une existence, sur le plan du système de la langue, indépendante de lui et. . . ils peuvent être saisis isolément.[17] (Guilbert 1969: 4–5)

Each dictionary entry is thought of as a unit, with its two forms (graphic and phonic) and its meaning—the basic Saussurean sign (Geeraerts 1989: 292). In the preparation stages of a dictionary, every word is picked, transported out of its natural milieu, and put under a microscope for examination. 'The necessities and traditions of the trade force . . . [the lexicographer] to extract a word from its context and thus to cut through the rich, multi-layered tissues which connect it with other words and keep it alive. For the sake of analysis he is obliged . . . to examine this lifeless thing out of its natural environment—discourse' (Moulin 1981: 180–1).

[17] 'Discourse can be cut up in segments that will be used as the entry-words of dictionaries and . . . to each of these segments corresponds a content which is the object of the dictionary article . . . discourse is seen as a concatenation of elements that have an existence of their own. They are in the language system, but they live independently and can be isolated from it.'

This impression that every word has an individual life of its own is particularly strong in dictionaries like the *OED*, where every word has a history, with a date of birth—a very important date—and various events until, in some cases, the word dies. Even the words that have changed meanings totally (for example *nice*) are still considered to have been the same word since 'their first recorded appearance', because the semantic evolution can be traced through texts, and even though the form may have changed dramatically over time. On the contrary, words that are 'felt' to be the same now are treated as different units on the basis of their history. Rundell mentions the examples of *bay*, *club*, and *drill* in two dictionaries for foreign learners, *ALD* and *LDOCE*, and he argues that the treatment of those words ultimately comes from the tradition of the 'word as an individual unit' in native speakers' dictionaries.

Most learners, for example, would probably see some connection between *bay*, in its meaning of 'an indentation in the coastline' and *bay*, when it means 'a recess' (as in *a loading bay* or *a bay window*); conversely, few learners would see any connection whatever between the two main meanings of *club* ('a society that people join' and 'a heavy stick used as a weapon'). Nevertheless, the historically-motivated (but counter-intuitive) organization of the native-speaker tradition has in general been carried over into the MLDs [i.e. the Monolingual Learners' Dictionaries], so that *bay* appears in LDOCE and ALD as five separate noun homographs, while *club* appears as just one. Even more confusingly, *drill* ('a tool for making holes') and *drill* ('a form of instruction based on repetition') are grouped together in one homograph, while *drill* ('an agricultural tool for planting seeds') is shown as a separate entry. (Rundell 1988: 129–30)

The problem is twofold: how far can one say that words are units, and, supposing they are indeed, how discrete are those units? The definition of a 'unit' is not obvious. Linguists have tended to say that something is a unit when it can enter into paradigmatic substitutions, and this applies to words to a certain extent, but two well-known phenomena blur the picture: what is felt to be a single unit can have different forms according to the syntagmatic environment, and the same form is sometimes intuitively attributed to different units. In both cases, it is difficult to support intuition with hard facts. The question is how far the common notion of a word, in everyday metalinguistics and in lexicography, corresponds to linguistic reality, and particularly to the mental lexicon, and this, again, has no ready-made answer.

6.2.4 *All words have meanings*

In the traditional dictionary, every single lexical item has a semantic content, a meaning of its own out of all context.

> La tradition, qui ne fait que conserver les moyens les plus commodes de satisfaire à un besoin social, confère à cette sémantique des dictionnaires un certain nombre de caractères, nullement pertinents sur le plan théorique, mais qu'il est nécessaire de connaître pour bien apprécier les caractères du "fait dictionnaire" (M. Cohen). C'est d'abord, et d'une manière très apparente, une *sémantique de l'unité lexicale*, mot ou lexie.[18] (Rey 1977: 15)

Some dictionaries treat function words differently, specifying their functions rather than their meanings, but there is always the underlying assumption that they have meanings as well as content words (Moon 1988). Some dictionaries also treat purely graphic items as if they had meaning: 'par traditionnalisme, on rencontre encore souvent des pseudo-unités imposées par l'écriture: *fur*, *hère*, etc.'[19] (Rey 1968: 69). *CED* defines *kith*, only used in *kith and kin*, as

> one's friends and acquaintances (esp. in the phrase *kith and kin*)

Sometimes, entry-words are forms that never appear in discourse and therefore hardly have any meaning: for example, the *Lexis*, like all other Larousse dictionaries, has an entry for *seoir*, the infinitive form of 'il sied que. . .', of which only the form *sied* is ever used (Guilbert 1969: 8). Many French dictionaries also have *gésir*, for the common phrase *ci-gît* used on tombstones. An English example is *couth*, or *hackles*, which is only ever used in the plural, and thus should be entered in the plural; the singular looks more satisfactory because it harmonizes the entry with all the others, but it does not correspond to any reality in usage, and therefore should not be described as having meaning.

[18] 'Tradition, whose object is only to preserve the most useful means to satisfy a social need, gives to that semantics of dictionaries a certain number of characteristics which have no theoretical value but which one must be well aware of if one is to appreciate the characters of the "fait dictionnaire" (Marcel Cohen). It is above all, in a very obvious way, a *semantics of the lexical unit*, whether word or phrase.'

[19] 'because of tradition, one still often comes across pseudo-units imposed by the writing system: *fur*, *hère*, etc.'

6.2.5 *Words are either polysemous or monosemous*

All linguists admit the existence of word meanings, and the fact that some words have only one (monosemy) while others have more than one (polysemy). But if one believes in the discreteness of the word, then one may wonder what the basic unit is: is the word a cluster of meanings, or is it the association of one form with one meaning?

The traditional dictionary distinguishes between monosemy and polysemy by using two types of entries: simple ones, with only one undivided paragraph explaining only one meaning for monosemous words, and complex ones, with more or less intricate subdivisions for polysemous words. But the fact that the same word can be treated as monosemous in one dictionary and polysemous in another (Atkins 1991) suggests that there is no clear limit. Recent research indicates that there are intermediate stages between monosemy and polysemy (Cruse 1986), but dictionaries, because of the constraints that bear upon the lexicographical text, find it difficult to represent the more subtle distinctions. Most dictionaries now have 'nested' polysemous entries, with more than one level of subdivision, but this 'nidification' (Hausmann 1989*b*: 221) may still not be enough to account for some types of polysemy. How can the dictionary represent a polysemous word with meanings clustering around a central one—as opposed to one with a string of meanings—if the text of the dictionary remains the traditionally linear type (Geeraerts 1989: 292; Atkins 1991: 181–2)?

6.2.6 *Word meanings are discrete*

Complex entries are lists of meanings for one form, suggesting that meanings can be clearly differentiated. But here again, different dictionaries adopt different solutions for the same word, and the same dictionary may have different solutions for similar words. Lexicographers do not agree on how many meanings words have and on what those meanings are (see below, 7.2); some indicate meanings that others do not have, and sometimes two dictionaries have the same meaning spectrum for the same word, but divided differently. Millions of examples could be given: *fasten* has only one undifferentiated entry in *LDOCE1*, and seven clearly marked meanings in *CED*; *expire* has five meanings in *COD7*, only three in *CED*; *line* (the noun) has five meanings in *COD5* and 33 in *COD6*.[20] This is because word meaning varies more or less according to context (see below, 7.1), and because many words have predictable applications that have a doubtful status (see below, 7.2.1.4). The traditional dictionary entry cannot do justice to all these subtle nuances: 'word meaning cannot be sliced up into distinct bundles, labelled (however carefully) and packaged into a dictionary entry' (Atkins 1991: 180). And the use of corpora has failed to clarify the situation. In fact, examining a corpus brings one to the conclusion that there are no discrete meanings: 'lexicographers who have worked with such corpora, and examined hundreds of individual citations minutely in an attempt to find objective evidence for the existence of dictionary senses, report that in many cases such objective evidence simply is not there' (Atkins 1991: 168; see also 179).

A consequence of the belief that word meanings are discrete is the belief that there is, for every word, a 'true' meaning, which is stored somewhere, which the lexicographer tries to reach, and which would be precise if only the definition were better.

> Une opinion couramment répandue est qu'il y a même un sens exact pour chaque mot (cf. les interrogations du type *Que signifie exactement ce mot?*). Opinion qu'accompagne le corollaire social de la *division du travail* (H. Putnam, 1975): si l'on ne sait pas exactement quel est le sens d'un mot, quelqu'un de plus instruit, dont c'est le rôle social, peut nous l'apprendre (cf. la confiance accordée aux dictionnaires).[21] (Kleiber 1988: 5 and 1990*a*: 27)

6.2.7 *Each word is a unit which is represented by a lemma*

The laws of lemmatization are purely conventional (Muller 1977: 6). They have only occasionally been challenged, for example by Matoré:

> le dictionnaire présente de la langue une image arbitraire. Cette image est déformée encore par l'adoption d'un certain nombre de pratiques dont

[20] Jean Tournier (personal communication). This is due in part to the fact that the sense divisions that used to be signalled by semicolons have been replaced by numbers.

[21] 'It is commonly believed that there is one exact meaning for each word (hence questions like *What exactly does that word mean?*). This is paralleled by the social corollary of the *division of labour* (Putnam 1975): if you do not know exactly what a word means, then somebody else, who is better educated and whose social role it is to do so, can tell you (hence the total confidence in dictionaries).'

l'ancienneté ne change pas le caractère contestable. Pourquoi présente-t-on les noms au masculin singulier (*lion* et non pas *lions*, *lionne* ou *lionnes*) et sans article? Pourquoi les verbes sont-ils toujours offerts sous la forme, relativement peu employée, de l'infinitif?[22] (Matoré 1968: 191)

But there is no linguistic reason to change the rules of lemmatization, if it is accepted that they are only arbitrary, but convenient, conventions. The lemma, when used as an entry-form, conventionally represents all the inflected forms of the unit, *umbrella* for *umbrella* and *umbrellas*, *take* for *take*, *takes*, *taking*, *taken*, and *took*, or *go* for *go*, *goes*, *going*, *gone*, and *went*: inflected forms are normally all treated together in the same entry, under the same entry-form. Some dictionaries spell out the different forms (only the irregular ones, or all), especially the new dictionaries with their information for encoding; others leave them for the user to retrieve with the help of the grammar.

When an inflected form is irregular, like *went*, it is normally also given a separate entry, with usually only a cross-reference to the main entry for the lemma. *Better* and *best* both must have separate entries if the dictionary is to be useful for decoding. Some forms however, like *I* and *me*, which are also, in a way, inflected forms, tend to be given full separate entries (Hudson 1988: 296).

Derivatives are normally distinguished from inflected forms, though the distinction is not always easy (Zgusta 1989*b*): *normal* and *normally* are derivatives of *norm*, not inflected forms. Some derivatives are omitted from the dictionary altogether, when their meanings are obvious, particularly in dictionaries for decoding (Geeraerts 1989: 289); some are included within the entry for the main form, either just listed, typically at the end of the entry (as opposed to inflected forms, which tend to be given at the beginning: Ilson 1984: 80), or with microstructural information of their own; some are given full entry status. What are the decisions based on? Practical considerations of space? Optimal usefulness for the users? Considerations on the nature of the lexical unit? Or a combination of those?

If the dictionary is to be a complete record of the language, it should include all derivatives; at least all the documented ones—

[22] 'The dictionary presents an arbitrary picture of the language. This is further accentuated by the adoption of a certain number of practices which may be debatable even though they are sanctioned by tradition. Why are nouns presented in the masculine singular form (*lion* rather than *lions*, *lionne*, or *lionnes*), with no article? Why are verbs always presented in the relatively little-used form of the infinitive?'

some say even the potential ones (Corbin and Corbin 1989). Most dictionaries refrain from that, because they would be cluttered with an enormous number of words (think of all the *un-* compounds). They choose just a few, and they justify the decision by saying that many derivatives are self-evident semantically. But a dictionary that does not list some words cannot be considered representative of the lexicon.

The decision to list derivatives in the entry for the base-form may be dictated by the need to save space. But the lexicographer who adopts that solution also says something to the user about the links between the base and the derivative. When dictionaries include derivatives as run-ons, without any definitions, the meaning distinctions between the base and the derivative are ignored. As we have seen, this is what happens sometimes with the feminine forms of words: *actress* may be the feminine form of *actor*, but *manageress* is not the feminine of *manager* (see above, 4.2.5.1). And there are many other cases where a regular morphological derivation hides some semantic irregularity, which the dictionary should account for: *lamely*, for example, is the adverb of only one meaning of *lame* (Hanks 1990).

On the whole, semantic relationships are not always satisfactorily represented in the traditional dictionary, because entries tend to focus on similarities of form rather than on similarities of meaning. For example, *strong* is the normal lemma for *stronger* and *strongest*, and usually also the entry-word for *strongly*. But *strength*, *strengthen*, *strengthening*, etc. are often other entries, without any obvious links with the first, and the entries will be all the more separated if the dictionary is a big one. *Thief* is the lemma of *thieves*, but is not always linked to *theft*. Scholfield (1979) even argued that the entry for *thief* should also contain *steal* etc.—a plea for a Robert-like analogical dictionary of English that has never been done. Also, the different meanings of a form tend to be separated in broad categories according to part of speech, so that similar meanings may be separated by several others, simply because they are not the same part of speech: sub-entry no. 4 of *head* in *COB* is 'head of a company', and sub-entry no. 17 is the verb *to head* 'a company', blurring the obvious semantic link. The same is true of *COD*, *CED*, *CTD*, etc.

Rules of lemmatization are one thing; but the basic problem is what constitutes a lexical unit. What do we store in our minds? Each form separately, with only one meaning, a form with all its meanings, a form with its inflections, or its derivatives, or both, a family of words? Lexicographers have no theory to go by, and they continue to write their entries in more or less traditional ways because there is nothing else they can do.

> What about pairs like *I* and *me*? Linguists have always been reluctant to take such different forms as part of the same lexical entry, but is this for any reason other than because this would be a departure from the model of traditional lexicography? Once again there is no general principle to which one can point as a guide to making these decisions, which suggests that reality—i.e. mental reality—is not in fact structured like that. (Hudson 1988: 296)

The traditional dictionary, because of the constraints on its organization, finds it difficult to represent word families, to differentiate between two lexical units which are totally unrelated, such as *green* and *sleep* for example, and two lexical units which are more or less closely related, such as *green* and *tree* or *green* and *evergreen* or *green* and *greenery* (Zgusta 1989*b*: 300). This gives an impoverished image of the organization of the lexicon.

> Indeed it is often assumed that to put two words in different lexical entries is to deny any connection at all between them, so that lexical relatedness is an all-or-none matter: either two words are related, in which case they will be shown in the same entry; or they are not related, and are in distinct entries. It seems unlikely, to say the least, that this is how our minds are structured; surely some words are more closely, or more obviously, related than others are, but there is no natural break in the scale of relatedness. (Hudson 1988: 296–7)

Experiments on word associations, or the study of language slips, indicate that links between words can be more or less direct and more or less strong. How this hierarchy could be indicated is an open question. Modern dictionaries use cross-references (Rey-Debove 1989*c*), but this does not do justice to the hierarchy in the semantic links evoked by Hudson. Perhaps the computer-accessible dictionary will offer new solutions.

Clearly, lexicographers have not yet fully exploited what psycholinguistics can contribute to dictionary-making, in terms of the different criteria according to which the mental lexicon seems to be organized and of the different keys that can give access to the lexical store.

6.2.8 *Words can be defined*

One of the fundamental tenets of traditional lexicography is that the meanings of all lexical items can be expressed by means of a paraphrase in the same language, the *definition*.[23]

La **définition du mot** consiste à donner une **paraphrase** qui lui soit **sémantiquement équivalente**: ceci signifie que, le contenu étant considéré comme invariant et, en quelque sorte, mis entre parenthèses, il existe *au moins deux "expressions"* qui peuvent le dénoter. Autrement dit, la définition lexicographique du mot implique l'existence d'un *universel sémantique*: il y a toujours au moins une **paire de synonymes** pour chaque terme de la langue, ce terme pouvant être un mot ou une phrase. On peut toujours substituer à un terme de la langue, un autre terme ou une autre phrase sans que le sens en soit modifié. . . Ainsi la lexicographie suppose que le concept de synonymie est primitif et que l'opération consistant à reconnaître des équivalences est un de ces universaux linguistiques, propriétés du langage humain.[24] (Dubois and Dubois 1971: 85)

If the definition 'works', that is if the user has, up to a point, some idea of the meaning of the word after having read the definition, it is not only because the two sides (word and definition) have the same meaning, but also because the right-hand side (the definition, or *definiens*) is more easily understandable than the left-hand side (the word, or *definiendum*). In the case of a true definition, as opposed to simple equivalence or synonymy, this means that decomposing the meaning of a word and 'spreading it out' on a longer and syntagmatically meaningful sequence of words makes it more accessible.

Nobody knows much about how a definition works. Some definitions look simpler than others, but the notion of simplicity for a definition is difficult to pinpoint: it may mean brevity, but it may also be that the longer a definition is the simpler it is, because it is more analytic—the meaning being distributed over a larger number of words. Long definitions in dictionaries tend to be encyclopedic or

[23] On the lexicographic definition, see Robinson (1954), Rey-Debove (1971), etc.

[24] 'The **definition of the word** is a **paraphrase** which is **semantically equivalent** to it: this means that, the content being considered as an invariant and being, so to speak, put between parentheses, there are *at least two ways* of expressing it. In other words, the lexicographical definition of a word presupposes the existence of a *semantic universal*: there is always at least **one synonym for each term** of the language, word or sentence. It is always possible to replace a word or a sentence by another without modifying the meaning . . . Thus lexicography assumes that the concept of synonymy is a primitive, and that the recognition of the equivalences is one of those linguistic universals which are the property of human language.'

difficult to read, and short definitions are usually dismissed by metalexicographers as not good enough. Is there an ideal length? Is there an ideal type of content?

The lexicographer assumes that it is always possible to define a word, and any evidence that a particular definition does not work tends to be attributed to the inadequacy of the writer. This is not an unreasonable view: paraphrase seems to be universal, and possible for all types of words, and definition is an everyday activity, which seems to work (see above, 5.2.2). But it is not at all certain that traditional dictionary definitions are possible for all words and all meanings. Some meanings might in fact be impossible to describe in linguistic terms, particularly within the constraints of the traditional lexicographical definition. Johnson expressed this quite clearly, in his Preface, about nuances of meaning in polysemous words: 'Ideas of the same race, though not exactly alike, are sometimes so little different, that no words can express the dissimilitude, though the mind easily perceives it' (Johnson's Preface, 1755). Another case where dictionary definitions fail to account for the full meaning of words is that of the names of animals: how can a dictionary definition help the user who has no idea of what a *platypus* or an *onager* is? The features of the concept are difficult, if not impossible, to express in linear discourse.

> Many critical semantic components may be perceptual and consequently may not be expressible in a spoken language. The general shape of a dog, for example, must be important in defining (in the wide sense) the concept [dog]. However, this shape cannot be described in English to any degree of satisfaction. (McNamara and Miller 1989: 358)

This is probably why many dictionary users say they want pictorial illustrations[25] (Tomaszczyk 1979: 114). Lexicographers point out how difficult it is to give a picture of a concept which is most of the time the name of a category of more or less different referents. Both Rey and Rey-Debove have argued that it is impossible to give a picture of a dog (Rey-Debove 1978: 148).

> Une illustration doit mettre en valeur les traits pertinents de la chose représentée, ce qui est en elle essentiel et non accidentel. . . Il est impossible par ces moyens de représenter un chien qui résume tous les chiens;

[25] On pictorial illustrations in dictionaries, see Ilson (1987*b*), Hupka (1989), and Stein (1991*a*).

impossible de représenter *le* chien; l'image renverra forcément à une race particulière.[26] (Rey 1982: 46–7)

This is perfectly true, and it is also true of the names of artefacts like *chair* or the famous *cup* (Wierzbicka 1985: 83), and of words like *green* or *walk*. It is true as well, to some extent, of general words like *animal* or *plant*, which can only be represented by several pictures. Prototype theory could have changed the practices of lexicography and made pictorial illustrations more fashionable, but this has not happened, so far at least, perhaps because the notion of prototype is not clear: it cannot be the 'real', most representative element of the category, or the prototype of *dog* would be, say, *poodle*, and the picture for *poodle* would be the same as the picture for *dog*; and if the prototype is an 'abstract bundle of features', then it is indeed difficult to represent as a picture.

However, the difficulties of pictorial illustrations also apply to the definition: 'Is there any reason—other than tradition or pious optimism—to believe that a dictionary entry gives a true account of what a native speaker knows about the semantic properties of a word?' (Atkins 1991: 169). Are we really certain that an imperfect definition works better than an imperfect illustration? When users consult the dictionary to find out the primary meaning of *dog*—a very improbable case; it takes a metalexicographer to do that—what do they really need? Don't they need only a vague idea of the concept of 'dog'? Is it really certain, in that case, that a picture does not work? The popularity of illustrations might be more than aesthetic or recreational. It might be that illustrations really help in the acquisition of word meanings in a way that has never been considered seriously in lexicography.

What is needed is more research in the psycholinguistics of the acquisition of meaning and of the mental processes of the dictionary user. What do we need to know about a lexical element when we are in the position of the dictionary user? Who says that a dictionary must 'give all the features' of an entry-word? Who knows what takes place in the users' minds when they read a definition or look at a picture? What does a definition have to contain to be good? Bolinger

[26] 'A pictorial illustration must underline the distinctive characteristics of the thing, what is essential and not accidental . . . It is impossible to represent a dog that would subsume all dogs; impossible to represent *the* dog; the picture must be of a particular kind of dog.'

might well be right when he writes: 'Dictionaries do not exist to define, but to help people grasp meanings' (Bolinger 1965: 572). The idea that we need 'all the features' of a category to be able to master it and name it does not coincide with what modern semantics tells us. If the language learner can categorize on the basis of sketchy evidence, why imagine that the dictionary user cannot?

6.2.9 *The analytic definition is always best*

Dictionary definitions are formulae with a limited number of subtypes that have not changed much over the centuries. They have now become so familiar to the users and to the lexicographers that it is difficult to break away from the tradition (Rey 1990: 21–2).

> What seems to have happened is that a whole range of conventional defining formulae has become 'ossified' in the almost liturgical domain of the dictionary: users accept such formulae, even expect them, in dictionary definitions, even though they would be considered deviant in most other environments. (Rundell 1988: 131)

The acceptance of the existing types of definition by dictionary users is all the more surprising, as they often find those definitions difficult to interpret (see above, 5.2.3.3). This is probably linked to the belief that there exists a true meaning for each word: the users think that if they do not understand a definition it is their own fault, not the fault of the dictionary. Also, perhaps a certain dose of inaccessibility gives the dictionary an extra aura of respectability.

The most prestigious type of definition is the analytic, intensional, Aristotelian definition. It is the one that lexicographers aim at as much as they can, and the one that is most often discussed in metalexicography (Iris *et al.* 1988: 241). Lexicographers see the Aristotelian definition as the hallmark of their trade: the best lexicographer is the person who can compose the best definitions of that type. The other types, the extensional (for example for words like *planet* or *ocean*), or the use of synonyms or antonyms, are used only when for one reason or another the analytic type does not work, and they are hardly ever discussed. Strictly speaking, the use of a synonym or of an antonym is not even a definition at all (Weinreich 1962: 40); it is used because it is economical, but it only sends the user back to another entry.

The reasons why the analytic definition is considered as the archetype are to be sought in the prestige of the work of some philosophers and logicians, since Plato, in the eyes of the lexicographers and of the dictionary users (Rey 1970*d*: 11). The dictionary definition has the same objectives as the definition of logicians and philosophers: maximal inclusion, and independence from the context.

Yet it is not obvious that an analytic definition is necessarily more effective in the transmission of the meaning of a word than another type. It might be worth while to re-examine other kinds of definition, even though they are not as prestigious. It would be a good idea to compare the relative efficacy of the different types, for different user groups and different word categories (Hausmann 1989*c*: 344). Maingay and Rundell (1987: 133–4) note that subjects, when asked to write sentences after having consulted dictionary definitions for rare words, tend to make the same errors on the same words. They give the following examples: for *reminisce*, most of the errors are syntactic, giving rise to such sentences as 'We stayed all morning reminiscing our childhood'; for *debris*, the errors are semantic: 'He always gives the debris of the meal to the dog'; and for *new-fangled*, the errors are connotative: 'My brother is crazy about new-fangled machines.' As a consequence, it is reasonable to argue that the techniques used for the explanation of meaning should vary with the type of word to be explained (see Hausmann 1990*a*: 232). No dictionary, given the present state of research, can prevent all the potential mistakes of the users, but some progress could be made if the techniques used for the explanation of meaning were adapted to the kind of word that is defined:

> many of the pitfalls are in fact highly predictable and to some extent preventable, and . . . some progress can be made towards dealing with them if the defining process is informed by an analysis of each headword on the basis of its semantic, stylistic, syntactic, and collocational features . . . This in turn argues for considerable flexibility and diversity, both in the way the various features of a word are distributed throughout the entry, and in the degree to which individual features may be singled out for special emphasis. (Maingay and Rundell 1987: 135)

E. L. Thorndike was probably the first lexicographer to use various types of explanations of meaning according to the type of word being defined.

> For very simple, axiomatic words he gives only a picture (e.g. *spoon*) or only illustrative sentences (e.g. *be*); for more advanced words he combines a

definition and a picture (e.g. *spur*) or uses a definition plus a sentence (e.g. *sputter*); for harder words that only more mature pupils will look up (e.g. *spell-bound*, *specification*), he is often content with a definition. (Barnhart 1949: 37)

This is only a rough categorization, but at least it acknowledges the fact that the definition might well be the most 'difficult' means of transmitting meaning, being the most abstract (Hausmann 1990*a*: 226).

There is a modern trend in English-language metalexicography towards writing definitions that would only go by the rule of 'maximal usefulness'.

If usefulness and usability of definitions are always in the forefront of the lexicographer's mind, as I believe they should be, he must be able to . . . transcend, or even break, the rules, in order to compose definitions that communicate, and are not merely dumb monuments to arcane speculations (Ayto 1983: 98; see also Allsopp 1987: 86–7).

A 'useful' definition would be, in Hanks's deliberately vague terms, 'a short statement about some features of the word or the object denoted by it, chosen by the lexicographer on the basis of his guess as to what a user might be doing when he is looking at that word for the definition' (Hanks 1973: 252). Of course, the problem is that it is difficult to gauge usefulness, and therefore to evaluate how useful —and how good—a definition is.

6.2.10 *The dictionary is closed*

The dictionary is said to be 'closed' if all the lexical items that are used in the microstructure are also elements of the macrostructure. This is a self-imposed rule in lexicography, partly to serve the image of the lexicon as a system, and also because it is useful to the user. It imposes a strict control of the defining vocabulary, to make sure that even the rare words used in the definitions will be defined in their own entries—a task next to impossible in the pre-computer era.

The rule of 'closedness' is difficult to observe (Neubauer 1989: 900). First, many dictionaries use words in their front matter, or their encyclopedic supplements, that are not defined in the main word-list. Allen (1986: 1) has noticed that the Fowler brothers, compilers of the first edition of the *COD* (1911), used the word *telegraphese* in the Preface to qualify their defining style, but forgot to define *telegraphese* in the main body of the dictionary. Also, observing the rule of 'closedness' may result in a dictionary that is actually worse, in a way, as a portrait of the language. For example, even small dictionaries have to use specialized metalinguistic words in the entries, like *preposition* or *transitive*, and those have to be defined, even though they would not qualify for inclusion by any other criteria. Similarly, the words used in the definitions in order to classify concepts have to be included in the macrostructure. The more 'scientific' a dictionary is in its definitions, the more difficult it is for the lexicographer to 'close it'. The problem is acute for the hyperonyms of words referring to animals or plants, which are normally used as genus words in analytic definitions. These hyperonyms are often much less frequent than the words they serve to define. For example, a dictionary that defines *duck* by saying that it belongs to the family Anatidae (a scientifically impeccable definition) will have to define the word *Anatidae* itself, although it is not clear whether it belongs in the dictionary or even whether it belongs to the English language at all (see below, 6.2.11).

6.2.11 *Words must be defined by more frequent words*

Defining words by words that are more frequent is a necessity if the definition is to be accessible to the users (Weinreich 1962: 37). But this is not possible if the word to be defined is very frequent, and it may not always be advisable in other cases. On the one hand, the more frequent a word is the more polysemous it is; this is one of the problems encountered by dictionaries, such as *LDOCE*, that use a limited defining vocabulary. On the other hand, a rare, scientific word is not only more precise, but it may also act as the trigger for the user to trace a 'chain' of concepts (van den Hurk and Meijs 1986: 112); thus, the users who find the word *Anatidae* in the definition for *duck* will look it up, then possibly another word that they will have found in the new entry, etc., and they will learn something of the taxonomy—if they are prepared to spend the time.

One solution to reconcile speed of consultation and accuracy of description would be to juxtapose two definitions, which can operate at two different levels, for different users or different circumstances: one would be scientifically accurate, with all the necessary indications as to the precise position of the referent in its taxonomy, and the other would be more easily accessible, with just a quick description, suitable for the user who is in a hurry, and who only needs a quick reminder. This is what Ilson (1984: 83) calls for, with the example of *shrimp*: some dictionaries define it with *decapod*, others with *10-legged*. The two are complementary: *10-legged* is easy to understand but difficult (in fact, probably impossible) to find in the macrostructure; *decapod* is easy to find but difficult to understand. If only *10-legged* was used, it would be impossible to find in the dictionary other animals that belong to the shrimp family; if only *decapod* was used, the user would almost always have to look it up as well. Ilson therefore suggests a 'two-speed' definition of *shrimp*:

any of numerous . . . decapod (10-legged) crustacean animals

Unfortunately, the technique does not equally apply to all words: for example, *crustacean* cannot be given a simple equivalent, because there is no common word to express the notion.

6.2.12 *Definitions must not be circular*

Non-circularity is a rule that lexicography has adopted in accordance with the well-known observation that one simply cannot, in theoretical or practical terms, define A by B and B by A. This dates back at least to Avicenna (Rey 1973: 80) and was formulated by Pascal. Quemada mentions the definition of *lumière* by 'un mouvement luminaire des corps lumineux',[27] which Pascal found amusing (Quemada 1968: 399).

The circularity of definitions seems to have preoccupied lexicographers mostly from the eighteenth century, particularly Diderot and D'Alembert (Auroux 1990: 37). The grossest form of circularity is when a definition uses the word to be defined, as in the example of *communism* in the Russian edition of *ALD* (see above, 4.2.5.1). This hardly ever happens in modern dictionaries, except in terminological dictionaries, but more common is the case of two definitions that echo each other, as when *COD* defines *glaze*, the verb, by 'cover (pottery, etc.) with glaze' and *glaze*, the noun, by 'substance used to glaze pottery'.

One solution proposed by linguists—given that circularity should be avoided—was to divide the lexicon into successive, independent strata, each stratum being used to define the next one (Weinreich

[27] 'a luminary movement of luminous bodies'.

1962: 37–8). But a strict application is impossible for obvious reasons: even if it were really possible to separate discrete strata, one would still have the problem of defining the 'last' stratum. Amsler (1980), having studied the definitions of the *Merriam-Webster Pocket Dictionary*, concluded that the chains of definitions are not as simple as could have been expected, particularly because some words (like *matter* or *being*) cannot be defined by 'higher' words (van den Hurk and Meijs 1986).

Leibniz, Locke, Wierzbicka, and a few others have proposed a set of *primitives* or 'logical atoms' which can be used to define other words but cannot themselves be defined (Auroux 1990: 31–2). Wierzbicka (1980) found thirteen: *want, don't want, think of, imagine, say, become, be part of, something, someone, I, you, world*, and *this*. Of course, her choice is heavily influenced by the nature of the definitions that she wants to produce. Yet another solution is a formalized language, like the one proposed by Mel'čuk in his Explanatory Combinational Dictionaries (ECD). But the signs of the formal language can only be semanticized through the natural language (Calzolari 1977).

Circularity is inevitable, particularly for the definitions of very frequent words, and especially of function words, as Samuel Johnson had already noticed in the Preface to his dictionary. The only thing the lexicographer can do is avoid the simplest types, like A = A, or A = B and B = A. The longer type, A = B, B = N, and N = A, is unavoidable and probably does not cause any practical problems either. Lexicographers may have been excessively rigorous about non-circularity. Littré was indignant when he found examples of circularity in dictionaries: 'Croit-on vraiment nous avoir appris quelque chose quand on définit *chaleur* par *qualité de ce qui est chaud*?'[28] But Rey has this comment: 'Littré ne voit pas que l'équivalence établie entre le contenu du morphème *-eur* et l'expression: *qualité de ce qui est*. . ., référant la forme du premier au concept "intelligible" exprimé par la seconde, est peut-être l'information la plus importante qu'apportent les dictionnaires unilingues'[29] (Rey

[28] 'Do they really think they have taught us something, when they have defined *chaleur* by *qualité de ce qui est chaud*?'

[29] 'Littré does not see that the equivalence between the contents of the *-eur* morpheme and the phrase *qualité de ce qui est* . . . , linking the form of the former and the "intelligible" concept expressed by the latter, may be the most fundamental piece of information provided by monolingual dictionaries.'

1970*c*: 310). Even in the example of *glaze* the definition says something to the user, if only the fact that the words that it uses belong to the code. If the noun *jump* is defined by 'act of jumping', the user will learn that there is a verb, and what that verb is: English does not have a noun *read* meaning 'act of reading'. After all, a dictionary definition has to use words, and cannot be understood if the user does not know what the words mean; there is a fundamental circularity in the genre of the monolingual general-purpose dictionary.

Finally, definitions are said to be circular when the same *form* occurs twice, or forms that are clearly related, but not when the relation is only semantic. How should one judge a definition of *ear* (the organ of hearing) that uses the verb *hear*? Or of *mouth* that contains *eat*? Can one define *mouth* without using *eat*? Can one imagine a user that would know one concept but not the other? Such definitions are never condemned, but they also exhibit a sort of semantic circularity.

6.2.13 *The definition can substitute for the word*

Lexicographers usually try to produce definitions that can be used in discourse in place of the words that they define, *salva veritate*. This is a relatively recent development; only some of Johnson's definitions, for example, are substitutable (Hanks 1987: 120). But it has become a rule since the eighteenth century, particularly under the influence of Leibniz (Rey 1973: 135; Hanks 1987: 119). It implies that the contents of the definiens and of the definiendum must be equal and that the definition should have the same syntactic constraints as the word.

The rule of substitutability is a strange rule. In many cases, it simply cannot be applied, as in the case of most function words: how can one find a definition for *the* that could be used in discourse in place of *the*? In other cases, it forces the lexicographer to adopt an unnatural defining language, as when defining adjectives with the help of formulae like *of*, or *pertaining to*, etc. (Ayto 1986; see also Gove 1968*a* and 1968*b*). This had led some linguists to doubt that it is at all possible to devise a definition that can substitute for the word in discourse: 'a claim of interchangeability between the term and its definition . . . is preposterous for natural languages' (Weinreich 1962: 39).

Also, and above all, it is not altogether clear that the rule of substitutability is necessary for the definition to 'work'. For example, the writing of a substitutable definition forces the lexicographer—at least in the analytic, Aristotelian type—to search for a genus word that will make the definiens the same part of speech as the definiendum. But folk definitions are unencumbered by such precautions. An (untraceable) example in authentic childish French is

— C'est quoi, un dictionnaire?
— C'est quand la maîtresse elle sait pas ce que ça veut dire un mot.[30]

Of course, such formulations can be explained by deletion: the defining noun (*un livre*, probably) is there, somewhere, in the deep structure of the definition; but the definition seems to work just as well in that shortened form. Here are a few English examples (from Manes 1980):

a. A: Stickball, . . .
B: That's just pitching the ball on one bounce and . . .
b. A: . . . warped . . .
B: It's when wood gets bent out of shape.
c. A: What's a coup?
B: When the military takes over.
d. A: What does irrelevant mean?
B: Something that you say, that it doesn't have anything to do with the subject.

In some of those cases, it is difficult to imagine a deep-structure genus noun. Yet such definitions certainly 'work' at least as well as the definitions one finds in dictionaries for the same words.

One of the results of the efforts made by lexicographers to adopt the rule of substitutability is that they tend to multiply the meanings of polysemous words and to see polysemy where there are only different contextual variations (see below, 7.2): 'in the interests of strict substitutability, a word like *shy* is given separate definitions to cover, on the one hand, *a shy person* and, on the other hand *a shy smile* ("showing the quality of shyness")' (Rundell 1988: 132). Such distinctions do not contribute to the effectiveness of the dictionary in the explanation of meaning (see below, 7.2).

30 — What's a dictionary?
— It's when the teacher doesn't know what a word means.

6.2.14 *Meaning and grammar can be separated*

The meaning of lexical items in dictionaries is always presented out of context, in isolation. But several researchers have recently challenged the idea that meaning and syntax can be neatly separated. In the Meaning → Text theory put forward by some Soviet linguists in the sixties (Apresjan *et al.* 1969; see also Mel'čuk 1988*a*, 1988*b*), for example, the two combine to produce text, and there is little meaning out of context. Some semanticists have started to include syntactic phenomena in their descriptions of discourse (see, for example, G. Lakoff 1987 and Wierzbicka 1988*b*), and some syntacticians are interested in the syntagmatic behaviour of individual words (see Hoekstra, Hudson, etc.). Some research indicates that there is a relationship between meaning and syntactic behaviour, so that the meanings of words can be predicted, to a certain extent, from their syntax, and vice versa. Levin, working on a large collection of English verbs, concludes that 'there is much evidence that the relationship between the meaning of verbs and their syntactic behaviour is governed by quite general principles, evidence coming from studies in both lexical semantics and syntax' (Levin 1991: 208), and she goes on to mention several pieces of research that support the conclusions. Lexicography will have to incorporate those findings soon, and this might challenge the traditional dictionary entry in which meaning is described as if it were totally de-contextualized (see below, 7.1).

6.2.15 *The textual conventions of the dictionary*

The style of dictionaries has become readily identifiable over centuries of dictionary-making, with its particular kind of discourse and its graphic conventions.

> In our days the presentation of lexicographical information has become rather conventionalized and one often wonders whether lexicographers are not just following suit without asking themselves what these conventions stand for . . . And the question that has been neglected but that is central to lexicography is whether there are any intrinsic interdependencies between the linguistic data given and the methods used to present them. (Stein 1984*a*: 124)

The dictionary text can be identified by many characteristics. For example, it is linear (Geeraerts 1989: 292), and this linearity has never been seriously challenged, even though it is probably not the ideal solution in all cases. Things would often be clearer if they could be presented in charts (Meier 1969), in taxonomies (Cowie 1979: 88), etc. Ilson (1987*b*) lists the different forms of presentation that could be used: partonomies, paradigms, cycles, chains, networks, frames, etc. These solutions have never been implemented in commercial dictionaries, for lack of space and, eventually, because the publishers do not want to upset the buyers by changing the traditions. Dubois discusses the uses of the verb *passer* and presents his results in a chart in his paper (1962), but this became a normal text in the final *DFC*.

The order in which the different pieces of information of the dictionary entry are given is also conventional. For instance, definitions almost always come before examples, if any,[31] even though in some cases the contrary would probably be more effective (Hausmann 1990*a*).

The dictionary text is elliptical: entries are like forms to be filled (Rey-Debove 1989*a*: 309). For example, the verb linking the definiendum and the definiens, either *be*, *refer to*, or *signify* (see above, 1.1.2.7), is never expressed. Definitions are one-sentence formulae that use rhetorical devices not used in other genres or having special meanings (Dubois and Dubois 1971: 42–6; Ilson 1984; Ahlswede and Evens 1988: 220): words and phrases like *relating*, *characterized*, *marked*, *stated*, *specified*, *of or pertaining to*, *as of*, etc. are typical, 'although it may well be that their full significance is lost on many readers' (Hanks 1987: 116). Parentheses have been used, at least since the *OED*, and are still heavily used in ways that are not immediately understandable, as in the examples of the entries for *fuse* in *LDOCE* or for *gallop* in *ALD* (mentioned by Hanks 1987: 116):

fuse: to (cause (metal) to) melt in great heat
gallop: (of a horse) to go at the fastest speed

In Hanks's words, 'it requires considerable sophistication to work out precisely what each set of parentheses is doing' (Hanks 1987: 116).

Many of the conventions of the dictionary text appeared in the

[31] Hausmann (1990*a*: 230–1) mentions the case of some words in the *Dictionnaire du français contemporain* (1967), of Gerhard Wahrig's *Deutsches Wörterbuch* (1966), and of Marcel Cohen's *Dictionnaire du français vivant* (1972), in which the examples are given before the definitions. Some children's dictionaries could have been added. See above, 2.2.5.

eighteenth century. Dictionaries before that time were much freer, much more discursive in style, but the eighteenth century imposed a kind of formalism that was thought to be indispensable to serious lexicography. The time may have come to attempt to standardize dictionary conventions (Collison 1982: 179; Stein 1984*b*). Ilson (1984) argues that the proliferation of new dictionaries with new conventions is one factor that contributes to the difficulties of the dictionary users. Re-evaluating those conventions in the light of recent linguistic and psycholinguistic research is an urgent task.

7

Whither Lexicography?

WHERE does lexicography go now? This is difficult to say. The answer is to be found partly in an examination of the innovative dictionaries that have been published recently—particularly (though not exclusively) those that have been or are now commercially successful (see above, 2.5), since the commercial success of a dictionary is the unmistakable sign that there is a need for it, and the evolution of lexicography is necessarily linked with this need. Other possible answers lie in the more theoretical writings of linguists on lexicography, in a domain that extends half-way between inapplicable theory and unfounded practice. The final pages of this book will be devoted to a survey of some of the most interesting research in theoretical linguistics from the point of view of the potential improvement of dictionaries.

7.1 LEXICOGRAPHY AND THE STUDY OF IDIOMATICITY

7.1.1 *The idiomaticity of discourse*

7.1.1.1 *The notion of idiomaticity*

In the major linguistic schools that have dominated the field over the last thirty years or so, mainly under the influence of generative grammar,[1] lexis was seen as an open list of elements that the encoder inserts one after the other in the appropriate slots in the syntagmatic chain. In such a view, syntax takes precedence over lexis, both in terms of relative importance and in terms of chronology in the process of encoding. In this context, idiomaticity, defined as that

[1] It is only at the cost of some oversimplification that one can speak of the 'major schools of linguistic thought', and sweeping statements, like flying planes, can indeed be dangerous. Yet it does seem fair to say that linguistics has been dominated over the last decades by the generativist transformationalist grammarians. For a similar view, see G. Lakoff (1987).

phenomenon according to which a string of several words is used to express a notion that is not analysable and distributable over the different words of the string, is seen as an anomaly of the system, since some of the slots have to be filled in by several words instead of one: for example, *kick the bucket* as opposed to *die*.[2]

In the recent past, some linguists have tried to break away from that view of language. Some British linguists, who had remained relatively indifferent to generative and transformational grammar, particularly specialists in the teaching of English as a foreign language, showed that the constraints of grammaticality were unable in themselves to account for some of the linguistic choices made by the encoder producing natural, spontaneous language—precisely the language that the learner tries to imitate. The notion of 'acceptability' that they used was linked to the notion of 'communicative competence' that had been used by some American sociolinguists for some time. Some linguistic choices are more appropriate than others in some contexts, it was said, according to certain elements of the general situation, regardless of the grammaticality of the message. Mastering the complex rules of acceptability and the no less complex but more clearly codified rules of grammaticality constitutes communicative competence.

More recently, some linguists have formulated the notion of 'naturalness' (McCarthy 1988*b*): some message forms are more natural than others, even though they may all be equally grammatical and acceptable. The notion may be the same as that of 'typicality' (Hanks 1988), which is something like prototype theory applied to discourse. Each element of language has typical uses which can be described in terms of syntactic and semantic environments, the whole thing being captured in a statistical study of text in terms of frequency.

One of the most interesting pieces of research published recently with direct relevance to lexicography is the work of Sinclair on idiomaticity (in Sinclair 1991), which was based on an examination of the Birmingham corpus. The general idea is that the traditional emphasis on syntax as a set of rules for the combination of words does not account for all the aspects of discourse, that discourse is not

[2] This is only an example: the Birmingham team working with their corpus have been able to demonstrate that the idiomatic phrases that have always been used as examples in the research on idiomaticity, like *kick the bucket* or *red herring*, are actually infrequent in spontaneous discourse (Moon 1988: 109). See below.

an empty syntactic structure into which the encoder inserts lexical elements one after the other, and that words are not inserted into those syntactic structures simply because of their categorization in terms of parts of speech. Words have 'built-in features', so that the choice of a word, or even of one particular sense of a word, entails the obligatory or preferential choice of some other words, or of some syntactic construction. This is an important observation in the context of the compilation of an encoding dictionary, if the dictionary is to equip the user with rules or recommendations that are precise enough to prevent any mistake, in terms not only of grammaticality but also of acceptability and naturalness, in the composition of text.

Lexical choices in text, Sinclair says, are constrained first of all by the relation between the language and the world. The names given to elements of the world that tend to appear together in reality will naturally tend to appear together in text. Typically, the special verbs used to refer to the sounds produced by animals will tend to occur in the vicinity of the names of these animals, *hypocoristic* will appear in a text about language, *gastritis* in a medical text, etc. That is sometimes evoked under the name of 'domain', or 'register'. The observation of such groupings is banal. But other constraints cannot be attributed to the relations between the language and the world: they are what Rey-Debove has called 'contrainte de signe', as opposed to 'contrainte de contenu' (Rey-Debove 1971: 211). Many of the lexical choices in a text entail some other choices, for purely linguistic—not extralinguistic—reasons, so that the encoder does not choose one word after the other but 'chunks' of text at the same time: 'much of language comes in pre-packaged strings which display a limited number of patterns, as opposed to . . . the classical linguistic notion that language consists of a series of syntactic "slots" into which lexical items may be deposited' (McCarthy 1988*b*: 56). This is what Sinclair calls the 'idiom principle' (Sinclair 1991: 110).

7.1.1.2 *The different types of idiomaticity*

Idiomaticity has been extensively discussed in twentieth-century linguistics. A powerful influence that is often mentioned in Britain is J. R. Firth, a linguist who was known through his students as much as through his writings and who has been an inspiration to linguists ever since the forties. Idiomaticity is present in all the multiword 'expressions' that are chosen 'at one go' by the language user, those that Bolinger (1976) calls 'pre-fabs' and Knowles (1990) 'cognitive units'. In some cases, there is absolutely no room for variation inside the chunk. This may be less frequent in real discourse than many linguists have thought, Sinclair says, but it does occur, apparently in all languages, for example in 'grammatical phrases' like *of course*. This functions in text as just one word, and the space between the two words has virtually no linguistic significance; it can be expected to disappear, exactly as in *maybe*, *anyway*, *everyone*, etc. (Sinclair 1991: 110). The language users do not choose *of* and then *course*: it is impossible to separate the two elements.[3] English has many similar examples, not only in the category of grammatical phrases but also in the domain of familiar expressions used in everyday conversation: *by all means*, *not at all*, *see you soon*, *pleased to meet you*, etc. By far the most frequent occurrences of words like *case* or *instance* have been found to occur in fixed constructions like *for instance*, *in many cases*, etc. (Moon 1988: 110).

There is also idiomaticity in many pre-packaged chunks like proverbs, sayings, or other set phrases and clichés (*it never rains but it pours*, etc.) and of course in the more clearly lexical idioms in the restricted sense: the *kick the bucket* type is by far the best known, having been the object of pages and pages of serious study, particularly in the English-speaking world (see especially Weinreich 1969, Fraser 1970, and Makkai 1972).[4] Such idioms admit contextual variations to some extent, as opposed to the first type above: *kick* in *kick the bucket* can appear as *kicks* or *kicked*, and the form *blow one's top* can take all the verbal and pronominal variations: *blows/blew/is blowing/are blowing*, etc., *my/your/his/her*, etc. In fact, they occur much more frequently in modified, truncated, or distorted form than in their canonical form: 'For example, the saying *you can't have your cake and eat it* typically occurs in a positive form' (Moon 1988: 109).

Another often-mentioned characteristic of idioms is the fact that each individual word that composes an idiom (in all these senses) tends to have a special 'meaning' when it is used in the pre-packaged

[3] If one excepts the admittedly totally jocular *Of fucking course!* On the playful use of language and its role in lexical creativity, see Tournier (1985: 384–407 and 1988: 168–74).

[4] The French lag behind the British and the Americans in the study of idioms. Most of the research carried out on the subject in France is very recent: see e.g. M. Gross (1981). There is also a vast body of research on idiomaticity and phraseology by Russian scholars that has been largely ignored in the West (see Weinreich 1969).

string. Leech (1974: 226) calls the process 'petrification'. The *of* in *of course*, Sinclair says, is not the preposition *of* as it is described in a dictionary entry, and the word *course* does not have one of the meanings that the normal dictionary entry for *course* describes (Sinclair 1991: 111). This feature has often been presented as the only definitional feature of *idiom*: a graphic string whose sense does not correspond to the addition of the senses of the words that compose it; the string has a 'synthetic', or non-compositional meaning. But this petrification is also true of many words that are made up of more than one recognizable constituent, like *cupboard* or *blackbird*.

Another, less well-studied, area of idiomaticity is that of the phenomenon of lexical affinities generally referred to under the name of 'collocations', at least since Firth discussed them in his *Papers in Linguistics 1934–1951*.[5] The concept of 'collocation', although introduced to the literature in the forties, has only recently been used by linguists. It is obviously an important idea for lexicography, particularly for dictionaries for encoding.

A collocation is a string of words bound together by a syntactic structure and that the language user 'recognizes' as a 'normal' construction. Typically, a collocation will be binary, like N+Adj, V+Adv, or Adj+Adv, but three-word collocations like N+Prep+N (or more) are also possible. A collocation is normally a sentence-constituent, but some N+V constructions are also treated as collocations by some authors (Hausmann 1989*e*: 1010). Collocations should be distinguished from compound words[6] on the one hand and from ordinary sentences on the other. The links between the words of a collocation are normally lexical ('contrainte de signe'), not semantic ('contrainte de contenu'), as Bally's famous example shows: although *gravement* and *grièvement* are synonyms, one can say *gravement malade* and *grièvement blessé*, but ?*gravement blessé* is dubious and **grièvement malade* is totally impossible.[7]

Cowie, in the front matter of *ODCIE2*, shows that there is no

[5] Zgusta (1971: 138–40) uses the word 'rections' for what is apparently the same phenomenon.

[6] Cowie (1978: 131) considers *tea service* or *marriage service* as collocations. It is indeed possible to use the word 'collocation' as an encompassing label for all the phenomena of idiomaticity. This is exactly what Crystal (1985: 55) does.

[7] In some cases, it is difficult to decide which type of 'contrainte' is at play, for example with the verbs used for animal cries mentioned above.

clear boundary between idioms and collocations. Collocations are not as syntactically rigid as idioms: typically, the same words will tend to be used together, but not necessarily always in the same order, and will allow some syntactic manipulation, such as passivization etc. Collocations are also more or less 'open', the degree of 'openness' corresponding to the number of different words that can fill the slot corresponding to each element of the combination. The openness of collocations is a measure of the predictability of the occurrence of each individual word that enters into their composition, or of the strength of the link between the different elements: 'the bond between *spick* and *span* is stronger than that between *letter* and *pillar-box*' (Crystal 1985: 55).

Cowie (1978: 133) proposes the following cline, from the more open to the less:

run a machine/car/army/team/business/scheme
explode a theory/claim/fallacy/case
foot the bill
fill the bill

The last example is in fact probably best classified as an idiom, since neither of the two words has its own 'normal' sense.[8] Thus, openness, predictability, and bond strength are connected with semantic depletion (Hausmann 1979; Benson 1989). The more semantically depleted a word is, the more it will make for a closed collocation, the more predictable its occurrence on the syntagmatic axis will be, and the stronger will be the link with the other element(s) of the collocation.

Collocations may be asymmetrical in two ways. Firstly, collocations may be asymmetrical in terms of the semantic depletion of their elements. In *torrential rain*, an Adj+N collocation, the number of substantives that can fit in with *torrential* is certainly not very high, but it is varied enough to allow the conclusion that *torrential* has kept a certain amount of semantic strength; one can speak, for example, of *torrential abuse*. The case of *deciduous tree* (perhaps a lexical item rather than a collocation) is different: the Birmingham corpus has 32 occurrences of *deciduous*, with 9 different collocates: *woodland/s* 8, *forest/s* 8, *trees* 3, *woods* 3, *shrubs* 3, *varieties* 2, *species* 2, *larch* 1, *block*

[8] Such classifications are always debatable. It could be argued, for example, that *run* actually has different meanings according to the collocate with which it is used.

(of woodland) 1 (one last context is impossible to interpret).[9] All are clearly members of the same set, which casts a certain doubt on the semantic autonomy of the adjective *deciduous*. This type of asymmetry is described by Hausmann in terms of 'base' and 'collocate' ('collocator' for Benson): the base is the word that remains semantically 'intact' in the collocation, thus *tree* is our last example. Other examples: ***sleep** soundly*, *trim **sails***, *heavy **drinker***, *sound **asleep***, etc.

In verb+noun collocations . . . the noun is the base, and the verb is the collocator. In adjective+noun collocations . . . the noun is once again the base, and the adjective is the collocator. In adverb+verb collocations . . . the verb is the base, and the adverb is the collocator. In adverb+adjective collocations the adjective is the base, and the adverb is the collocator. (Benson 1989: 6)

Collocations are also asymmetrical in terms of the frequency of their elements (Sinclair 1991: 115): taking each word of a text in turn and calling it the 'node' of the collocation, one obtains two categories: when the node is less frequent than the collocate, the collocation is an 'upward collocation'; if the node is more frequent the collocation is 'downward'.

Idioms and collocations are relatively well known. But Sinclair identified many other types of co-occurrences which indicate that some sort of idiomaticity is at play in cases where it had never been described before.

It is well known that many verbs take only some types of nouns as subjects or as objects: for example, *laugh* will typically take only human subjects—apart from *hyena*. But the choice of a particular word often influences the choice of more words than one. The choice of the verb *set eyes on*, for example, Sinclair says, tends to go together with the auxiliary *has*, the use of a pronoun as subject of the verb, as well as the use of an indication of time, typically an adverb like *never* or a phrase like *the moment*, *the first time*, etc. (Sinclair 1991: 111). Similarly for the verb *strike* in the sense of 'appear to': 'there are 125 occurrences of the word . . . Of these 125, no less than 109 have a pronoun as the direct object. *Me* is overwhelmingly the most frequent' (McCarthy 1988*b*: 55). The verb *set about* is generally preceded by *to*, and followed by a transitive verb in the *-ing* form; *how* is often in the immediate vicinity of the word, generally to the

[9] Moon: personal communication.

left, and the context is generally that of 'problem-solving' (Sinclair 1991: 75–6).

Such choices are obviously not obligatory, but if the corpus is reasonably carefully distributed to avoid idiosyncrasies the observations must reflect tendencies in the encoding of text by native speakers. These tendencies are part of the mastery of the language, and therefore eligible for inclusion in a dictionary. 'Such data can never be exhaustive, but it makes the very clear point that there are preferred sequences and that these sequences are finely balanced combinations of lexico-syntax' (McCarthy 1988*b*: 55). Sinclair's conclusion is that the 'idiom principle' is necessary to account for much of what goes on in discourse (Sinclair 1991: 110).

7.1.1.3 *The importance of idiomaticity*

One can hypothesize that idiomaticity facilitates communication because the linguistic expressions that are associated with recurrent situations can be acquired, stored, and used as more or less solid wholes, thus ensuring the rapidity of reaction described by Fodor (1983). This is supported by the observation that the more 'ordinary' texts are also the more idiomatic.

Other observations seem to confirm the hypothesis of 'extended idiomaticity'. For example, it seems that intonation patterns correspond to groups of words and that some of the pronunciation difficulties experienced by foreign learners could be explained by their inability to encode in chunks large enough to support those intonation patterns. Bolinger (1976), having examined some experimental studies, concludes that children learn their mother tongue by first analysing the syntagmatic sequences in which they have found each individual word, and that they subsequently keep memories of the sequences as well as of the individual words (see also Greenbaum 1974: 89 and Cowie 1981: 234). Many other researchers have come up with evidence that idiomatic strings are not an obstacle for the interpretation of discourse, some even saying that in at least some cases the message is first interpreted synthetically, analytical interpretation following only if it proves necessary (Gibbs 1986).

The fact that many idiomatic strings tend to occur in discourse in distorted forms is not a counter-argument: the distorted forms can function in discourse only because there are 'canonical' forms in the language that the receiver of the message knows as such. A distorted idiom is 'metadiscursive': it is a comment on normal discourse as the receiver expects it.

The idiomaticity of language as described by Sinclair does not mean that encoders have no choice. In many cases, they have a choice between the most frequent, common, ordinary form, and some more original variant, between a marked and an unmarked form. If an encoder chooses a prefabricated form, the receiver will consciously or unconsciously concentrate on the subject matter, but if unexpected forms are chosen, then the attention of the receiver will be drawn towards the form as well as the content. Literary language tends to favour the marked forms, and scientific and didactic languages prefer the unmarked forms: in legal language, particularly, or in some areas of experimental medicine and pharmacology, discourse seems to proceed by whole pre-packaged chunks at a time.

Some misunderstandings may occur when the same message is interpreted differently by different receivers: according to whether or not one assumes that the message is idiomatic or not, one will reach different conclusions. Ruhl (1978: 375) mentions the examples of *out of patience* and *out of sympathy*: each has a literal interpretation as well as an idiomatic one. And this applies to 'pure' idioms as well. Moon (1988: 107) quotes from Tom Stoppard's play *Rosencrantz and Guildernstern are Dead*:

Guildernstern: How do you know?
Player: I keep my ear to the ground
Guildernstern: One day someone will step on your head.[10]

7.1.1.4 *Idiomaticity and word meaning*

The idiomaticity of language has at least one consequence on word meaning: many word meanings are difficult to pinpoint out of the contexts in which they normally occur. Many words do not even have meaning at all in some contexts. For example, *take* in *take a look at this* is only a 'copula' verb which supports the word *look*, putting it, so to speak, in the limelight (Wierzbicka 1982; Stein 1991*b*; Stein and Quirk 1991). The structure *take a look at this*, as opposed to *look at this*, puts special emphasis on the noun, gives it special prominence by allowing it to assume its substance as a noun.

[10] It even applies to compound nouns. When Tristan Bernard was arrested and taken away by the police because he was a Jew, a friend of his asked him: 'Maître, avez-vous besoin d'un vêtement?', and his answer was: 'J'aurais eu besoin d'un cache-nez' ('Master, do you need any clothes?' . . . 'I would have needed a scarf') (*scarf* in French is *cache-nez*, literally 'hide-nose').

The word *take* in *take a look* cannot be defined in a dictionary out of the context *take a look*.

Sinclair remarks that the most frequent meaning of a polysemous word is very often not an 'independent' meaning, but one which is typically context-bound (Sinclair 1991: 112). For example, the word *time* is relatively infrequent in its 'central' sense in the Birmingham corpus, and most uses of *time* are in more or less petrified expressions (Moon 1988: 114). Similarly, 'the commonest use of *take* in English is delexical' (Hanks 1990: 35). The most frequent meaning of the form *back* ('in, to, or towards the original starting point, place, or condition') is defined in *CED* at no. 47, whereas no. 1 in the same dictionary ('the posterior part of the human body extending from the neck to the pelvis') is rare in the corpus. Similarly, the most frequent meaning of the verb *pursue* ('to apply oneself to (one's studies, hobbies, interests, etc.)') is no. 5 in *CED*, where no. 1 is 'to follow (a fugitive) in order to capture or overtake', which seems to be much less frequent in discourse. Yet, Sinclair argues, the ordering of meanings in *CED* is not particularly objectionable. It is probably the ordering that any literate native speaker would propose intuitively—and virtually all dictionaries have the same.[11]

The most frequent meanings tend to be more delexicalized than the less frequent ones, just as are the more frequent words compared with the less frequent. The preposition *back* certainly does not have as clear a semantic content as the noun *back*. The verb *pursue* in *pursue one's studies* is strongly delexicalized; the whole phrase is virtually the equivalent (semantically if not stylistically) of *to study*. *Pursue* is a supportive verb just like *take* in *take a look*. All this points towards the following conclusions: the most frequent words, and the most frequent uses of polysemous words, whatever their frequency, seem to tend to have meanings that are less clear, less independent than rarer words, or rarer uses of the same words: meanings tend to lose their autonomy over time and as frequency increases (Cowie 1988: 135). The highly frequent words like *give*, *head*, *heavy*, *place*, *time*, etc. (Moon 1988; Cowie 1988: 130) are often difficult, or

[11] For *back*, dictionaries like *ALD* and *LDOCE2* have different entries for the noun, the preposition, the verb, etc. *PED* and *CTD* have exactly the same sort of ordering as *CED*. For *pursue*, *ALD*, *LDOCE2*, *PED*, and *COD* have the same as *CED*; only *CTD* has a first meaning 'harass, persecute, persist in opposing or seeking to injure' and the meaning 'to follow in order to overtake and capture or kill' in third position.

impossible, to define out of the typical contexts in which they occur idiomatically. But when the language users think of a word out of context, it cannot be the delexicalized meaning that comes to their minds first, so that the 'foremost' meaning cannot be the most frequent. Sinclair (1991: 113) hypothesizes that it could be 'the most frequent independent sense'.

The relation between the observations on the meanings of words in discourse and those on idiomaticity is clear enough. The words used in the stretches of discourse that are characterized by a high degree of idiomaticity tend to be at the same time the most frequent and the most clearly context-bound.

This, however, should not be construed as evidence for the Wittgensteinian idea that words do not have meaning, that 'the meaning of a term is its use in the language'. This, as Weinreich observed, is untenable: 'This slogan of British linguistic philosophy may offer an escape from certain lexicographic impasses in connection with polysemy, but as a general theory it would require us to renounce dictionaries and to be satisfied, at most, with concordances' (Weinreich 1962: 29). It is meaningless to say that words do not have meaning, as Kleiber (1990*b*) has convincingly argued, and saying, for example, that adjectives take on different meanings according to the words with which they are used makes sense only if one defines exactly what is meant by 'meaning' and therefore by 'different meanings' (Gross and Miller 1990: 266). If words combine to form chunks, it is precisely because they have something to contribute to the chunks to which they belong.

> The choice of *any* word at any point in a discourse raises the question, what is the special contribution of that word to the discourse? Much of what is contributed will depend on the context into which the term is introduced, among other matters. But at core, each term in a language has a particular set of potentials for contributing meaning to discourse. (Hanks 1988: 45)

Some or even most of the semantic content may be absent in ordinary discourse, but it is rarely totally lost in the language, and can be retrieved by the language users if necessary, as in the accidental or deliberate literal, compositional interpretation of idioms.

7.1.2 *Lexicographical applications*

Sinclair's observations on the idiomaticity of discourse have fairly clear potential lexicographical applications. If word meanings can be described only in context, the definitions should indicate the typical contexts. The lexis of a language is not a list of forms, but a complex set of rules that specify the ways in which each of these forms must, or should, be used: 'lexical units are *complexes* of various kinds more often than the traditional organization of the dictionary has prepared us to believe or reductionist images of the lexicon encourage us to suppose' (Cowie 1981: 233).

7.1.2.1 *The traditional treatment of idiomaticity*

Traditional dictionaries have always laid the emphasis on words in isolation: words were decontextualized as much as possible. 'Statements are made about what the words mean, but very little is said about how they are used' (Hanks 1987: 121).

Multi-word units tend to be even less well treated than simple words. They are not always listed, and the criteria used by the lexicographer are far from being obvious. Rey-Debove (1971: 113) wonders: 'Pourquoi des syntagmes figurent-ils comme entrées, et pourquoi ceux-là plutôt que d'autres?'[12]

Collocations are difficult to collect as well, because they are in an ill-defined area between *langue* and *parole*.

> Rien n'est plus délicat dans un dictionnaire monolingue que de décrire de manière convenable la phraséologie, car il faut donner la part belle aux collocations légitimes (faits de langue) plutôt que stylistiques (faits de parole), et rendre compte du même coup du phénomène de la lexicalisation (syntagme libre devenant progressivement figé).[13] (Gorcy 1989: 909)

In traditional dictionaries, they are only indicated when they are necessary for a definition (Frawley 1988: 191). For example, some transitive verbs cannot be defined if one does not mention the nouns that are used as their objects, and some adjectives cannot be defined if one does not mention the nouns that they qualify: *torrential* can be defined in itself, but *deciduous* cannot be defined without the concept of 'tree', just as *feather* cannot be defined if one does not use the concept of 'bird', or *pregnant* cannot be defined without 'woman'

[12] 'Why do dictionaries have some syntagms as entry-forms, and why those particular ones rather than others?'

[13] 'Nothing is more difficult in a monolingual dictionary than to give an adequate description of phraseology: proper attention must be given to legitimate collocations (those that are in "langue") rather than to stylistic ones (those that are in "parole"), and the phenomenon of lexicalization (the free syntagm becoming frozen little by little) must be accounted for.'

(Mackenzie and Mel'čuk 1988). Typically, the normal collocates will be indicated in parentheses within the definition itself, in what Hanks (1988: 43) calls the 'contorted style of modern dictionaries'.

claim: vt. Demand as one's due or property (recognition, etc., to be, that one should be, recognized, etc.) (*COD7*)
throw: to be subjected to (a fit) (*CED*)
buxom: adj. (of women) plump and healthy-looking; having a large bosom (*ALD4*)

The indication of the more elusive elements of context is even weaker. For example, the dictionary which defines *egg* as 'person' (as in 'a bad egg') authorizes sentences like 'Yesterday an egg tried to sell me a stolen watch' (McCawley 1973: 167). The sixth definition of *place* in *CED* is 'a house or living quarters'. This could give rise to sentences like 'There are five places on that street'. Obviously, if the dictionary is to be used for encoding, the definition should carry a warning that this meaning of *place* must be preceded by a possessive. Similarly, most dictionary definitions of *budge* (*CTD* has 'to move or stir') fail to account for the fact that it can only be used in the negative (McCawley 1986: 4–5). The verb *like* and the adverb *much* can only co-occur if the verb is in the negative form: one can say *I don't like him much*, but not **I like him much* (McCarthy 1988*b*: 54; this is also true of other verbs).

Modern dictionaries have made progress in the area of the contextualization of meaning, but they are still better with paradigmatic than with syntagmatic relations. There is as yet no systematic approach to the treatment of multi-word units, and even less of the broader aspects of idiomaticity as analysed by Sinclair. 'Some of those facts are traditionally described in grammar-books, and dealt with more haphazardly by dictionary-makers, often simply in the form of examples' (Frawley 1988: 197).

7.1.2.2 *Towards a new treatment of idiomaticity*

Collocations are now better treated in English lexicography than they used to be. Some dictionaries, like *BBI* in some of its entries, have begun to indicate them in the entry for the base, for encoding, as well as in the entry for the collocate for decoding (Benson 1989: 7). What remains to be done is a dictionary of collocations based on the study of a corpus, and eventually the incorporation of collocative information into general-purpose dictionaries.

Before that, some of the problems of the indication of collocations will have to be resolved, such as the sort of metalanguage that can be used. One possibility is to indicate the broad semantic traits of the group of collocates: thus, +HUMAN+MALE+ADULT, etc., but this is applicable only when the collocates constitute a category, and is probably too abstract for the average user. It is simpler to use real collocates, as does *ODCIE*, but the problem is what status those words have and how far, and in what direction, the user can go beyond the list. When the dictionary says, for example, of the phrase *enough to make one weep*,

S: destruction, slaughter; smell, sight; neglect. V: . . . be, become, find sth,

should one conclude that *catastrophe* can be used as a subject, or *discover* as a verb?

Some of the looser sequences of discourse are treated in the combinatory dictionaries of Russian, English, and French of the Mel'čukian school, particularly the *Dictionnaire explicatif et combinatoire du français contemporain* (*DEC*), currently published at the Université de Montréal (vol. 1: 1984; vol. 2: 1987; vol. 3: 1992. The dictionary contents are accessed through words, as in all dictionaries, but those words are meant to serve as keys to the description of discourse. Each entry contains a set of syntagmatic and paradigmatic associations (the 'lexical functions') that are necessary for the use of the word in encoding text. 'An ECD [i.e. Explanatory Combinatorial Dictionary] is PRODUCTION-ORIENTED. It is intended to supply all the information which is conveyed by individual lexical units and which is necessary to express a given meaning in a completely idiomatic way' (Mel'čuk 1988*a*: 167). The system is still experimental (volume 2 has only 107 entries) and too complicated at this stage for the average user, but many researchers are now trying to adapt it to design bilingual and monolingual general-purpose dictionaries (see Steele 1986 and Lépinette 1989).

The most notable step forward in the direction of the lexicographical treatment of idiomaticity is the *COB* mode of definition, which systematically inserts the word into a syntagmatic sequence that represents its typical environment (see above, 2.3.2.1). A typical *COB* definition is a sentence in two parts separated by a joining verb. To the left is the entry-word in its typical context, and to the right is a defining periphrasis that re-expresses in a different way what the first half of the sentence containing the entry-word said. Thus, in the entry for *budge*, it is not *budge* that is defined, but 'someone/something will not budge' and 'someone cannot budge something'. The entry for *hackles* runs: 'a dog that has its hackles up is one that is angry or ready to fight'.

COB uses several defining patterns, according to the nature of the word and sequence to be defined.

For nouns:

— (a/an/0/the) X is (a/an/0/the/someone) . . . Examples: *passageway*, *passer-by*, *passion-fruit*, *passion play*, etc.
— If (you/someone/something) + V + X (+ Prep) (someone/something), you . . . Example: *pasting*.
— if you are a X, . . . Example: *past master*.
— your X is . . . Examples: *pate*, *patella*.
— if a man has X, . . . Example: *paternity leave*.

For adjectives:

— (a man/someone/something) (who/that) is X + V . . . Examples: *passionate*, *passé*.
— (a/an/0/the) X + N is/relates to, etc. Examples: *pastel*, *pastoral*, *paternalistic*.
— if (something/someone) is X, it is . . . Example: *patchy*.

For verbs:

— to X (someone/something) means to . . . Example: *bewitch*.[14]
— (when/if) you X (someone/something), you . . . Example: *passivize*.
— when (someone/something) is Xed, . . . Example: *pasteurize*.
— (someone/something) (who/that/which) Xs . . . Example: *peddle*.

In addition, the *COB* compilers used a variety of explicitly metalinguistic formulations, like 'If you say X you mean Y', 'If you describe/refer to something/someone as X, you mean Y', for words like *abject*, *ablutions*, *actually*, *blues*, *deep*, *bridal*, *rascal*, etc.

The difference between *you*, *someone*, *a man*, etc. is not totally

[14] It has not been possible to find an example of this type of definition in the letter P where all the other examples were taken from. The *bewitch* example I owe to Fillmore (1989: 61). Perhaps the policies of the lexicographical team had changed between the letter B and the letter P. Or else, different members of the team simply had slightly different techniques.

clear. It seems that the authors tried to avoid associating disagreeable things or actions with the pronoun *you*. Also, the choice of one formulation rather than another is not wholly explained. Fillmore (1989: 63) observes with a chuckle that *cunt* is defined as 'a cunt is a very rude and offensive word that refers to a woman's vagina'—a strange example of the mixing-up of the word and the thing. Generally speaking, the explicitly metalinguistic formulations seem to be used for function words and for those words that require a register or style label. The fact that a word is typical of a certain register, or a certain style, is considered to be part of the semantics of the word, and is consequently included in the left-hand part of the defining formula.

This technique brings to the fore a distinction that is always present, though rarely mentioned: the distinction between the unit of treatment and the unit of classification. The unit of classification in *COB* remains the graphic word, for obvious practical reasons, but the unit that is defined in the entry goes much beyond the unit of classification.

One drawback of the technique is that it requires a different definition for each different construction in which the word is used. If a definition tries to pack too much into a single sentence, it soon becomes unmanageable. Fillmore (1989: 59) compares the treatment of *rhyme* in *COB* and in *LDOCE2*:

rhyme: (with) (of words or lines of poetry) to end with the same sound, including a vowel. (*LDOCE2*)
rhyme: if one word rhymes with another, or if two words rhyme, they have a very similar sound. (*COB*)

If one disregards for the time being the fact that the *COB* definition is so vague as to be almost wrong, it is clear that *LDOCE2* has more information, and that for *COB* to have the same amount of information would have required several definitions, or a still more cumbersome formulation like 'If one word or line of poetry rhymes with another or if two words or two lines of poetry rhyme, etc.' The compilers sometimes chose that solution. Hausmann and Gorbahn (1989: 48) have found the following:

throw . . . 12: if something throws light or a shadow on a particular thing or area, it causes that thing or area to have light or a shadow on it.

It remains to be seen how the information will be processed by the dictionary user, and specifically how the user will be able to tell what is possible beyond what is indicated. One of the basic assumptions of more traditional lexicography is that the users can use the words simply by applying the rules of grammar. *COB*, to a certain extent, 'replaces' the grammar, but does not say how much room there is for variation. In the *hackles* example, the dictionary does not say if the word can be used of a wolf, a cat, a human being, etc. The dictionary does not say whether other verbs than *have . . . up* can be used with *hackles*. What about *make*, *set*, *put*, etc.? Not that traditional definitions do any better; but *COB* gives the user a sense of security that might at times be counter-productive. This is the problem of all dictionaries for encoding. It is strange to think that the more accurately descriptive a dictionary is, the more we feel the need for a 'theoretical', 'generative' dictionary indicating how far language can go.

The defining technique of *COB* is the only existing technique that does some justice to the idiomaticity of language. It is useful for decoding, since words are defined as they are really used, and also for encoding, since the user is provided with all sorts of contextual information. Much remains to be done to explore the advantages and disadvantages of the technique. Time will tell whether it has revolutionized lexicography, or whether it is just another variation on the theme of lexicographical definition.

7.2 WORD MEANING AND LEXICOGRAPHY

Research on word meaning, particularly on how many meanings a word has, and how these meanings can be differentiated and described, has been the staple question of linguistic philosophy and semantics since at least Aristotle. The questions are disarmingly simple for the non-specialist: anyone who wants to know how many meanings a word has, for example, need only turn to the dictionary, and the answers will be accepted as revealed truth rather than educated guesses. For the linguist, however, the questions turn out to be maddeningly complicated, as Lyons said with marked understatement: 'it is not as easy to say how many meanings a word has as casual reflection might suggest' (Lyons 1981: 22).

Any attempt at anchoring meaning in reference is defeated by the fact that the referent varies with each new use of a word (Kleiber 1990*a*: 139): this was expressed by Heraclitus as 'One cannot step into the same river twice'. And the different linguistic contexts in which a word is used also induce semantic variations that are difficult to classify. For example, *her* in 'Fill her up' at the service station refers to the car in general, and to the tank of the car in particular. The context is clear, but should the dictionary record 'the tank of a car' as one of the meanings of *car*? Intuitively, the answer is no, but there are many other similar cases where the limit between what seems intuitively to be a meaning and what does not is flimsy. Even proper names have contextual interpretations: *Shakespeare* in 'I have all Shakespeare on this shelf' means 'the books containing all the writings of Shakespeare', not 'the man Shakespeare' or even 'Shakespeare the playwright'. Should the dictionary record 'the books containing the writings of Shakespeare' as one of the 'meanings' of *Shakespeare*? The problem for lexicographers is that they cannot make do with just a statement about how difficult the question is; they have to come up with some sort of solution, however imperfect.

Research on word meaning has been reinvigorated recently, particularly on the delineation and description of the concept, and on polysemy and contextual interpretations. The relevance to lexicography of such research need not be emphasized. Even what psychologists envisage as 'thought categorization' translates easily in terms of word meaning: a word is the name of a category, and what is true of mental categories must be true of linguistic categories as well.

The treatment of polysemy is certainly the most difficult thing general-language lexicographers have to deal with. They are not doing very well: *COB* has a contents meaning for *carafe*, *bucket*, *glass*, and *pail*, but not for *pitcher*. No two dictionaries have exactly the same meanings for such 'simple' words as *book*, *horse*, *door*, or *red*, most of the differences arising from different interpretations of the influence of context on 'meaning' that Cruse (1986) calls 'modulation' (see also Atkins 1991: 179).

7.2.1 *Polysemy and ambiguity*

Polysemy has often been described as an unfortunate corruption of the language, pulling it away from the Humboldtian ideal of 'one form ↔ one meaning' (see Geeraerts 1985*b*). It is now clear that, as Leibniz said (Rey 1973: 129), it is a fundamental, indispensable trait that, together with modifiers (such as adjectives and adverbs), makes it possible for the limited resources of language to cope with the unlimited variations of reality. Languages could not do without it: 'Si elles [i.e. les langues] possédaient autant de formes différentes qu'il y a de notions, d'objets et de relations entre eux dans le monde extérieur à la langue, elles seraient inutilisables, à cause de la charge énorme qu'elles imposeraient à la mémoire'[15] (Hagège 1985: 126).

The traditional treatment of polysemy is descriptive: specialists of the historical development of language, as well as lexicologists and others, have described how the name of a category can be applied to another category through metaphor and metonymy. Recently, however, linguists have been trying to discover some sort of internal structure in the lexicon, and to find out the rules that govern the creation and use of word meanings.

7.2.1.1 *The detection of polysemy*

The title of Cruse (1986), *Lexical Semantics*, is representative of an area that is attracting more and more research. The book is partly about the detection of ambiguity—an important area for lexicography because an ambiguous word will normally be treated in a polysemous entry. Cruse, like many before him, devised several sorts of tests that can be used in order to establish whether a form corresponds to only one meaning or to more than one. Some of those are only sophisticated versions of what lexicographers have always tried to do intuitively. For example, the preface of the *TLF* says: 'deux sémèmes constituent des acceptions d'un même signe . . . s'il est possible de les relier par l'un des indicateurs sémantiques suivants: *en partic.*, *p. ext.*, *p. méton.*, *p. anal.*, *au fig.*'[16] But Cruse tries to go beyond that: he inserts the word in a stretch of discourse, and observes what happens. The most interesting of his tests is no doubt the zeugma test, which purports to measure the compatibility of two meanings on the syntagmatic axis. For example, it is possible to say

My cousin, who is pregnant, was born on the same day as Arthur's, who is the father

[15] 'If they [i.e. languages] had as many different forms as there are notions, objects, or relations among them in the world outside the language, they would be impossible to use, because of the enormous burden they would impose on our memories.'

[16] 'two sememes are meanings of one and the same sign . . . if they can be connected by means of one of the following semantic indicators: *partic.*, *by ext.*, *meton.*, *by anal.*, *fig.*'

because *cousin* is not marked for sex, and, from that point of view at least, has only one meaning (Cruse 1986: 62). But you can't say

*John and his driving licence expired last Thursday

because *expire* is marked for 'type of subject', and can thus be taken as having more than one meaning (Cruse 1986: 61).

However, none of the tests is totally convincing, and for some words different tests give contradictory results. There are many borderline cases, like *mouth* or *book*, for which it is impossible to say whether they are ambiguous or not. Zwicky and Sadock (1975) had come to the same conclusions.

Several researchers have been working recently on the automatization of the distinction between the different meanings of polysemous words, particularly with a view to machine translation and artificial intelligence in general (see for example Cottrell 1989; Boguraev and Briscoe 1989; etc.). From the point of view of lexicography, much of that research may appear circular, since it typically starts from a dictionary and its word-meaning divisions. Yet the comparison of how a certain number of dictionaries distinguish multiple meanings is potentially interesting.

7.2.1.2 *The explanation of polysemy*

The work of Guillaume (1964) deserves to be better known abroad, though it is not always easy to interpret, particularly because of the use of a highly idiosyncratic set of terms. Guillaume's treatment of polysemy is particularly interesting: he tries to systematize the phenomenon in terms of the functioning of the human mind in general. For him, the most 'fundamental' meaning of any polysemous word is the more abstract, and the meaning shifts towards the concrete according to a limited number of possible patterns. Picoche (1986), using Guillaume's ideas, describes the different meanings of *hôtel*, *bureau*, etc.

7.2.1.3 *The elimination of polysemy*

Some semanticists, since at least the early sixties, have been arguing that many of the 'meanings' in dictionaries are only contextual applications, and that many more words are monosemous than has been traditionally thought. According to them, a word like *good*, for example, which is usually presented as highly polysemous, can be said to have only one meaning (Hines 1978; Seppänen 1984).

It is a well-known fact that polysemy does not correspond to extension (Ducrot and Todorov 1972: 303–4): a word can be 'general', it can refer to many different concepts, and still be sufficiently unified in meaning to be considered monosemous. A word like *plant*, for example, has a large extension but is fairly well defined, at least in its vegetal sense: 'in ordinary English the word *plant* is not even polysemous, as has sometimes been suggested (cf Casson 1981: 78). Linguistic evidence shows that in ordinary English it has only one meaning' (Wierzbicka 1985: 155). Verbs like *take*, *give*, *come*, *go*, *break*, and *hit*, and even words like *thing*, or the verb *be* (Catford 1983), can be said to have one 'general' meaning. Words like *expire*, *recognize*, and *realize* (Bäcklund 1981: 410), *well* (Hines 1978), *break*, *cut*, *tear* (Ruhl 1980), which are traditionally presented as polysemous, 'are monosemic, and are judged as polysemic by dictionaries and linguists because their essential, general meanings are confused with contextual, inferential meanings' (Ruhl 1979: 93).

Most lexicographers—not only in English-language dictionaries[17]—have tended to be 'splitters' rather than 'lumpers' (Moon 1987: 177; Zgusta 1971: 274–5), perhaps because of a desire to be exhaustive, or because of an excessive attention to the rule of the substitutability of the definition (see above, 6.2.13). Johnson had five pages and 88 sections for *set*. Murray, the 'arch-splitter', had 341 different meanings for *take* in the *OED* (Moon 1987: 177). Most dictionaries distinguish *door* 'the space' from *door* 'the thing that closes up that space' (see Schelbert 1988: 65)—a distinction never applied to *window*—and sometimes even *door* 'the door of a public building'. *CED* sees two meanings for *child*:

1.a. a boy or girl between birth and puberty. b. . . . 2. a baby or infant

It also has a 'special' meaning for each noun when it is used as a modifier (here 1.b.). We have seen that *LDOCE1* assigned two meanings to the verb *walk*: one for creatures with two legs and another one for creatures with four legs or more (see above, 2.3.2.1). *COD7* has a *horse* (sub-)meaning 'representation of horse'. 'An expression like *sing the baby to sleep* is used to generate a separate "meaning" of *sing* along the lines of "bring someone into the specified state by singing" (eg W9 . . .)' (Rundell 1988: 132).[18] As

[17] Rey-Debove (1971: 255–6) says the same about French dictionaries.
[18] W9 = *NCD9*.

for American dictionaries, their tendency to distinguish meanings that are only contextually bound uses—what Saporta (1961: 283) calls 'the extreme contextualist position'—is even more marked.

Moon (1987: 173) uses the label *quasi-monosemous* for words like *top* or *mouth* that are traditionally treated as polysemous in dictionaries but have a somewhat unified meaning. The word *mouth* can alternatively designate:

(1) the opening: He took the cigarette out of his mouth
(2) the lips: She had a wide and smiling mouth
(3) the cavity: He put the meat into his mouth (Moon 1987: 174)

Yet there is no reason to consider that those are different meanings, since the right interpretation is clearly indicated by the context.

The potential applications to dictionaries of such research are portentous. If there is indeed some sort of semantic unity in the meanings or interpretations of words, this unity should be indicated by the dictionary. This could be done by giving a broad definition whenever possible, which could be followed by examples for the different applications, or sub-definitions. The idea of indicating general meanings was discussed by many grammarians in the eighteenth century (see the entry for *sens* in the French *Encyclopédie*), and implemented in some dictionaries, for example in Passow's Greek–English dictionary (1831), in Richardson's dictionary (1836–7), in Grimm's *Deutsches Wörterbuch* (1854), and to some extent in the *OED*, etc. (see Zgusta 1989*c*). Most lexicographers have regarded the solution as less than satisfactory. The status of the general definition is not clear: is it the 'central' definition of the basic meaning from which all the others can be derived (as in the case of *back*; see above, 7.1.1.4), or is it only a bundle of semantic features that is shared by all the meanings but does not correspond to any word in particular? Also, there are cases where there are no features common to all the meanings, as in 'linear' polysemy where meaning B is connected to meaning A and meaning C is connected to B but not to A—the 'family resemblances' of Wittgenstein (1953: 31–2) (at least if I understand them correctly). The common features could become so vague as to be of no practical utility (Kleiber 1988: 4–5). Take the simple example of *empress*. *COB* says:

. . . a woman who rules an empire; also used to refer to the wife of an emperor

How can one give a broad definition that would encompass those two meanings? Should one say something like 'woman *who is connected* to an emperor'?

On the whole, the 'monosemy movement' has provided an interesting discussion of the distinctions between meanings and contextual applications. There may already be a tendency in modern dictionaries to avoid 'splitting up' meanings as much as before: for example, *COD8* has eliminated the meaning of *horse* 'representation of horse'. But the decision on how many meanings a word has and what those meanings are is still done very much intuitively.

This is a very difficult area, where it would be foolish to expect a revolution in lexicographical practice. One element that has to be taken into consideration is the fact that the dictionary treatment of a word is not necessarily an attempt at describing what the word is 'really' like, but an explanation of the meaning for a user. A word might be considered monosemous or quasi-monosemous by semanticists and yet be split up into different meanings in the dictionary on the grounds that this is more useful for whoever will consult the dictionary.

7.2.1.4 *The prediction of polysemy*

Nunberg (1978), Norrick (1981), Ross (1981), and many others have raised the question of the regularity of semantic relationships between the different meanings of a polysemous word. Nunberg came to the conclusion that any application of a word to a new category is predictable by very general rules, given the characteristics of the word or of the original category. This predictability of polysemous developments is an extremely interesting idea for lexicography, because it could provide templates to be used by lexicographers for the compilation of their polysemous entries. Nunberg argues that a lexicon of the language (not a dictionary) can be reduced by the omission of the senses that are predictable.

Lehrer (1990) uses an extended definition of polysemy, 'to refer to all cases where there is phonological and orthographic identity of forms wherever there is a semantic relationship' (Lehrer 1990: 208); in other words, for her, polysemy crosses the traditional part-of-speech boundaries. After having put Nunberg's contention to the test with several different categories of words (nouns, adjectives, prepositions, verbs), she comes to the conclusion that there are very few rules that have no exceptions; one example is 'the rule that states that a representation of a thing can be called by the same term as the thing depicted' (Lehrer 1990: 238). Lehrer says that polysemous senses and even changes of part of speech for a given form can be explained, so to speak *a posteriori*, but can hardly be predicted.

This is similar to the conclusion reached by G. Lakoff (1987). Lakoff was one of the early converts to prototype theory (see Rosch 1973 and following years), but he soon realized that polysemy was not easily accounted for in prototype theory. Roughly speaking, he starts from the observation that lexical categories go much beyond what is normally thought of as categories of referents in the real world. For example, some Australian aborigines use the same word (*bayi*) to refer to such an unlikely group as: 'Men, kangaroos, possums, bats, most snakes, most fishes, some birds, most insects, the moon, storms, rainbows, boomerangs, some spears, etc.' (G. Lakoff 1987: 92). Similarly, Casson (1981: 182) had mentioned Kannada, where the word *amma* means mother, woman, goddess, smallpox, and is additionally used as a cry for help. Such groupings call for an explanation. Lakoff argues that polysemy is neither arbitrary nor predictable, but 'motivated': it cannot be predicted, but it is not totally arbitrary either. Every new meaning can be explained by a connection to at least one of the others that preceded it, through metaphor or metonymy.

> Deux attitudes sont interdites: opter pour l'arbitraire ou opter pour la prédictibilité totale. G. Lakoff (1986, p. 28) propose la voie de la *motivation*. Les différents emplois ou sous-catégories sont motivés, dans le sens où ils peuvent être "expliqués". Le passage de *veau*-'animal' à *veau*-'viande' est motivé par la relation de métonymie qui unit les deux. S'il s'agissait de prédictibilité absolue, tous les animaux devraient donner lieu à une telle métonymie, ce qui n'est pas le cas. S'il s'agissait simplement d'une convention arbitraire, il n'y aurait pas de lien à restituer. La polysémie est donc fondamentalement envisagée comme un phénomène de convention motivée.[19] (Kleiber 1988: 53)

[19] 'Two attitudes are equally untenable: choosing arbitrariness, and choosing total predictability. G. Lakoff (1986: 28) proposes the concept of *motivation*. Different uses and sub-uses are motivated in the sense that they can be "explained". The shift from *veau* (the animal) to *veau* (the meat) is motivated by the relation of metonymy that links the two. If there were total predictability, all animals would give rise to such metonymies, which is not the case. If it were only an arbitrary convention, there would be no link between the two. Thus, polysemy is fundamentally seen as a phenomenon of motivated convention.'

Kleiber's example is probably a bad one. If all other animals do not produce the same metonymic shift as *veau*, it is purely for extralinguistic reasons, because there are animals that we do not eat; this has nothing to do with the language as such. If we started eating chimpanzees or caterpillars no doubt the same metonymy from the name of the animal to the name of its meat would apply.[20] Yet the point remains: there is a certain amount of regularity in polysemy. This is because, says Lakoff, the mind works with a relatively small number of basic building blocks, like space and the human body ('ICMs', or idealized cognitive models), and all the adventures of polysemy can be eventually reduced to man's interaction with his environment.

Lakoff's ideas have received little attention in metalexicography so far. They argue for a more 'reasoned' presentation of polysemy, with more explicit links between the different meanings than has been done so far. A more systematic use of anaphora to indicate the connections between the different parts of an entry might be helpful (Marello 1988). The benefits for the dictionary as an instrument for teaching the language would be immense.

Some semanticists have recently taken up ideas expressed in the seventies by a few 'dissident' grammarians (McCawley, Fillmore), and in Apresjan's seminal 1973 paper on 'Regular polysemy'. They have been trying to draw up lists of regular 'meaning shifts' that, in dictionaries, are sometimes treated as cases of polysemy and sometimes totally ignored because they are too obvious. This includes changes in form or in part of speech. For example, there is a rule in English that can be formulated as 'Material → Adjective', according to which the noun used for a material gives rise to an adjective formed by the noun plus an *-en* suffix: *gold* → *golden*, *wood* → *wooden*, etc. Atkins has drawn up a list of about 130 such shifts, under the form of rules that suffer some exceptions (Ostler and Atkins 1991).

It is not clear whether those rules are part of the lexicon or whether they are extralinguistic knowledge brought to bear on the context by the language user. Ostler and Atkins argue that since there are different rules in different languages, and even in different dialects of the same language, the rules must be part of the description of the lexicon.

[20] Unless some other phenomenon prevents the application of the rule, like the existence of the words *pork*, *beef*, *veal*, and *mutton* in English, or the use of special words for some kinds of fur (euphemisms; one does not wear 'rat'), or fish used as food.

Meaning shifts offer an interesting insight into lexical semantics, and bear directly upon lexicography. Atkins's list was prepared deliberately to streamline the work of dictionary compilers. A better knowledge of the patterns of meaning shifts makes the preparation stage faster and more consistent, particularly if the templates can be fed into a computer. It also makes it possible to arrange the meanings in a more meaningful way in the entry, and to make the dictionary better on the principle that the more faithfully a dictionary reflects the organization of the mental lexicon the better a chance it has of being understandable and exploitable by the users.

One question still must be answered: should all regularities, whether they be meanings or just interpretations, be omitted from the dictionary on the basis that the user can predict them? The question is the same as that of the inclusion of derivatives (see above, 6.2.7) or nominal compounds (Levi 1983). Some regularities are traditionally omitted: for example, no dictionary records the sense of direction (for a train) that all city names can take in phrases like 'the London train'; others tend to be included, like the verb that all names of dances produce (*waltz* → *to waltz*) (Ostler and Atkins 1991). For others still, practice varies. Ilson (1990*a*) observes that the verbal regularities (the transitive use of an intransitive verb, for example, as in 'These apples bake well') tend to be included as long as they imply a change in syntactic pattern, whereas shifts of meaning in nouns are very inconsistently treated.

On the one hand, it is arguable, in a 'Bloomfieldian' lexicography, that the dictionary should indicate only what is specific to each word, as opposed to what applies to several and is best regarded as belonging to the grammar. If for practical reasons the dictionary does record such regularities, it should record them all, or it will be misleading, particularly for encoding. But 'the complete representation of all such regularities would swell real dictionaries to an unmanageable size, with material much of which would be of doubtful use' (Ilson 1990*a*: 130). And among the regularities, not all are actually used, and some are more frequent than others. The question does not have a clear answer, because it brings us back to a more basic question: what is the dictionary, after all? A storehouse of the language as it is actually used? A thesaurus of the potentialities of the language, or of the idiosyncrasies of words? An instrument for encoding, or for decoding?

7.2.2 *Prototype theory*

As we have seen (6.1.2.1), prototype theory has not had much impact yet on lexicographical practice. Lexicographers received it as a mixed blessing when it appeared. They were comforted, at first, by the observation that in prototype theory it was possible to remain vague in the definition of a word, since categories were said to be fuzzy. This removed some of their feeling of guilt at writing definitions that they never found good enough. Here was justification, after all, for that vagueness in dictionary definitions that lexicographers had never known what to do with (Kleiber 1990*a*: 109). But the excessive interpretations of prototype theory, that categories have no clear boundaries, soon had to be corrected.

> Cette flexibilité ne s'exerce toutefois pas librement, car s'il en allait ainsi on pourrait catégoriser un nouvel élément n'importe comment, et, chose plus grave, une telle liberté signifierait en fait la ruine de toute catégorisation possible: une chaise ne se distinguerait plus d'un fauteuil, puisque, dans cette hypothèse, l'on pourrait appeler l'un aussi bien que l'autre *chaise* ou *fauteuil*, ou *pouf*, ou encore *vélo*.[21] (Kleiber 1988: 23)

On the other hand, prototype theory—at least in its earlier versions—argued that meaning was not perceived in features but as wholes, that it was an illustration of Gestalt theory. Such a vision of meaning would pose a serious threat to definition in the traditional lexicographical sense: if the whole is simpler than its parts, then it might well be useless to describe the meaning of a word in a paraphrase. The latest versions of prototype theory are less clear on that point, and semanticists now argue that prototype theory is not even incompatible with a compositional view of meaning (Wierzbicka 1985: 18; Kleiber 1990*a*). Better still, the idea that features can no longer be separated neatly into linguistic on the one hand and encyclopedic on the other as they used to be, but that they rather constitute a cline, some features being more central than others, reinforces the traditional practice of lexicography, which has always tended to mix the two kinds of features. The writers of definitions need no longer attempt to produce merely contrastive definitions, as the structuralists wanted them to, but can feel free to produce

[21] 'However, this flexibility is not totally free, because, if it were, a new element could be characterized in all sorts of ways and—more seriously—such freedom would be the end of all categorization: a *chaise* would not be different from a *fauteuil* since, in that case, either could be called *chaise* or *fauteuil*, as well as *pouf* or even *vélo*.'

'positive' ones, as they have always wanted to. 'Il ne s'agit plus seulement de dire ce qui distingue un chien d'un chat, mais de décrire positivement ce qu'est un chien et ce qu'est un chat'[22] (Kleiber 1990*a*: 74). This is a fundamental evolution, not yet implemented in commercial lexicography, from the Leibnizian—if not Aristotelian—ideal of what a good dictionary definition should be like.

7.2.3 *The limits of the linguistic concept*

Wierzbicka (1985) starts from Labov's (1973) discussion of the meaning of *cup*. She argues that the difference between *cup* and *mug* lies in the function of the object, that is to say in the nature of human interaction with the category. She accepts the compositionality of meaning, and she says that the use of introspection makes it possible to reach good descriptions of the concepts associated with words, in more or less detail, from the concept minima to the concept maxima. As in the traditional approaches to word meaning she distinguishes two sorts of features: the linguistic (she calls them 'conceptual') and the encyclopedic; but as in prototype theory she argues that definitions can, and sometimes should, contain features that are less central than others. Her definitions distinguish between what is 'essential' and what is 'typical'. They are much longer than ordinary dictionary definitions, partly because they avoid circularity through the use of a set of primitives. For example, her definition for *cup* runs over two pages:

<u>CUPS</u>
A KIND OF THING THAT PEOPLE MAKE
IMAGINING THINGS OF THIS KIND PEOPLE WOULD SAY
THESE THINGS ABOUT THEM:

they are made for people to use repeatedly for drinking hot liquids from such as tea or coffee <u>PURPOSE</u>
one person from one thing of this kind
being able to put them down on something else . . . (Wierzbicka 1985: 33–4)

Wierzbicka's definitions aim at describing the concept that most language users 'have in their minds' when they think of the word. For her, the concept that corresponds to a word is what each

[22] 'The aim is not so much to say what distinguishes a dog from a cat, but positively to describe what a dog is and what a cat is.'

language user assumes that the other members of the same linguistic community have in their minds about the same concept. This is a far cry from views like Putnam's (1975), for whom the 'true' meaning of a word is held only by the specialist. Of course, Wierzbicka's definitions are much too long and complex to be used in commercial lexicography, but they provide a basis on which dictionary definitions might be revised and corrected.

Conclusion

A BRIEF review of some of the recent research in linguistics that could be relevant to lexicography could not hope to be exhaustive. Surely the ideas outlined above will be of varying usefulness in future lexicography. But dictionaries will be improved, and the improvements will arise from research by linguists of all kinds, semanticists, lexicologists, syntacticians, psycholinguists, or sociolinguists. The challenge facing lexicographers is clear: dictionaries will have to evolve, at the same time improving the quality of their description of language as it is used and maintaining a reasonable accessibility of the information that they provide, refining their evaluation of the dictionary user's needs and skills, and at the same time refusing to be guided exclusively by the desire to be accessible.

Bibliography

Ahlswede, T., and Evens, M. (1988), 'Generating a relational lexicon from a machine-readable dictionary', *International Journal of Lexicography* 1/3: 214–37.

Aitchison, J., and Gilchrist, A. (1972), *Thesaurus Construction: A Practical Manual* (London: ASLIB).

Aitken, A. J. (1987), 'The period dictionaries', in Burchfield (ed.), 94–116.

Algeo, J. (1987), 'A dictionary of briticisms', *Dictionaries* 6: 164–78.

—— (1989*a*), 'Dictionaries as seen by the educated public in Great Britain and the USA', in Hausmann *et al.* (edd.), 28–34.

—— (1989*b*), 'The image of the dictionary in the mass media: USA', in Hausmann *et al.* (edd.), 34–7.

—— (1990*a*), review of John Ayto, *The Longman Register of New Words*, in *International Journal of Lexicography* 3/3: 211–18.

—— (1990*b*), 'American lexicography', in Hausmann *et al.* (edd.), 1987–2009.

Allen, R. E. (1986), 'A concise history of the COD', in Hartmann (ed.), 1–11.

Allsopp, R. (1987), '"Like if say you see a jumbie or a duppy": problems of definitional differentiae in a complex of anglophone cultures', in Bailey (ed.), 75–98.

Aman, R. (1985), 'Offensive words in dictionaries', *Maledicta* 8: 123–53.

Amsler, R. A. (1980), 'The structure of the Merriam-Webster Pocket Dictionary' (Ph.D. Thesis; Austin: The University of Texas).

Anglin, J. M. (1970), *The Growth of Word Meaning* (Cambridge, Mass.: MIT Press).

Antal, L. (1963), 'A new type of dictionary', *Linguistics* 1: 75–84.

Apresjan, J. D. (1973), 'Regular polysemy', *Linguistics* 124: 5–39.

—— Mel'čuk, I. A., and Žolkovskij, A. K. (1969), 'Semantics and lexicography: towards a new type of unilingual dictionary', in F. Kiefer (ed.), *Studies in Syntax and Semantics* (Dordrecht: Reidel), 1–33.

Ard, J. (1982), 'The use of bilingual dictionaries by ESL students while writing', *ITL Review of Applied Linguistics* 58: 1–27.

Aresca, N. (1989), 'Il dizionario monolingue per studenti di inglese (o *Learner's Dictionary*): che informazioni contiene e come sfruttarle', in Prat Zagrebelsky (ed.), 93–154.

Arnaud, P. J. L., and Béjoint, H. (edd.) (1991), *Vocabulary and Applied Linguistics* (London: Longman).

Atkins, B. T. (1985), 'Monolingual and bilingual learners' dictionaries: a comparison', in Ilson (ed.), 15–24.

—— (1987), 'Semantic ID tags: corpus evidence for dictionary senses', in *The Uses of Large Text Databases* (Proceedings of the Second Annual Conference of the UW Centre for the New OED, Waterloo, Canada).

—— (1991), 'Building a lexicon: the contribution of lexicography', *International Journal of Lexicography* 4/3: 167–204.

—— and Knowles, F. E. (1990), 'Interim report on the EURALEX AILA research project into dictionary use', in Magay and Zigany (edd.), 381–92.

—— Lewis, H., Summers, D., and Whitcut, J. (1987), 'A research project into the use of learners' dictionaries', in Cowie (ed.), 29–43.

—— Kegl, J., and Lèvin, B. (1988), 'Anatomy of a verb entry: from linguistic theory to lexicographic practice', *International Journal of Lexicography* 1/2: 84–126.

Auroux, S. (1990), 'La Définition et la théorie des idées', in Centre d'Etudes du Lexique, 30–9.

Ayto, J. R. (1983), 'On specifying meaning: semantic analysis and dictionary definitions', in Hartmann (ed.), 89–98.

—— (1986), 'Of or pertaining to dictionaries', *English Today* 6: 39–40.

—— (1988), 'Fig. leaves. Metaphor in dictionaries', in Snell-Hornby (ed.), 49–54.

Bäcklund, U. (1981), 'Pregnant and specific objects: a collocational investigation of *Recognize* and *Realize*', in J. E. Copeland and P. W. Davis (edd.), *The Seventh LACUS Forum* (Columbia, SC: Hornbeam Press), 399–411.

Bailey, R. W. (ed.), (1987) *Dictionaries of English: Prospects for the Record of our Language* (Ann Arbor: The University of Michigan Press).

Bareggi, C. (1989), 'Gli studenti e il dizionario: un'inchiesta presso gli studenti di inglese del Corso di Laurea in Lingue e Letterature Straniere della Facoltà di Lettere di Torino', in Prat Zagrebelsky (ed.), 155–90.

Barnhart, C. L. (1949), 'Contributions of Dr. Thorndike to lexicography', *Teachers College Record* 51/1: 35–42.

—— (1962/1975), 'Problems in editing commercial monolingual dictionaries', in Householder and Saporta (edd.), 161–81.

—— (1969), 'General dictionaries', *American Speech*, Fall 1969, 173–8.

Barnhart, R., and Barnhart, C. (1990), 'The dictionary of neologisms', in Hausmann *et al.* (edd.), 1159–66.

Battenburg, J. D. (1989), 'A study of English monolingual learner's dictionaries and their users' (Ph.D. Dissertation, Purdue University).

—— (1991), *English Monolingual Learners' Dictionaries: A User-Oriented Study* (Tübingen: Niemeyer).

Baxter, J. (1980), 'The dictionary and vocabulary behavior: a single word or a handful?', *TESOL Quarterly* 14/3: 325–36.

Beaujot, J. P. (1989), 'Dictionnaire et idéologie', in Hausmann *et al.* (edd.), 79–88.

Béjoint, H. (1980), 'La Représentation de l'étranger dans le lexique américain', *Revue française d'études américaines* 9: 107–16.

—— (1981*a*), 'The foreign student's use of monolingual English dictionaries: a study of language needs and reference skills', *Applied Linguistics* 2/3: 207–22.

—— (1981*b*), 'Les Américanismes dans les dictionnaires britanniques récents', *Trema* 7: 19–34.

—— (1981*c*), 'Les Marques d'usage dans les dictionnaires de langue anglaise', *Trema* 7: 69–74.

—— (1985), review of *Le Robert méthodique*, in *Dictionaries* 6: 261–8.

—— (1988), 'Scientific and technical words in general dictionaries', *International Journal of Lexicography* 1/4: 354–68.

—— (1989*a*), '"Codedness" and lexicography', in G. C. James (ed.), *Lexicographers and their Works* (Exeter: University of Exeter), 1–4.

—— (1989*b*), 'The teaching of dictionary use', in Hausmann *et al.* (edd.), 208–15.

Benbow, T., Carrington, P., Johanessen, G., Tompa, F., and Weiner, E. (1990), 'Report on the New Oxford English Dictionary User Survey', *International Journal of Lexicography* 3/3: 155–203.

Benson, M. (1989), 'The structure of the collocational dictionary', *International Journal of Lexicography* 2/1: 1–14.

—— (1990), 'Collocations and general-purpose dictionaries', *International Journal of Lexicography* 3/1: 23–34.

Bensoussan, M., Sim, D., and Weiss, R. (1981), 'The effect of dictionary usage on EFL test performance compared with student and teacher attitudes and expectations', in B. Sigurd and J. Svartvik (edd.), *AILA 81, Proceedings I* (Lund University). Also in *Reading in a Foreign Language* (1984), 2/2: 262–76.

Besterman, T. (1943), 'On a bibliography of dictionaries', *Proceedings of the British Society for International Bibliography* 4: 63–73.

Black, A. (1985), 'The effects on comprehension and memory of providing different types of defining information for new vocabulary' (Cambridge: MRC Applied Psychology Unit).

Bloomfield, L. (1933), *Language* (New York: Holt, Rinehart & Winston).

Bogaards, P. (1988), 'A propos de l'usage du dictionnaire de langue étrangère', *Cahiers de lexicologie* 52: 131–52.

—— (1990), 'Où cherche-t-on dans le dictionnaire?', *International Journal of Lexicography* 3/2: 79–102.

Boguraev, B., and Briscoe, T. (edd.) (1989), *Computational Lexicography for Natural Language Processing* (London: Longman).

Boisson, C. (1990), 'La Place de l'image mentale en sémantique', *RANAM* 23: 1–12.

—— Kirtchuk, P., and Béjoint, H. (1991), 'Aux origines de la lexicographie: les premiers dictionnaires monolingues et bilingues', *International Journal of Lexicography* 4/4: 261–315.

Bolinger, D. (1965), 'The atomization of meaning', *Language* 41: 555–73.

—— (1973), 'Getting the *Words* in', in McDavid and Duckert (edd.), 8–13.

—— (1976), 'Meaning and memory', *Forum Linguisticum* 1/1: 1–14.

—— (1980), *Language, the Loaded Weapon: The Use and Abuse of Language Today* (London: Longman).

Boulanger, J.-C. (1986), *Aspects de l'interdiction dans la lexicographie française contemporaine* (Tübingen: Niemeyer).

Bray, L. (1986), *César-Pierre Richelet (*1626–1698*) Biographie et œuvre lexicographique* (Tübingen: Niemeyer).

Bujas, Z. (1975), 'Testing the performance of a bilingual dictionary on topical current texts', *Studia Romanica et Anglica Zagrabiensia* 39: 193–204.

Burchfield, R. W. (1972), 'Four-letter words and the Oxford English Dictionary', *Times Literary Supplement*, 13 Oct. 1972, p. 1233. Also in Scholler and Reidy (edd.) (1973), 84–9.

—— (1973), 'The treatment of controversial vocabulary in the *Oxford English Dictionary*', *Transactions of the Philological Society*, 1973, 1–28.

—— (1980), 'Dictionaries and ethnic sensibilities', in L. Michaels and C. Ricks (edd.), *The State of the Language* (Berkeley: University of California Press), 15–23.

—— (1986), 'The Oxford English Dictionary', in Ilson (ed.), 17–27.

—— (1987*a*), 'The *Supplement to the Oxford English Dictionary*: the end of the alphabet', in Bailey (ed.), 11–21.

—— (1987*b*), *Studies in Lexicography* (Oxford: The Clarendon Press).

Burkett, E. M. (1979), *American Dictionaries of the English Language before 1861* (Metuchen, NJ: Scarecrow Press).

Burnett, L. S. (1988), 'Making it short: the Shorter Oxford English Dictionary', in Snell-Hornby (ed.), 229–33.

—— (1989), 'A number of problems for the *New Shorter Oxford English Dictionary*', *Dictionaries* 11: 139–47.

Burrill, M. F., and Bonsack, E., Jr. (1962/1975), 'Use and preparation of specialized glossaries', in Householder and Saporta (edd.), 183–200.

Buzon, C. (1979), 'Dictionnaire, langue, discours, idéologie', *Langue française* 43: 27–44.

—— Descamps, J.-L., and Lamizet, B. (1980), 'Un exercice dictionnairique (I): les données du problème', *Cahiers de lexicologie* 36: 111–18.

Cahiers de linguistique, d'orientalisme et de slavistique, 11. *La Structure du mot*, juillet 1978, Université de Provence.

Calzolari, N. (1977), 'An empirical approach to circularity in dictionary definitions', *Cahiers de lexicologie* 31/2: 118–28.

Carey, S. (1978), 'The child as a word learner', in M. Halle, J. Bresnan, and G. A. Miller (edd.), *Linguistic Theory and Psychological Reality* (Cambridge, Mass.: MIT Press), 264–93.

Carter, R. A. (1989), review of *COBUILD Dictionary of the English Language*, *International Journal of Lexicography* 2/1: 30–43.

—— and McCarthy, M. (edd.) (1988), *Vocabulary and Language Teaching* (London: Longman).

Cassidy, F. G. (1987*a*), 'The *Dictionary of American Regional English* as a resource for language study', in Burchfield (ed.), 117–35.

—— (1987*b*), 'The *Oxford English Dictionary* and the *Dictionary of American Regional English*: some differences of practice', in Bailey (ed.), 22–9.

Casson, R. W. (1981), *Language, Culture and Cognition: Anthropological Perspectives* (New York: Macmillan).

Catford, J. C. (1983), 'Insects are free: reflections on meaning in linguistics', *Language Learning* 33/5: 13–32.

Centre d'Etudes du Lexique (1990), *La Définition* (Paris: Larousse).

Channell, J. (1990), 'Vocabulary acquisition and the mental lexicon', in Tomaszczyk and Lewandowska-Tomaszczyk (edd.), 21–30.

Clarke, D. D., and Nerlich, B. (1991), 'Word-waves: a computational model of lexical semantic change', *Language and Communication* 11/3: 227–38.

Collignon, L., and Glatigny, M. (1978), *Les Dictionnaires—initiation à la lexicographie* (Paris: Cedic).

Collison, R. L. (1971), *Dictionaries of English and Foreign Languages: A Bibliographical Guide to both General and Technical Dictionaries with Explanatory Notes and References*, 2nd edn. (New York: Hafner Publishing Co.).

—— (1982), *A History of Foreign-Language Dictionaries* (London: André Deutsch).

Congleton, J. E., Gates, J. E., and Hobar, D. (edd.) (1979), *Papers on Lexicography* (Indiana State University: The Dictionary Society of North America).

Connor Ferris, D. (1990), 'An example of interaction between syntax and semantics', in Tomaszczyk and Lewandowska-Tomaszczyk (edd.), 113–21.

Cook, D. (1959), 'A point of lexicographical method', *American Speech* 34: 20–5.

Cop, M. (1989), 'Linguistic and encyclopedic information not included in the dictionary articles', in Hausmann *et al.* (edd.), 761–7.

Corbin, D., and Corbin, P. (1989), 'Sélection et description des dérivés et composés dans le dictionnaire monolingue', in Hausmann *et al.* (edd.), 937–46.

Corneri, A. (1990), 'Il *Dictionnaire* di P. Richelet (1680): un secolo e un autore', in Deslex (ed.), 13–52.

Cottrell, G. W. (1989), *A Connectionist Approach to Word-Sense Disambiguation* (London: Pitman).

Cowie, A. P. (1978), 'The place of illustrative material and collocations in the design of a learner's dictionary', in Strevens (ed.), 127–39.

—— (1979), 'The treatment of polysemy in the design of a learner's dictionary', in Hartmann (ed.), 82–8.

—— (1981), 'The treatment of collocations and idioms in learners' dictionaries', *Applied Linguistics* 2/3: 223–35.

—— (1983), 'The pedagogical/learner's dictionary: English dictionaries for the foreign learner', in Hartmann (ed.), 135–44.

—— (ed.) (1987), *The Dictionary and the Language Learner* (Tübingen: Niemeyer).

—— (1988), 'Stable and creative aspects of vocabulary use', in Carter and McCarthy (edd.), 126–39.

Cruse, D. A. (1986), *Lexical Semantics* (Cambridge: Cambridge University Press).

Crystal, D. (1985), *A Dictionary of Linguistics and Phonetics*, 2nd edn. (London: André Deutsch). First edn. 1980.

—— (1986), 'The ideal dictionary, lexicographer and user', in Ilson (ed.), 72–81.

—— (1988), *The English Language* (Harmondsworth: Penguin Books).

D'Alembert, J. Le Rond (1763), *Discours préliminaire de l'Encyclopédie*, 1965 edn. (Paris: Gonthier).

Delbridge, A. (1983), 'On national variants of the English dictionary: the English dictionary in different parts of the world', in Hartmann (ed.), 23–40.

Descamps, J.-L., and Vaunaize, R. (1983), 'Le Dictionnaire au jour le jour en milieu adulte: une pré-enquête', *Etudes de linguistique appliquée* 49: 89–109.

Deslex, M. G. (ed.) (1990), *Società allo specchio: Ideologie nei dizionari francesi* (Turin: Tirrenia Stampatori).

Diab, T. (1990), *Pedagogical Lexicography* (Tübingen: Niemeyer).

Di Sciullo, A.-M., and Williams, E. S. (1987), *On the Definition of Word* (Cambridge, Mass.: MIT Press).

Dixon, A. W. (1967), 'Dr. Johnson and Emily Post', in Gove (ed.), 19–21.

Dolezal, F. (1986), 'How abstract is the English dictionary?' in Hartmann (ed.), 47–55.

Drysdale, P. D. (1979), 'Aspects of Canadian lexicography', in Congleton *et al.* (edd.), 37–45.

Dubois, J. (1962), 'Recherches lexicographiques: esquisse d'un dictionnaire structural', *Etudes de linguistique appliquée* 1: 43–8.

—— (1981), 'Models of the dictionary: evolution in dictionary design', *Applied Linguistics* 2/3: 236–49.

—— and Dubois, C. (1971), *Introduction à la lexicographie: Le Dictionnaire* (Paris: Larousse).

Ducháček, O. (1959), 'Sur le problème de la structure du lexique et de son évolution', *Cahiers de lexicologie* 1: 89–98.

Ducrot, O., and Todorov, T. (1972), *Dictionnaire encyclopédique des sciences du langage* (Paris: Editions du Seuil).

Dykema, K. W. (1967), 'Cultural lag and reviewers of *Webster iii*', in Gove (ed.), 43–50.

Ellegård, A. (1978), 'On dictionaries for language learners', *Moderna Språk* 72/3: 225–42.

Fay, D. A., and Cutler, A. (1975), 'You have a dictionary in your head, not a thesaurus', *Texas Linguistic Forum* 1: 27–40.

Feldman, J. (1981), *La Sexualité du Petit Larousse ou Le Jeu du dictionnaire* (Paris: Editions Tierce).

Fernando, C., and Flavell, R. (1981), *On Idiom: Critical Views and Perspectives* (Exeter: University of Exeter).

Fillmore, C. J. (1969), 'Types of lexical information', in F. Kiefer (ed.), *Studies in Syntax and Semantics* (Dordrecht: Reidel), 109–37.

—— (1989), review of *COBUILD Dictionary of the English Language*, in *International Journal of Lexicography* 2/1: 57–83.

Finkenstaedt, T., and Wolff, D. (1973), *Ordered Profusion: Studies in Dictionaries and the English Lexicon* (Heidelberg: Carl Winter, Universitätsverlag).

Firth, J. R. (1957), *Papers in Linguistics 1934–1951* (Oxford: Oxford University Press).

Flaherty, M. C. (1923), *How to Use the Dictionary* (New York: Ronald Press).

Fodor, J. A. (1983), *The Modularity of Mind* (Cambridge, Mass.: MIT Press).

Follett, W. (1962), 'Sabotage in Springfield: Webster's third edition', *The Atlantic* 209: 73–7. Also in Sledd and Ebbitt (edd.) (1962), 111–19.

Forgue, G. J. (1979), 'Neologisms in American English since 1945: indicators of cultural change?', in Hartmann (ed.), 127–33.

—— (1981), 'Postwar americanisms and cultural change', *Trema* 7: 89–97.

Fraser, B. (1970), 'Idioms within a transformational grammar', *Foundations of Language* 6/1: 22–42.

Frawley, W. (1981), 'In defence of the dictionary: a response to Haiman', *Lingua* 55/1: 53–61.

—— (1988), 'New forms of specialized dictionaries', *International Journal of Lexicography* 1/3: 189–213.

—— and Steiner, R. (edd.) (1986), *Advances in Lexicography*, 2 vols. (Edmonton, Alberta: Boreal).

Friend, J. H. (1967), *The Development of American Lexicography 1798–1864* (The Hague: Mouton).

Gak, V. G. (1970), 'La Langue et le discours dans un dictionnaire bilingue', *Langages* 19: 103–15.

Galisson, R. (1983), 'Image et usage du dictionnaire chez les étudiants (en langue) de niveau avancé', *Etudes de linguistique appliquée* 49: 5–88.

—— (1987), 'De la lexicographie de dépannage à la lexicographie d'apprentissage: pour une politique de rénovation des dictionnaires monolingues de FLE à l'école', *Cahiers de lexicologie* 51/2: 95–118.

Gates, J. E. (1988), 'The treatment of multiword lexemes in some current dictionaries of English', in Snell-Hornby (ed.), 99–106.

Geeraerts, D. (1984), 'Dictionary classification and the foundations of lexicography', *ITL Review of Applied Linguistics* 63: 37–63.

—— (1985*a*), 'Les Données stéréotypiques, prototypiques et encyclopédiques dans le dictionnaire', *Cahiers de lexicologie* 46: 27–43.

—— (1985*b*), 'Polysemization and Humboldt's principle', *Cahiers de l'Institut de Linguistique de Louvain* 11/3–4: 29–50.

—— (1987), 'Types of semantic information in dictionaries', in Ilson (ed.), 1–10.

—— (1989), 'Principles of monolingual lexicography', in Hausmann *et al.* (edd.), 287–96.

Gershuny, L. H. (1977), 'Sexism in dictionaries and texts: omissions and commissions', in A. P. Nielsen *et al.* (edd.), *Sexism and Language* (Urbana, Ill.: NCTE), 143–59.

Gibbs, R. W., Jr. (1980), 'Spilling the beans on understanding and memory for idioms in conversation', *Memory and Cognition* 8: 449–56.

—— (1986), 'Skating on thin ice: literal meaning and understanding idioms in conversation', *Discourse Processes* 9: 17–30.

Girardin, C. (1979), 'Contenu, usage social et interdits dans le dictionnaire', *Langue française* 43: 84–99.

Gleason, H. A. (1962/1975), 'The relation of lexicon and grammar', in Householder and Saporta (edd.), 85–102.

Gold, D. L. (1974), 'New perspectives in English lexicography', *Babel* 20: 188–96.

—— (1975), 'New Perspectives in North American lexicography', *Babel* 21: 21–9.

—— (1979), 'The ordering of lexemes in a dictionary', in Michell (ed.), 51–80.

—— (1981), 'Ordering the senses in a monolingual dictionary entry', in Y. Anderson (ed.), *Papers of the Dictionary Society of North America, 1981*, 42–9.

—— (1985), 'The debate over *Webster's Third* twenty-five years later: winnowing the chaff from the grain', *Dictionaries* 7: 225–36.

—— (1989), review of *A Dictionary of South African English*, 3rd edn. (1987), in *Dictionaries* 11: 242–60.

Gorcy, G. (1989), 'Différenciation des significations dans le dictionnaire monolingue: problèmes et méthodes', in Hausmann *et al.* (edd.), 905–17.

Görlach, M. (1990), 'The dictionary of transplanted varieties of languages: English', in Hausmann *et al.* (edd.), 1475–99.

Gove, P. B. (1961), 'Linguistic advances in lexicography', *Word Study* 37: 3–8. Also in Sledd and Ebbitt (edd.) (1962), 65–74, and in Wilson *et al.* (edd.) (1963), 28–9.

—— (1964), '"Noun often attributive" and "adjective"', *American Speech* 39: 163–75.

—— (1966), 'Self-explanatory words', *American Speech* 41: 182–98.

—— (1967*a*), 'The dictionary's function', in Gove (ed.), 5–8.

—— (ed.) (1967*b*), *The Role of the Dictionary* (Indianapolis: The Bobbs-Merrill Company).

—— (1968*a*), 'On defining adjectives, part I', *American Speech* 43: 5–32.

—— (1968*b*), 'On defining adjectives, part II', *American Speech* 43: 243–67.

—— (1972), 'English dictionaries of the future', in Weinbrot (ed.), 152–68.

Graham, A. (1975), 'The making of a non-sexist dictionary', *ETC: A Review of General Semantics* 31: 57–64. Also in B. Thorne and N. Henley (edd.), *Language and Sex: Difference and Dominance* (Rowley, Mass.: Newbury House), 57–63.

Greenbaum, S. (1974), 'Some verb-intensifier collocations in American and British English', *American Speech* 49/1–2: 79–89.

—— (1977), 'The linguist as experimenter', in R. Eckman (ed.), *Current Trends in Linguistics* (Washington: Hemisphere Publishing Corp.).

—— Meyer, C. F., and Taylor, J. (1984), 'The image of the dictionary for American college students', *Dictionaries* 6: 31–52.

Greenberg, J. H. (1954), 'The word as a linguistic unit', *IJAL* 20/4; also in C. A. Osgood and T. A. Sebeok (edd.), *Psycholinguistics* (Bloomington and London: Indiana University Press, 1965), 66–71.

Grice, H. P. (1975), 'Logic and conversation', in P. Cole and J. L. Morgan (edd.), *Syntax and Semantics*, 3. *Speech Acts* (New York: Academic Press), 41–58.

Griffin, P. J. (1985), 'Dictionaries in the ESL classroom' (MA Thesis; Carbondale, Ill.: Southern Illinois University).

Gross, D., and Miller, K. J. (1990), 'Adjectives in WordNet', *International Journal of Lexicography* 3/4: 265–77.

Gross, G. (1981), 'Lexicographie et grammaire', *Cahiers de Lexicologie* 39: 35–46.

—— (1989), 'Le Dictionnaire et l'enseignement de la langue maternelle', in Hausmann *et al.* (edd.), 174–80.

Gross, M. (1981), 'Les Bases empiriques de la notion de prédicat sémantique', *Langages* 63: 7–52.

Guilbert, L. (1969), 'Dictionnaires et linguistique: essai d'une typologie des dictionnaires monolingues français contemporains', *Langue française* 2: 4–29.

Guillaume, G. (1964), *Langage et science du langage* (Paris: Nizet).

Haas, M. R. (1962/1975), 'What belongs in a bilingual dictionary?', in Householder and Saporta (edd.), 45–50.

Haebler, T. (1989), 'The reception of the Third *New International Dictionary*', *Dictionaries* 11: 165–218.

Hagège, C. (1985), *L'Homme de paroles* (Paris: Fayard).

Haiman, J. (1980), 'Dictionaries and encyclopedias', *Lingua* 50: 329–57.

—— (1982), 'Dictionaries and encyclopedias again', *Lingua* 56: 353–5.

Hallig, R., and Von Wartburg, W. (1952), *Begriffssystem als Grundlage für die Lexicographie* (Berlin: Akademie). Second edn. 1963.

Hamers, J. F., and Blanc, M. (1983), *Bilingualité et bilinguisme* (Brussels: Pierre Mardaga).

Hanks, P. (1973), 'Discussion', in McDavid and Duckert (edd.), 251–2.

—— (1979), 'To what extent does a dictionary definition define?', in Hartmann (ed.), 32–8.

—— (1987), 'Definitions and explanations', in Sinclair (ed.), 116–36.

—— (1988), 'Typicality and meaning potentials', in Snell-Hornby (ed.), 37–47.

—— (1989), 'How common is "common"?', *The Collins Dictionary Diary* 1989, 2–12.

—— (1990), 'Evidence and intuition in lexicography', in Tomaszczyk and Lewandowska-Tomaszczyk (edd.), 31–41.

Hanon, S. (1990), 'La Concordance', in Hausmann *et al.* (edd.), 1562–7.

Harris, R. (1981), *The Language Myth* (London: Duckworth).

Hartmann, R. R. K. (ed.) (1979), *Dictionaries and their Users* (Exeter: University of Exeter).

—— (1981), 'Dictionaries, learners, users: some issues in lexicography', *Applied Linguistics* 2/3: 297–303.

—— (1982*a*), 'Das zweisprächige Wörterbuch im Fremdsprachenwerb', in H. E. Wiegand (ed.), *Studien zur neuhochdeutschen Lexikographie* 2 (Hildesheim: Olms), 73–86.

—— (1982*b*), 'Dictionaries for lexicographers? For linguists? For laymen?', *Dictionaries* 4: 270–3.

—— (1983*a*), 'On theory and practice: theory and practice in dictionary-making', in Hartmann (ed.), 3–11.

—— (1983*b*), 'The bilingual learner's dictionary and its uses', *Multilingua* 2/4: 195–201.

—— (ed.) (1983*c*), *Lexicography: Principles and Practice* (London: Academic Press).

—— (ed.) (1984), *LEXeter '83 Proceedings* (Tübingen: Niemeyer).

—— (1985), 'Dictionaries of English: the user's perspective', manuscript.

—— (ed.) (1986), *The History of Lexicography: Papers from the Dictionary Research Centre Seminar at Exeter, March* 1986 (Amsterdam: Benjamins).

—— (1987*a*), 'Four perspectives on dictionary use: a critical review of research methods', in Cowie (ed.), 11–28.

—— (1987*b*), 'Dictionaries of English: the user's perspective', in Bailey (ed.), 121–35.

—— (1988), 'The learner's dictionary: Traum oder Wirklichkeit?', in Hyldgaard-Jensen and Zettersten (edd.) (1988*a*), 215–35.

—— (1989), 'Sociology of the dictionary user: hypotheses and empirical studies', in Hausmann *et al.* (edd.), 102–11.

Hatch, E. M. (1983), *Psycholinguistics: A Second Language Perspective* (Rowley, Mass.: Newbury House).

Hatherall, G. (1984), 'Studying dictionary use: some findings and proposals', in Hartmann (ed.), 183–9.

Haugen, E. (1985), 'Lexicography and language planning', in K. R. Jankowsky (ed.), *Scientific and Humanistic Dimensions of Language* (Amsterdam: Benjamins), 571–80.

Hausmann, F. J. (1977), *Einführung in die Benutzung der neufranzösischen Wörterbücher* (Tübingen: Niemeyer).

—— (1979), 'Un dictionnaire de collocations est-il possible?', *Travaux de linguistique et de littérature* 17/1: 187–95.

—— (1984), 'Trois paysages dictionnairiques: la Grande-Bretagne, la France et l'Allemagne. Comparaisons et connexions', *Lexicographica* 1: 24–50.

—— (1986), 'The training and professional development of lexicographers in Germany', in Ilson (ed.), 101–10.

—— (1989*a*), 'Dictionary criminality', in Hausmann *et al.* (edd.), 97–101.

—— (1989*b*), 'Pour une histoire de la métalexicographie', in Hausmann *et al.* (edd.), 216–24.

—— (1989*c*), 'Component parts and structures of general monolingual dictionaries: a survey', in Hausmann *et al.* (edd.), 328–60.

—— (1989*d*), 'Wörterbuchtypologie', in Hausmann *et al.* (edd.), 968–81.

—— (1989*e*), 'Le Dictionnaire de collocations', in Hausmann *et al.* (edd.), 1010–19.

—— (1990*a*), 'La Définition est-elle utile?', in Centre d'Etudes du Lexique, 225–35.

—— (1990*b*), 'Le Dictionnaire analogique', in Hausmann *et al.* (edd.), 1094–9.

—— and Gorbahn, A. (1989), review of *COBUILD Dictionary of the English Language*, in *International Journal of Lexicography* 2/1: 44–56.

—— Reichmann, O., Wiegand, H. E., and Zgusta, L. (edd.) (1989 for vol. 1; 1990 for vol. 2; 1991 for vol. 3), *International Encyclopedia of Lexicography* (Berlin: Walter de Gruyter).

Hayashi, T. (1978), *The Theory of English Lexicography 1530–1791* (Amsterdam: Benjamins).

Heath, D., and Herbst, T. (1985), 'Wer weiss schon, was im Wörterbuch steht?—Plädoyer für mehr Wörterbucharbeit im Englischunterricht', *Die Neueren Sprachen* 84/6: 580–95.

Henne, H. (1976), 'Prinzipien einsprachiger Lexikographie', in H. Moser (ed.), *Probleme der Lexikologie und Lexikographie* (Düsseldorf: Schwann), 95–117.

Herbst, T. (1986), 'Defining with a controlled defining vocabulary in foreign learners' dictionaries', *Lexicographica* 2: 101–19.

—— (1990), 'Dictionaries for foreign language teaching', in Hausmann *et al.* (edd.), 1379–85.

—— and Stein, G. (1987), 'Dictionary-using skills: a plea for a new orientation in language teaching', in Cowie (ed.), 115–27.

Hill, A. A. (1970), 'Laymen, lexicographers and linguists', *Language* 46: 245–58.

Hines, C. P. (1978), 'Lexical integrity: *good, great, and well*', in W. Wölck and P. L. Garvin (edd.), *The Fifth LACUS Forum* (Columbia, SC: Hornbeam Press), 134–41.

Hiorth, F. (1955), 'Arrangement of meanings in lexicography', *Lingua* 4: 413–24.

Hjelmslev, L. (1958), 'Dans quelle mesure les significations des mots peuvent-elles être considérées comme formant une structure?', in Sivertsen (ed.), 636–54.

Hobar, D. (ed.) (1982), *Papers of the Dictionary Society of North America 1977* (Terre Haute, Ind.: Indiana State University).

Hoekstra, T., van den Hulst, H., and Moortgat, M. (edd.) (1980), *Lexical Grammar* (Dordrecht: Foris).

Hoenigswald, H. M. (1962/1975), 'Lexicography and Grammar', in Householder and Saporta (edd.), 103–10.

Hoss, N. (1974), 'Words: lexicography in America or why Texans don't shit', *Penthouse*, Jan. 1974, pp. 36–8.

Householder, F. W., and Saporta, S. (edd.) (1962), *Problems in Lexicography* (Bloomington, Ind.: Indiana University). New edn. 1975.

Hudson, R. A. (1981), 'Some issues on which linguists can agree', *Journal of Linguistics* 17: 333–43.

—— (1984), *Word Grammar* (Oxford: Blackwell).

—— (1988), 'The linguistic foundations for lexical research and dictionary design', *International Journal of Lexicography* 1/4: 287–312.

Hulbert, J. R. (1955), *Dictionaries: British and American* (London: André Deutsch). New edn. 1968.

Hultin, N. C., and Logan, H. M. (1984), 'The *New Oxford English Dictionary* project at Waterloo', *Dictionaries* 6: 166–98.

Hupka, W. (1989), 'Die Bebilderung und sonstige Formen der Veranschaulichung im allgemeinen einsprachigen Wörterbuch', in Hausmann *et al.* (edd.), 704–26.

Hyldgaard-Jensen, K., and Zettersten, A. (edd.) (1985), *Symposium on Lexicography II* (Tübingen: Niemeyer).

—— —— (edd.) (1988*a*), *Symposium on Lexicography III* (Tübingen: Niemeyer).

—— —— (edd.) (1988*b*), *Symposium on Lexicography IV* (Tübingen: Niemeyer).

Ilson, R. F. (1984), 'The communicative significance of some lexicographic conventions', in Hartmann (ed.), 80–6.

—— (1985*a*), 'The linguistic significance of some lexicographic conventions', *Applied Linguistics* 6/2: 162–72.

—— (ed.) (1985*b*), *Dictionaries, Lexicography and Language Learning* (Oxford: Pergamon Press).

—— (1986*a*), 'Introduction', in Ilson (ed.), pp. xii–xiv.

—— (1986*b*), 'British and American Lexicography', in Ilson (ed.), 51–71.

—— (1986*c*), 'General English dictionaries for foreign learners: explanatory techniques in dictionaries', *Lexicographica* 2: 214–22.

—— (1986*d*), 'Lexicographic archaeology: comparing dictionaries of the same family', in Hartmann (ed.), 127–36.

—— (ed.) (1986*e*), *Lexicography: An Emerging International Profession* (Manchester: Manchester University Press).

—— (1987*a*), 'Towards a taxonomy of dictionary definitions', in Ilson (ed.), 61–73.

—— (1987*b*), 'Illustrations in dictionaries', in Cowie (ed.), 193–212.

—— (ed.) (1987*c*), *A Spectrum of Lexicography: Papers from AILA Brussels* 1984 (Amsterdam: Benjamins).

—— (1990*a*), 'Semantic regularities in dictionaries', in Tomaszczyk and Lewandowska-Tomaszczyk (edd.), 123–32.

—— (1990*b*), 'Present-day British lexicography', in Hausmann *et al.* (edd.), 1967–83.

Iqbal, Z. (1987), 'Aspects of the learner's dictionary with special reference to advanced Pakistani learners of English' (Ph.D. Dissertation, University of Aston at Birmingham).

Iris, M. A., Litowitz, B. E., and Evens, M. W. (1988), 'Moving towards literacy by making definitions', *International Journal of Lexicography* 1/3: 238–52.

Jackson, H. (1985), 'Grammar in the dictionary', in Ilson (ed.), 53–9.

—— (1988), *Words and their Meaning* (London: Longman).

Jain, M. P. (1981), 'On meaning in the foreign learner's dictionary', *Applied Linguistics* 2/3: 274–86.

Jansen, J., Mergeai, J. P., and Vanandroye, J. (1987). 'Controlling LDOCE's controlled vocabulary', in Cowie (ed.), 78–94.

Jeffries, L., and Willis, P. (1982), review of T. McArthur, *Longman Lexicon of Contemporary English*, in *English Language Teaching Journal* 36/4: 277–8.

Jones, S., and Sinclair, J. McH. (1974), 'English lexical collocations', *Cahiers de Lexicologie* 24/1: 15–61.

Jongen, R. (ed.) (1985), *La Polysémie: Lexicographie et cognition* (Louvain: Cabay).

Kachru, B. (1980), 'The new Englishes and old dictionaries: directions in lexicographical research on non-native varieties on English', in Zgusta (ed.), 71–101.

Kahane, H., and Kahane, R. (1962/1975), 'Problems in modern Greek lexicography', in Householder and Saporta (edd.), 249–62.

Katre, Sumitra (1965), *Lexicography* (Annamalainagar: Annamalai University).

—— (1980), 'Current trends in Indian lexicography', in Zgusta (ed.) (1980), 177–89.

Kauffman, C. A. (1980), 'A survey of Russian obscenities and invective usage', *Maledicta* 4/2: 261–89.

Kaye, G. (1989), '*The Oxford English Dictionary* on CD-ROM', *International Journal of Lexicography* 2/1: 84–7.

Kharma, N. N. (1985), 'Wanted: a brand-new type of learner's dictionary', *Multilingua* 4: 85–90.

Kipfer, B. A. (1982), 'Bibliography of computer applications in lexicography and lexicology', *Dictionaries* 4: 202–37.

—— (1984), *Workbook on Lexicography: A Course for Dictionary Users* (Exeter: University of Exeter).

—— (1985), 'Dictionaries and the intermediate student: communicative needs and the development of user reference skills' (M.Phil. Dissertation, University of Exeter).

—— (1986), 'Computer applications in lexicography—Summary of the state-of-the-art', in Frawley and Steiner (edd.), i. 139–84.

—— (1987), 'Dictionaries and the intermediate student: communicative needs and the development of user reference skills', in Cowie (ed.), 44–54.

Kirkpatrick, B. (1985), 'A lexicographical dilemma: monolingual dictionaries for the native speaker and for the learner', in Ilson (ed.), 7–13.

—— (1989), 'User's guides in dictionaries', in Hausmann *et al.* (edd.), 754–61.

Kister, K. F. (1977), *Dictionary Buying Guide: A Consumer Guide to General English-Language Wordbooks in Print* (New York: R. R. Bowker).

Kleiber, G. (1988), 'Prototype, stéréotype: un air de famille?', *DRLAV* 38: 1–61.

—— (1990*a*), *La Sémantique du prototype* (Paris: PUF).

—— (1990*b*), 'Sur la définition sémantique d'un mot—Les Sens uniques conduisent-ils à des impasses?', in Centre d'Etudes du Lexique, 125–48.

Knowles, F. E. (1983), 'Towards the machine dictionary: "mechanical" dictionaries', in Hartmann (ed.), 181–93.

—— (1984), 'Dictionaries and computers', in Hartmann (ed.), 301–14.

—— (1990), 'The computer in lexicography', in Hausmann *et al.* (edd.), 1645–72.

Knudsen, T., and Sommerfelt, A. (1958), 'Principles of unilingual dictionary definitions', in Sivertsen (ed.), 92–8, plus discussion 98–115.

Kremin, H., and Koskas, E. (1984), 'Données de la pathologie sur la dénomination', *Langages* 76: 31–75.

Kristeva, J. (1981), *Le Langage, cet inconnu* (Paris: Editions du Seuil). First edn. under the name of Julia Joyaux (Paris: SGPP, 1969).

Kruisinga, E. (1931), 'Grammar and the dictionary', *English Studies* 13: 7–14.

Labov, W. (1972), *Sociolinguistic Patterns* (Philadelphia: University of Pennsylvania Press).

—— (1973), 'The boundaries of words and their meanings', in C. J. Bailey and R. Shuy (edd.), *New Ways of Analyzing Variation in English* (Washington: Georgetown University Press), 340–73.

Laird, C. G. (1970), *Language in America* (New York: World Publishing Company).

Lakoff, G. (1973), 'Lexicography and generative grammar I: Hedges and meaning criteria', in McDavid and Duckert (edd.), 144–53.

—— (1986), 'Classifiers as a reflexion of mind', in C. Craig (ed.), *Noun Classes and Categorization* (Amsterdam: Benjamins), 13–51.

—— (1987), *Women, Fire and Dangerous Things* (Chicago: The University of Chicago Press).

Lakoff, R. (1973), 'Lexicography and generative grammar II: context and connotation in the dictionary', in McDavid and Duckert (edd.), 154–64.

Lamy, M.-N. (1985), 'Innovative practices in French monolingual learners' dictionaries as compared with their English counterparts', in Ilson (ed.), 25–34.

Landau, S. I. (1974), 'Scientific and technical entries in American dictionaries', *American Speech* 49/3–4: 241–4.

—— (1984), *Dictionaries: The Art and Craft of Lexicography* (New York: Charles Scribner's Sons).

—— (1985), 'The expression of changing social values in dictionaries', *Dictionaries* 7: 261–9.

Lara, L. F. (1989), 'Dictionnaire de langue, encyclopédie et dictionnaire encyclopédique: le sens de leur distinction', in Hausmann *et al.* (edd.), 280–7.

Laughlin, R. M. (1972), 'Prescriptivism, psychology and THAT dictionary',

in L. M. Davis (ed.), *Studies in Honor of Raven I. McDavid Jr.* (The University of Alabama Press), 377–95.
Leech, G. (1974), *Semantics* (London: Pelican Books).
Lehmann, A. (1984), 'Graphes et description des renvois dans le dictionnaire: le traitement du vocabulaire de l'appareil génital dans le *Petit Larousse Illustré* de 1948 à 1980', *Cahiers de lexicologie* 45: 47–60.
—— (1990), 'De définition à définition—L'interprétation dans le dictionnaire par le jeu des renvois', in Centre d'Etudes du Lexique, 208–24.
—— and Beaujot, J.-P. (1978), 'Dictionnaire, langue, idéologie: le discours tenu sur *femme* et *fille* dans le *Petit Larousse Illustré* de 1906 à 1978', *Bulletin du Centre d'Analyse du Discours* 3 (Université de Lille III), 1–175.
Lehrer, A. (1968), 'Semantic cuisine', *Journal of Linguistics* 5: 39–56.
—— (1974*a*), 'Homonymy and polysemy: measuring similarity in meaning', *Language Sciences* 3: 33–9.
—— (1974*b*), *Semantic Fields and Lexical Structure* (Amsterdam: North-Holland).
—— (1990), 'Polysemy, conventionality, and the structure of the lexicon', *Cognitive Linguistics* 1/2: 207–46.
Lemmens, M., and Wekker, H. (1986), *Grammar in English Learner's Dictionaries* (Tübingen: Niemeyer).
—— (1991), 'On the relationship between lexis and grammar in English learners' dictionaries', *International Journal of Lexicography* 4/1: 1–14.
Lépinette, B. (1989), 'Vers un dictionnaire explicatif et combinatoire bilingue', *Cahiers de lexicologie* 1/54: 105–62.
Leschiera, S. (1990), 'Le lessie "homme" e "femme" nelle microstrutture dei dizionari francesi dal Cinquecento all'epoca contemporanea', in Deslex (ed.), 53–109.
Levi, J. N. (1983), 'Complex nominals: new discoveries, new questions', in S. Hattori and K. Inoue (edd.), *Proceedings of the XIIIth International Congress of Linguists* (Tokyo), 183–97.
Levin, B. (ed.) (1985), *Lexical Semantics in Review* (Cambridge, Mass.: MIT Press).
—— (1991), 'Building a lexicon: the contribution of linguistics', *International Journal of Lexicography* 4/3: 205–26.
—— (forthcoming), 'Approaches to lexical semantic representation', in D. Walker, A. Zampolli, and N. Calzolari (edd.), *Automating the Lexicon* 1 (Oxford: Oxford University Press).
Lewis, R., and Pugmire, M. (1980), *How to Use your Dictionary* (Cambridge: National Extension College).
Lipka, L. (1990), *An Outline of English Lexicology* (Tübingen: Niemeyer).
Lloyd, D. J., and Warfel, H. R. (1963), 'The development of the American dictionary', in Wilson *et al.* (edd.), 7–12.

Lurquin, G. (1982), 'The orthophonic dictionary', in J. Goetschalckx, and L. Rolling (edd.), *Lexicography in the Electronic Age* (Amsterdam: North-Holland), 99–107.

Lyons, J. (1981), *Language, Meaning and Context* (London: Fontana).

McAdam, E. L., and Milne, G. (edd.) (1963), *Johnson's Dictionary: A Modern Selection* (Victor Gollancz). Second edn. 1982 (London: Papermac).

McArthur, T. (1986*a*), 'Thematic lexicography', in Hartmann (ed.), 125–7.

—— (1986*b*), *Worlds of Reference* (Cambridge: Cambridge University Press).

McCarthy, M. (1988*a*), 'Questions of naturalness in language', in McCarthy (ed.), 47–60.

—— (ed.) (1988*b*), *Naturalness in Language* (*ELR Journal* 2).

McCawley, J. D. (1973), 'Discussion paper', in McDavid and Duckert (edd.), 165–8.

—— (1986), 'What linguists might contribute to dictionary making if they could get their act together', in P. Bjarman and V. Raskin (edd.), *The Real-World Linguist* (Norwood, NJ: Ablex), 1–18.

McCluskey, J. (1989), 'Dictionaries and labeling of words offensive to groups, with particular attention to the second edition of the *OED*', *Dictionaries* 11: 111–23.

McDavid, R. I., Jr. (1971), 'False scents and cold trails: the pre-publication criticism of the Merriam *Third*', *Journal of English Linguistics* 5: 101–21.

—— (1973*a*), 'Opening remarks', in McDavid and Duckert (edd.), 5–7.

—— (1973*b*), 'Go slow in ethnic attributions: geographical mobility and dialect prejudices', in R. W. Bailey and J. L. Robinson (edd.), *Varieties of Present-Day English* (New York: Macmillan), 258–73.

—— (1979), 'The social role of the dictionary', in Congleton *et al.* (edd.), 17–28. Also in R. I. McDavid, Jr. (ed.) (1980), *Varieties of American English* (Stanford, Calif.: Stanford University Press), 296–309.

—— (1981), 'The American linguistic chastity since H. L. Mencken', *Trema* 7: 5–18.

—— and Duckert, A. R. (edd.) (1973), *Lexicography in English* (New York: New York Academy of Sciences).

MacFarquhar, P. D., and Richards, J. C. (1983), 'On dictionaries and definitions', *RELC Journal* 14/1: 111–24.

Mackenzie, I., and Mel'čuk, I. (1988), 'Crossroads of obstetrics and lexicography: a case study', *International Journal of Lexicography* 1/2: 71–83.

Mackin, R. (1978), 'On collocations: words shall be known by the company they keep', in Strevens (ed.), 149–65.

McNamara, T. P., and Miller, D. L. (1989), 'Attributes of theories of meaning', *Psychological Bulletin* 106/3: 355–76.

Magay, T., and Zigany, J. (edd.) (1990), *BudaLEX'88: Proceedings of the Third EURALEX Congress* (Budapest: Akadémiai Kiadó).

Maingay, S., and Rundell, M. (1987), 'Anticipating learners' errors—implications for dictionary writers', in Cowie (ed.), 128–35.

Makkai, A. (1972), *Idiom Structure in English* (The Hague: Mouton).

—— (1976), 'Toward an ecological dictionary of English', in P. A. Reich (ed.), *The Second LACUS Forum* (Columbia, SC: Hornbeam Press), 52–9.

—— (1977), 'Idioms, psychology, and the lexemic principle', in R. J. Di Pietro and E. L. Blansitt (edd.), *The Third LACUS Forum* (Columbia, SC: Hornbeam Press), 467–78.

—— (1980), 'Theoretical and practical aspects of an associative lexicon for 20th-century English', in Zgusta (ed.), 125–46.

Malakhovski, L. V. (1987), 'Homonyms in English dictionaries', in Burchfield (ed.), 36–51.

Malkiel, Y. (1962/1975), 'A typological classification of dictionaries on the basis of distinctive features', in Householder and Saporta (edd.), 3–24.

—— (1980), 'The lexicographer as a mediator between linguistics and society', in Zgusta (ed.), 43–58.

Mallinson, G. (1979), 'The dictionary and the lexicon: a happy medium?', in Hartmann (ed.), 10–18.

Malone, K. (1962/1975), 'Structural linguistics and bilingual dictionaries', in Householder and Saporta (edd.), 111–18.

Manes, J. (1980), 'Ways of defining: folk definitions and the study of semantics', *Forum Linguisticum* 5/2: 122–38.

Marckwardt, A. H. (1963), Dictionaries and the English language', *English Journal* 12: 336–45. Also in Gove (ed.) (1967), 31–8.

—— (1973), 'The dictionary as an English teaching resource', *TESOL Quarterly* 7/4: 369–79.

Marello, C. (1988), 'Anaphora and deixis as cohesive devices in lexicography', in Snell-Hornby (ed.), 117–23.

—— (1990), 'The thesaurus', in Hausmann *et al.* (edd.), 1083–94.

Markowitz, J., and Franz, S. K. (1988), 'The development of defining style', *International Journal of Lexicography* 1/3: 253–67.

Martin, R. (1969), 'Le *Trésor de la Langue Française* et la méthode lexicographique', *Langue française* 2: 44–5.

—— (1989), 'L'Exemple lexicographique dans le dictionnaire monolingue', in Hausmann *et al.* (edd.), 599–607.

—— (1990), 'La Définition "naturelle"', in Centre d'Etudes du Lexique, 86–95.

Martin, S. E. (1962/1975), 'Selection and presentation of ready equivalents in a translation dictionary', in Householder and Saporta (edd.), 153–9.

Martinet, A. (1975), 'Le Mot', *Diogène* 51: 39–53.

Mathiot, M. (1973), 'Grammatical problems in lexicography: grammatical versus lexical status', in McDavid and Duckert (edd.), 39–44.

—— (1979), 'Folk definitions as a tool for the analysis of lexical meaning', in M. Mathiot (ed.), *Ethnolinguistics: Boas, Sapir and Whorf Revisited* (The Hague: Mouton), 121–260.

Matoré, G. (1968), *Histoire des dictionnaires français* (Paris: Larousse).

Mazière, F. (1981), 'Le Dictionnaire et les termes', *Cahiers de lexicologie* 39/2: 79–104.

Meara, P. (1980), 'Vocabulary acquisition: a neglected aspect of language learning', *Language Teaching and Linguistics: Abstracts* 13: 221–46.

—— (1983), 'Word associations in a foreign language: a report on the Birkbeck Vocabulary Project', *Nottingham Linguistics Circular* 11/2: 29–38.

Meier, H. H. (1969), 'Lexicography as applied linguistics', *English Studies* 50: 141–51.

Mel'čuk, I. A. (1988*a*), 'Semantic description of lexical units in an explanatory combinatorial dictionary: basic principles and heuristic criteria', *International Journal of Lexicography* 1/3: 165–88.

—— (1988*b*), 'Paraphrase et lexique dans la théorie linguistique Sens-Texte', in G. G. Bès and C. Fuchs (edd.), *Lexique et paraphrase* (*Lexique*, special issue; Lille: Presses Universitaires de Lille), 13–54.

—— Iordanskaja, L., and Arbatchewsky-Jumarie, N. (1981), 'Un nouveau type de dictionnaire: le dictionnaire explicatif et combinatoire du français contemporain', *Cahiers de lexicologie* 38/1: 3–34.

Mellor, C. J. (1979), 'Jacob Grimm's inclusion of loanwords and compounds in the *Deutsches Wörterbuch*', *Dictionaries* 1: 69–86.

Meschonnic, H. (1991), *Des mots et des mondes: Dictionnaires, encyclopédies, grammaires, nomenclatures* (Paris: Hatier).

Michell, G. (ed.) (1979), *Papers of the Dictionary Society of North America* (London, Ontario: The University of Western Ontario).

Michiels, A., and Moulin, A. (1983), 'The "Longman Lexicon of Contemporary English": a tentative appraisal', *Grazer Linguistische Studien* 19: 106–23.

—— and Noël, J. (1984), 'The pro's and con's of a controlled defining vocabulary in a learner's dictionary', in Hartmann (ed.), 385–94.

Milic, L. T. (1990), review of *The Oxford English Dictionary* on compact disk (1987), in *Dictionaries* 12: 155–60.

Miller, C., and Swift, K. (1979), *Words and Women* (Harmondsworth: Penguin). First edn. 1976 (Anchor Press).

Miller, G. A., and Gildea, P. M. (1985), 'How to misread a dictionary', manuscript. Also in *Proceedings of Coling 84*, p. 462.

—— —— (1987), 'How children learn words', *Scientific American*, Sept. 1987, pp. 94–9.

—— Beckwith, R., Fellbaum, C., Gross, D., and Miller, K. J. (1990), 'Introduction to WordNet: an on-line lexical database', *International Journal of Lexicography* 3/4: 235–44.

Milroy, J., and Milroy, L. (1985), *Authority in Language* (London: Routledge & Kegan Paul).
Mitchell, E. (1983), *Search-Do Reading: Difficulties in Using a Dictionary* (Aberdeen: College of Education).
Mitterand, Henri (1963), *Les Mots français* (Paris: Presses Universitaires de France).
Moon, R. (1987), 'Monosemous words and the dictionary', in Cowie (ed.), 173–82.
—— (1988), '"Time" and idioms', in Snell-Hornby (ed.), 107–15.
—— (1989), 'Objective or objectionable: ideological aspects of dictionaries, or The subversive dictionary', *English Language Research* 3: 59–94.
Moortgat, M., van den Hulst, H., and Hoekstra, Teun (edd.) (1981), *The Scope of Lexical Rules* (Dordrecht: Foris).
Morton, H. C. (1989), 'Gove's rationale for illustrative quotations in Webster's Third *New International*', *Dictionaries* 11: 153–64.
Moulin, A. (1981), 'The treatment of "Dialect" and "Register" in dictionaries for advanced learners of English', *Grazer Linguistische Studien* 15: 166–83.
Muller, C. (1963), 'Le Mot, unité de texte et unité de lexique en statistique lexicologique', *Travaux de linguistique et de littérature* 1: 155–73.
—— (1975), 'Peut-on estimer l'étendue d'un lexique?', *Cahiers de lexicologie* 27/2: 3–29.
—— (1977), *Principes et méthodes de statistique lexicale* (Paris: Hachette).
Murray, K. M. E. (1977), *Caught in the Web of Words: James A. H. Murray and the Oxford English Dictionary* (New Haven, Conn.: Yale University Press).
Nesi, H. (1984), 'Dealing with lexical errors' (M.Sc. Dissertation, University of Aston at Birmingham).
Neubach, A., and Cohen, A. D. (1988), 'Processing strategies and problems encountered in the use of dictionaries', *Dictionaries* 10: 1–19.
Neubauer, F. (1984), 'The language of explanation in monolingual dictionaries', in Hartmann (ed.), 117–23.
—— (1987), 'How to define a defining vocabulary', in Ilson (ed.), 49–59.
—— (1989), 'Vocabulary control in the definitions and examples of monolingual dictionaries', in Hausmann *et al.* (edd.), 899–905.
Nida, E. A. (1958), 'Analysis of meaning and dictionary making', *International Journal of American Linguistics* 24: 279–92. Also in E. A. Nida (1975), *Exploring Semantic Structure* (Munich: Wilhelm Fink), 117–35, and in A. S. Dill (ed.) (1975), *Language Structure and Translation* (Stanford, Calif.: Stanford University Press), 1–23.
Norrick, N. (1981), *Semiotic Principles in Semantic Theory* (Amsterdam: Benjamins).
Nowakowski, M. (1990), 'Metaphysics of the dictionary *versus* the lexicon', in Tomaszczyk and Lewandowska-Tomaszczyk (edd.), 3–19.

Nunberg, G. (1978), *The Pragmatics of Reference* (Bloomington, Ind.: Indiana University Linguistics Club).

O'Brien, T., and Jordan, R. R. (1985), *Developing Reference Skills* (London: Collins).

Opitz, K. (1979), 'Technical dictionaries: testing the requirements of the professional user', in Hartmann (ed.), 89–95.

O'Rourke, J. P. (1974), *Towards a Science of Vocabulary Development* (The Hague: Mouton).

Országh, L. (1969), 'Wanted: better English dictionaries', *English Language Teaching* 23/3: 216–21.

Osselton, N. E. (1958), *Branded Words in English Dictionaries before Johnson* (Groningen: Wolters).

—— (1983), 'On the history of dictionaries: the history of English-language dictionaries', in Hartmann (ed.), 13–21.

—— (1988), 'The dictionary label "figurative": modern praxis and the origins of a tradition', in Hyldgaard-Jensen and Zettersten (edd.) (1988*a*), 239–50.

—— (1989), 'The history of academic dictionary criticism with reference to major dictionaries', in Hausmann *et al.* (edd.), 225–30.

—— (1990), 'English lexicography from the beginning up to and including Johnson', in Hausmann *et al.* (edd.), 1943–53.

Ostler, N., and Atkins, B. T. S. (1991), 'Predictable meaning shift: some linguistic properties of lexical implication rules', manuscript.

Ostyn, P., and Godin, P. (1985), 'RALEX: an alternative approach to language teaching', *Modern Language Journal* 69/4: 346–55.

Pawley, A., and Syder, F. H. (1983), 'Two puzzles for linguistic theory: nativelike selection and nativelike fluency', in J. C. Richards and R. W. Schmidt (edd.), *Language and Communication* (London: Longman), 191–227.

Pergnier, M. (1986), Le Mot (Paris: Presses Universitaires de France).

Peters, A. M. (1983), *The Units of Language Acquisition* (Cambridge: Cambridge University Press).

Picoche, J. (1986), *Structures sémantiques du lexique français* (Paris: Fernand Nathan).

Pottier, B. (1965), 'La Définition sémantique dans les dictionnaires', *Travaux de linguistique et de littérature* 3/1: 33–9.

Powell, F. V. (1935), *Better Dictionary-Work Habits* (Springfield, Mass.: Merriam-Webster).

Prat Zagrebelsky, M. T. (ed.) (1989), *Dal dizionario ai dizionari* (Turin: Tirrenia Stampatori).

Putnam, H. (1975), 'The meaning of meaning', in H. Putnam, *Mind, Language and Reality* (Cambridge: Cambridge University Press), 215–71.

Quemada, B. (1968), *Les Dictionnaires du français moderne 1539–1863: Etude de leur histoire, leurs types et leurs méthodes* (Paris: Didier).

—— (1972), 'Lexicology and lexicography', in T. A. Sebeok (ed.), *Current Trends in Linguistics* 9/1 (The Hague: Mouton), 395–475.

—— (1987), 'Notes sur *lexicographie* et *dictionnairique*', Cahiers de lexicologie 51/2: 229–42.

Quine, W. V. O. (1973), 'Vagaries of definition', in McDavid and Duckert (edd.), 247–50.

Quirk, R. (1972), *The English Language and Images of Matter* (Oxford: Oxford University Press).

—— (1973), 'The social impact of dictionaries in the U.K.', in McDavid and Duckert (edd.), 76–88. Also as 'The image of the dictionary', in R. Quirk (ed.) (1974), *The Linguist and the English Language* (London: Edward Arnold), 148–63.

—— (1986), 'Opening remarks', in Ilson (ed.), 1–6.

—— *et al.* (1985), *A Comprehensive Grammar of the English Language* (London: Longman).

Ramson, W. S. (1987), '*The Australian National Dictionary*: a foretaste', in Burchfield (ed.), 137–55.

Rastier, F. (1987), *Sémantique interprétative* (Paris: Presses Universitaires de France).

Read, A. W. (1934), 'An obscenity symbol', *American Speech* 9/4: 264–78.

—— (1962/1975), 'The labeling of national and regional variation in popular dictionaries', in Householder and Saporta (edd.), 217–27.

—— (1973*a*), 'Approaches to lexicography and semantics', in T. A. Sebeok (ed.), *Current Trends in Linguistics* 10/1 (The Hague: Mouton), 145–205.

—— (1973*b*), 'The social impact of dictionaries in the United States', in McDavid and Duckert (edd.), 69–75.

—— (1979), 'The war of the dictionaries in the Middle West', in Congleton *et al.* (edd.), 3–16.

—— (1986), 'The history of lexicography', in Ilson (ed.), 28–50.

—— (1987), 'A dictionary of the English of England: problems and findings', *Dictionaries* 9: 149–63.

Reif, J. A. (1987), 'The development of a dictionary concept: an English learner's dictionary and an exotic alphabet', in Cowie (ed.), 146–58.

Renouf, A. J. (1987), 'Lexical resolution', in W. Meijs (ed.), *Corpus Linguistics and Beyond* (Amsterdam: Rodopi), 121–31.

Rey, A. (1968), 'Les Bases théoriques de la description lexicographique du français: tendances actuelles', *Travaux de linguistique et de littérature* 6/1: 55–72.

—— (1970*a*), 'Un texte compromettant: le dictionnaire', *Critique* 273: 163–81.

—— (1970*b*), 'Typologie génétique des dictionnaires', *Langages* 19: 48–68.

—— (1970*c*), *Littré, l'humaniste et les mots* (Paris: Gallimard).

—— (1970*d*), *La Lexicologie: Lectures* (Paris: Klincksieck).

—— (1972), 'Usages, jugements et prescriptions linguistiques', *Langue française* 16: 4–28.

—— (1973), *Théories du signe et du sens*, vol. 1; (1976), vol. 2 (Paris: Klincksieck).

—— (1977), *Le Lexique: images et modèles. Du dictionnaire à la lexicologie* (Paris: Armand Colin).

—— (1982), *Encyclopédies et dictionnaires* (Paris: Presses Universitaires de France).

—— (1985), 'La terminologie dans un dictionnaire général de langue française: le *Grand Robert*', *TermNet News* 14: 5–7.

—— (1987*a*), 'Le Dictionnaire culturel', *Lexicographica* 3: 3–50.

—— (1987*b*), 'La Notion de dictionnaire culturel et ses applications', *Cahiers de lexicologie* 51/2: 243–56.

—— (1990), 'Polysémie du terme *définition*', in Centre d'Etudes du Lexique, 13–22.

—— and Delesalle, S. (1979), 'Problèmes et conflits lexicographiques', *Langue française* 43: 4–26.

Rey-Debove, J. (1966), 'La Définition lexicographique: recherches sur l'équation sémique', *Cahiers de lexicologie* 8/1: 71–94.

—— (1967), 'La Définition lexicographique: bases d'une typologie formelle', *Travaux de linguistique et de littérature* 5/1: 141–59.

—— (1969*a*), 'Le Dictionnaire comme discours sur la chose et discours sur le signe', *Semiotica* 1/2: 185–95.

—— (1969*b*), 'Les Relations entre le signe et la chose dans le discours métalinguistique', *Travaux de linguistique et de littérature* 7/1: 113–29.

—— (1970*a*), 'Le Domaine du dictionnaire', *Langages* 19: 3–34.

—— (ed.) (1970*b*), *La Lexicographie* (*Langages* 19; Paris: Didier/Larousse).

—— (1971), *Etude linguistique et sémiotique des dictionnaires français contemporains* (The Hague: Mouton).

—— (1978), *Le Métalangage* (Paris: Le Robert).

—— (1989*a*), 'La Métalangue lexicographique: formes et fonction en lexicographie monolingue', in Hausmann *et al.* (edd.), 305–12.

—— (1989*b*), 'Le Traitement analogique dans le dictionnaire monolingue', in Hausmann *et al.* (edd.), 635–40.

—— (1989*c*), 'Les Systèmes de renvois dans le dictionnaire monolingue', in Hausmann *et al.* (edd.), 931–7.

Riegel, M. (1987), 'Définition directe et indirecte dans le langage ordinaire: les énoncés définitoires copulatifs', *Langue française* 73: 29–53.

Robins, R. H. (1987), 'Polysemy and the lexicographer', in Burchfield (ed.), 52–75.

Robinson, J. (1982), 'The dictionary as witness', *Dictionaries* 4: 110–17.

Robinson, R. (1954), *Definition* (Oxford: Oxford University Press).

Roe, K. (1982), 'A survey of the encyclopedic tradition in English dictionaries', in Hobar (ed.), 16–23.

Roggero, J. (1977), 'Des rouges et des lueurs', *Sigma* 2: 147–70.

Rosch, E. (1973), 'Natural categories', *Cognitive Psychology* 4: 328–50.

—— (1977), 'Human categorization', in N. Warren (ed.), *Studies in Cross-Cultural Psychology*, 1 (London: Academic Press), 1–49.

—— (1978), 'Principles of categorization', in E. Rosch and B. B. Lloyd (edd.), *Cognition and Categorization* (Hillsdale: Lawrence Erlbaum), 27–48.

—— and Mervis, C. B. (1975), 'Family resemblances: studies in the internal structure of categories', *Cognitive Psychology* 7: 573–605.

Ross, J. D. (1981), *Portraying Analogy* (Cambridge: Cambridge University Press).

Rossner, R. (1985), 'The learner as lexicographer: using dictionaries in second language learning', in Ilson (ed.), 95–102.

Ruhl, C. (1978), 'Two forms of reductionism', in M. Paradis (ed.), *The Fourth LACUS Forum* (Columbia, SC: Hornbeam Press), 370–83.

—— (1979), 'Alleged idioms with HIT', in W. Wölck and P. L. Garvin (edd.), *The Fifth LACUS Forum* (Columbia, SC: Hornbeam Press), 93–107.

—— (1980), 'The semantic field of *break*, *cut* and *tear*', in W. C. McCormack and H. J. Izzo (edd.), *The Sixth LACUS Forum* (Columbia, SC: Hornbeam Press), 200–14.

—— (1981), 'The noun *ice*', in J. E. Copeland and P. W. Davis (edd.), *The Seventh LACUS Forum* (Columbia SC: Hornbeam Press), 257–69.

Rundell, M. (1988), 'Changing the rules: why the monolingual learner's dictionary should move away from the native-speaker tradition', in Snell-Hornby (ed.), 127–37.

Russell, I. W. (1962), '*Webster's Third New International Dictionary*: an essay-review', in Sledd and Ebbitt (edd.), 221–6.

Sagarin, E. (1963), *The Anatomy of Dirty Words* (New York: Lyle Stuart).

Sands, D. B. (1981), 'Engaged lexicography: comment on an East German dictionary', *Dictionaries* 3: 39–51.

Saporta, S. (1961), *Psycholinguistics: A Book of Readings* (New York: Holt, Rinehart and Winston).

Sappler, P. (1990), 'Der Index', in Hausmann *et al.* (edd.), 1567–73.

Schäfer, J. (1980), *Documentation in the O.E.D.: Shakespeare and Nash as Test Cases* (Oxford: The Clarendon Press).

—— (1984), 'Documentation in the *OED*: a plea for supplementary studies', *Dictionaries* 6: 145–9.

Schelbert, T. (1988), 'Dictionaries—Too many words?', in Snell-Hornby (ed.), 63–70.

Scherba, L. V. (1940), 'Opyt obščej teorii leksikografii', *Izvestija Akademii Nauk SSSR* 3: 89–117. English summary by P. Garvin in *Word* 3 (1947), 129–30.

Scholfield, P. J. (1979), 'On a non-standard dictionary definition schema', in Hartmann (ed.), 54–62.

—— (1982), 'Using the English dictionary for comprehension', *TESOL Quarterly* 16/2: 185–94.

Scholler, H., and Reidy, J. (edd.) (1973), *Lexicography and Dialect Geography* (Wiesbaden: Franz Steiner).

Schur, N. (1980), *English English* (Essex, Conn.: Verbatim).

Scott, F. S. (1986), review of *The New Zealand Pocket Oxford Dictionary*, in *Dictionaries* 8: 317–26.

Sebeok, T. A. (1962), 'Materials for a typology of dictionaries', *Lingua* 11: 363–74.

Seppänen, A. (1984), 'Lexical integrity or semantic diversity: *good*, *great* and *well*', *English Studies* 65/6: 534–49.

Shapiro, F. R. (1986), '*Webster's Ninth* and historical lexicography', *Dictionaries* 8: 169–73.

Sherman, D. (1978), 'Special purpose dictionaries', *Cahiers de Lexicologie* 32/1: 82–102.

Simpson, J. A. (1988), 'Computers and the new OED's new words', in Snell-Hornby (ed.), 437–44.

—— (1990), 'English lexicography after Johnson to 1945', in Hausmann *et al.* (edd.), 1953–66.

Sinclair, John McH. (1987*a*), 'Grammar in the dictionary', in Sinclair (ed.), 104–15.

—— (1987*b*), 'The nature of the evidence', in Sinclair (ed.), 150–9.

—— (ed.) (1987*c*), *Looking Up: An Account of the COBUILD Project in Lexical Computing* (London: Collins).

—— (1991), *Corpus, Concordance, Collocation* (Oxford: Oxford University Press).

Singh, R. A. (1982), *An Introduction to Lexicography* (Mysore, India: Central Institute of Indian Languages).

Sivertsen, E. (ed.) (1958), *Proceedings of the Eighth International Congress of Linguists* (Oslo: Oslo University Press).

Sledd, J. H. (1972), 'Dollars and dictionaries: the limits of commercial lexicography', in Weinbrot (ed.), 119–37.

—— and Ebbitt, W. R. (edd.) (1962), *Dictionaries and That Dictionary: A Casebook on the Aims of Lexicographers and the Targets of Reviewers* (Chicago: Scott, Foresman and Co.).

—— and Kolb, G. J. (1955), *Dr. Johnson's Dictionary* (Chicago: University of Chicago Press).

Smith, J. W. (1979), 'A sketch of the history of the dictionary of English usage', in Congleton *et al.* (edd.), 47–58.

Smith, R. N. (1986), 'Conceptual primitives in the English lexicon', in Frawley and Steiner (edd.), i. 99–137.

Snell-Hornby, M. (ed.) (1988), *ZüriLEX'86 Proceedings: Papers read at the EURALEX International Conference* (Tübingen: Francke Verlag).

Sommerfeldt, A. (1958), 'Principles of unilingual dictionary definitions', in Sivertsen (ed.), 92–8.

Sparck-Jones, K. (1986), *Synonymy and Semantic Classification* (Edinburgh: Edinburgh University Press).

Spears, R. A. (1989), 'Historical principles in dictionaries of non-standardized vocabularies', *Dictionaries* 11: 97–109.

Stark, M. P. (1990), *Dictionary Workbooks* (Exeter: Exeter University Press).

Starnes, D. T., and Noyes, G. E. (1946), *The English Dictionary from Cawdrey to Johnson (1604–1755)* (Chapel Hill, NC: University of North Carolina Press). New edn. 1991 with introduction and new bibliography by G. Stein (Amsterdam–Philadelphia).

Steele, J. (1986), 'A lexical entry for an explanatory-combinatorial dictionary of English (*hope II.1*)', *Dictionaries* 8: 1–54.

Stein, G. (1979), 'The best of British and American lexicography', *Dictionaries* 1: 1–23.

—— (1984*a*), 'Towards a theory of lexicography: principles and/vs practice in modern English dictionaries', in Hartmann (ed.), 124–30.

—— (1984*b*), 'Traditio delectat: or no change at OUP', *Anglia* 102: 392–405.

—— (1984*c*), 'The English dictionary: past, present, and future', *Occasional Publication of the Dictionary Research Centre, Exeter*, 1–17.

—— (1985), *The English Dictionary before Cawdrey* (Tübingen: Niemeyer).

—— (1990), 'The emerging role of English in the dictionaries of Renaissance Europe', *Folia Linguistica Historica* 9/1: 29–138.

—— (1991*a*), 'Illustrations in dictionaries', *International Journal of Lexicography* 4/2: 99–127.

—— (1991*b*), 'The phrasal verb type "to have a look" in Modern English', *IRAL* 29: 1–29.

—— and Quirk, R. (1991), 'On having a look in a corpus', in K. Aijmer and B. Altenberg (edd.), *English Corpus Linguistics: Studies in Honour of Jan Svartvik* (London: Longman), 197–203.

Steiner, R. J. (1980), 'Putting obscene words into the dictionary', *Maledicta* 4/1: 23–37.

—— (1984), 'Guidelines for reviewers of bilingual dictionaries', *Dictionaries* 6: 166–81.

—— (1990), review of *The Penguin Canadian Dictionary*, in *Dictionaries* 12: 139–46.

Strevens, P. (ed.) (1978), *In Honour of A. S. Hornby* (Oxford: Oxford University Press).

Summers, D. (1988), 'The role of dictionaries in language learning', in Carter and McCarthy (edd.), 111–25.

Swanson, D. C. (1962/1975), 'Recommendations on the selection of entries for a bilingual dictionary', in Householder and Saporta (edd.), 63–77.

Sweet, H. (1899), *The Practical Study of Languages* (London: Dent) New edn. 1964 (Oxford: Oxford University Press).

Swinney, D., and Cutler, A. E. (1979), 'The access and processing of idiomatic expressions', *Journal of Verbal Learning and Verbal Behavior* 18: 523–34.

Thorndike, E. L. (1928), 'The psychology of the school dictionary', *Bulletin of the School of Education 4 (Indiana University)*, 24–31.

—— and Lorge, I. (1944), *The Teacher's Word Book of 30,000 Words* (Columbia, SC: Columbia University Press).

Tollenaere, F. de (1960), 'Lexicographie alphabétique ou idéologique', *Cahiers de lexicologie* 2: 19–29.

Tomaszczyk, J. (1979), 'Dictionaries: users and uses', *Glottodidactica* 12: 103–19.

—— (1988), 'The bilingual dictionary under review', in Snell-Hornby (ed.), 289–97.

—— and Lewandowska-Tomaszczyk, B. (edd.) (1990), *Meaning and Lexicography* (Amsterdam: Benjamins).

Tono, Y. (1984), 'On the dictionary user's reference skills' (B.Ed. Dissertation, University of Tokyo).

—— (1987), 'Which word do you look up? A Study of dictionary reference skills' (M.Ed. Dissertation, University of Tokyo).

Tournier, J. (1985), *Introduction descriptive à la lexicogénétique de l'anglais contemporain* (Paris–Geneva: Champion–Slatkine).

—— (1988), *Précis de lexicologie anglaise* (Paris: Nathan).

Trench, R. C. (1857), 'On Some Deficiencies in our English Dictionaries', in *Transactions of the Philological Society* (London), 1–70.

Underhill, A. (1980), *Use your Dictionary* (Oxford: Oxford University Press).

—— (1985), 'Working with the monolingual learners' dictionary', in Ilson (ed.), 103–14.

Urdang, L. (1963), review of *Problems in Lexicography*, in *Language* 39: 586–94.

—— (1975), review of L. Zgusta, *Manual of Lexicography*, in *Language* 51: 220–30.

—— (1979), 'Meaning: denotative, connotative, allusive', in Hartmann (ed.), 47–52. Also in *ITL: Review of Applied Linguistics* 45/46 (1979), 47–52.

van den Hurk, I., and Meijs, W. (1986), 'The dictionary as corpus: analyzing LDOCE's definition-language', in Aarts and Meijs (edd.), *Corpus Linguistics* (Amsterdam: Rodopi), 99–125.

Wadsworth, R. W. (1989), 'Lexicographers as closet authoritarians', *Dictionaries* 11: 81–95.

Wagner, R.-L. (1967), *Les Vocabulaires français*, 1. *Définitions. Les Dictionnaires* (Paris: Didier).

—— (1970), *Les Vocabulaires français*, 2. *Les Tâches de la lexicologie synchronique. Glossaires et dépouillements. Analyse lexicale* (Paris: Didier).

—— (1975), 'Réflexions naïves à propos des dictionnaires', *Cahiers de lexicologie* 27: 81–106.

Wahrig, G. (1969), 'The syntagma as the fundamental unit of lexicon entries', *Zeitschrift für Dialektologie und Linguistik* 36: 257–68.

Wakelin, M. F. (1987), 'The treatment of dialect in English dictionaries', in Burchfield (ed.), 156–77.

Wandruszka, M. (1973), 'Le Mot: connotations et indices socio-culturels', *Travaux de linguistique et de littérature* 11: 53–61.

Warburton, Y. (1986), 'Finding the right words: an account of research for the supplements to the *Oxford English Dictionary*', *Dictionaries* 8: 94–111.

Weinbrot, H. D. (1972), 'Samuel Johnson's *Plan* and Preface to the *Dictionary*: the growth of a lexicographer's mind', in Weinbrot (ed.), 73–94.

—— (ed.) (1972), *New Aspects of Lexicography* (Carbondale, Ill.: Southern Illinois University Press).

Weiner, E. S. C. (1986), 'The new *Oxford English Dictionary* and world English', *English Worldwide* 7: 256–66.

—— (1987), 'The *New Oxford English Dictionary*: progress and prospects', in Bailey (ed.), 30–48.

Weinreich, U. (1962/1975), 'Lexicographic definition in descriptive semantics', in Householder and Saporta (edd.), 25–44. Also in W. Labov and B. S. Weinreich (edd.) (1980), *On Semantics* (Philadelphia: University of Pennsylvania Press), 295–314.

—— (1964), '*Webster's Third*: a critique of its semantics', *International Journal of American Linguistics* 30/4: 405–9. Also in Labov and Weinreich (edd.) (1980), *On Semantics* (Philadelphia: University of Pennsylvania Press), 361–7.

—— (1968), 'Lexicography', in T. A. Sebeok (ed.), *Current Trends in Linguistics* 1 (The Hague: Mouton), 60–93. Also in Labov and Weinreich (edd.) (1980), *On Semantics* (Philadelphia: University of Pennsylvania Press), 315–57.

—— (1969), 'Problems in the analysis of idioms', in J. Puhvel (ed.), *Substance and Structure of Language* (Berkeley and Los Angeles: University of California Press), 23–81.

Wells, R. A. (1973), *Dictionaries and the Authoritarian Tradition* (The Hague: Mouton).

West, M. (1936/1953), *A General Service List of English Words* (London: Longman).

Whitcut, J. (1979), *Learning with LDOCE* (London: Longman).

—— (1984), 'Sexism in dictionaries', in Hartmann (ed.), 141–4.

—— (1986), 'The training of dictionary users', in Ilson (ed.), 111–22.

Whittaker, K. (1966), *Dictionaries* (London: Clive Bingley).

Wiegand, H. E. (1977), 'Nachdenken über Wörterbücher: aktuelle Probleme', in G. Drosdowski, H. Henne, and H. E. Wiegand (edd.), *Nachdenken über Wörterbücher (Mannheim: Bibliographisches Institut)*, 51–102.

—— (1984), 'On the structure and contents of a general theory of lexicography', in Hartmann (ed.), 13–30.

Wierzbicka, A. (1972), *Semantic Primitives* (Frankfurt: Athenäum).

—— (1980), *Lingua Mentalis: The Semantics of Natural Language* (Sydney: Academic Press).

—— (1982), 'Why can you *have a drink* when you can't **have an eat?*', *Language* 58: 753–99.

—— (1985), *Lexicography and Conceptual Analysis* (Ann Arbor: Karoma Publishers Inc.).

—— (1988*a*), 'The semantics and lexicography of "Natural Kinds"', in Hyldgaard-Jensen and Zettersten (edd.) (1988*a*), 155–82.

—— (1988*b*), *The Semantics of Grammar* (Amsterdam: Benjamins).

Wilks, Y., Fass, D., Guo, C., McDonald, J., Plate, T., and Slator, B. (1989), 'A tractable machine dictionary as a resource for computational semantics', in Boguraev and Briscoe (edd.), 193–228.

Wilson, K. G., Hendrickson, R. H., and Taylor, P. A. (edd.) (1963), *Harbrace Guide to Dictionaries* (New York: Harcourt, Brace and World).

Winer, L. (1983), 'Methodological considerations in the *Dictionary of Trinidadian English*', *Dictionaries* 5: 36–57.

Wittgenstein, L. (1953), *Philosophical Investigations* (Oxford: Blackwell).

Yorkey, R. (1969), 'Which desk dictionary is best for foreign students of English?', *TESOL Quarterly* 3/3: 257–70.

Zgusta, L. (1971), *Manual of Lexicography* (The Hague: Mouton).

—— (ed.) (1980), *Theory and Method in Lexicography: Western and Non-Western Perspectives* (Columbia, SC: Hornbeam Press).

—— (1986*a*), 'Summation', in Ilson (ed.), 138–46.

—— (1986*b*), 'The lexicon and the dictionaries: some theoretical and historical observations', in Frawley and Steiner (edd.), ii. 67–81.

—— (1989*a*), 'The role of dictionaries in the genesis and development of the standard', in Hausmann *et al.* (edd.), 70–9.

—— (1989*b*), 'The influence of scripts and morphological language types on the structure of dictionaries', in Hausmann *et al.* (edd.) 296–305.

—— (1989*c*), 'The *Oxford English Dictionary* and other dictionaries', *International Journal of Lexicography* 2/3: 188–230.

—— and Farina, M. T. C. (1988), *Lexicography Today* (Tübingen: Niemeyer).

Zurif, E. B., and Blumstein, S. E. (1978), 'Language and the brain', in

M. Halle, J. Bresnan, and G. A. Miller (edd.), *Linguistic Theory and Psychological Reality* (Cambridge, Mass.: MIT Press), 229–45.

Zwicky, A., and Sadock, J. M. (1975), 'Ambiguity tests and how to fail them', in J. P. Kimball (ed.), *Syntax and Semantics* 4 (New York: Academic Press), 1–36.

Index